The Periodicals Collection

By the same author

Academic and legal deposit libraries
Bibliographic control
Commercial information: a source handbook

The Periodicals Collection

Donald Davinson

Revised and Enlarged Edition

Westview Press/Boulder, Colorado

Published in 1978 in the United States of America by
Westview Press, Inc.
5500 Central Avenue
Boulder, Colorado 80301
Frederick A. Praeger, Publisher

First published in 1969 by
André Deutsch Limited
105 Great Russell Street, London WC1

Second revised edition 1978

Library of Congress Cataloging in Publication Data

Davinson, Donald Edward.
  The periodicals collection.

  (Grafton books on library and information science)
  Edition of 1964 published under title: Periodicals.
  Includes index.
  1. Serials control systems. I. Title. II. Series.
Z692.S5D34 1978   025.3'4'302854   78–17873
ISBN 0–89158–833–7

Printed in Great Britain by
Ebenezer Baylis & Son Limited
The Trinity Press, Worcester, and London

Contents

Introduction

What is a periodical? It would be pleasant to be able to supply a short, neat, all-embracing definition that is unquestioningly accepted universally. It is not possible to do so. To dip even the most tentative of toes into the definitional water is to risk drowning in a sea of conflicting interpretations and variations in terminology. An inspection of the literature soon produces a large number of definitions of the term 'periodical' whilst also introducing others which are synonyms or which are considered by some to be super-ordinate or subordinate terms. 'Serial' is the term most frequently met with; it is considered by some to be synonymous to, by others superior to, and by still others totally distinct from, the term 'periodical'. 'Magazine', 'organ', 'review', 'journal' and, indeed, 'newspaper' also come into the reckoning in a full consideration of terminological problems.

Authorities who have attempted to define a clear cut distinction between the two terms 'periodical' and 'serial' have rarely given the appearance of convincing even themselves that it can be done. Their arguments tend to be based upon attempts to restrict the term serial to items such as reports, monographic works appearing under the same general editorship and entitled a 'series', for example the *Mariners Library* series. By this type of definition items like the British Government publications *Command Papers* and *House of Commons Papers* issued irregularly but numbered consecutively would be defined as serials as might annuals, directories and yearbooks.

The exclusive and separate definition of the term 'serial' as distinct from 'periodical' is not really a possibility given the way in which the two terms are employed. The more realistic issue is that of deciding whether the two terms are synonymous or not. In European, and especially British, practice it is usual to find periodical as the blanket term used to describe publications issued under the same title in parts produced at regular intervals, in a sequence with no foreseeable end. In other parts of the world and especially in North America, the term serial is used for the same purpose in the common parlance of librarians but usually with the important addition that they consider it to be all-embracing and less open to misinterpretation. The lack of a single term which satisfies everyone is a considerable inconvenience and the source of a number of difficulties in using reference works dealing with periodicals, serials, magazines, newspapers or whatever.

In using works like *Ulrich's international periodicals directory* (New York: Bowker) or *Guide to current British periodicals* (London: Library Association), the *British union catalogue of periodicals* (London: Butterworth 1955–1958, 4 vols with supplements and cumulations) and *Union list of serials* (New York: H. W. Wilson, 3rd ed., 1965) in order to clarify the titles or other aspects of the bibliographic citation of items, it is obviously going to be difficult if the checker is unsure whether lack of success in finding details arises from using inaccurate data in the first instance, or from the fact that the several editors of such works have defined periodical or serial in a way which excludes the item sought. Being forewarned, therefore, that there are likely to be variations of inclusion in lists and reference works devoted to periodicals and serials is an essential preliminary to using them. It is absolutely essential to check the definition of the scope of individual reference works in any cases of doubt. It is usual for editors of union lists, directories and bibliographies to define the field of their inclusion in an introductory statement. It is rare to find two editors in agreement as to their fields of coverage!

Andrew D. Osborn[1] in a comprehensive analysis of the definitional jungle comes down hard in favour of serial as befits an author entitling his book *Serial publications*. He regards the term as covering more than periodical and argues a persuasive case, pointing out especially that it is widely applied in North America and is used as part of the titles of major works of bibliography like the Library of Congress's *New serial titles* and the *Union list of serials*. Osborn's argument for wide applicability to North American practice might be shaken by reference to *Ulrich's international periodicals directory* and the *Coden for periodical titles* of the American Society for Testing and

Materials, as examples of other major North American bibliographic activities using the alternative term. Bowker and Company, who publish *Ulrich's*, thoroughly confuse the issue by publishing a companion volume entitled *Irregular serials and annuals* and a supplement to both entitled *Serials bibliography supplement*! In general, however, Osborn's claim to the near universality of the term serial in North American practice is a fair one and he obviously believes that it deserves to be adopted world wide as standard:

> The great advantage which the inclusive term 'Serial' enjoys is that it is not ambiguous, even though in some respects it may, of necessity, be vague. 'Periodical', on the other hand, is decidedly ambiguous in addition to being somewhat vague.

Osborn's claim is based upon the belief that serial will comfortably embody everything, including monograph series, issued in numbered volumes, directories, annuals and year-books, which the term periodical certainly does not. His overwhelming rejection of the European (and especially British) preference for the term periodical culminates in the reminder that the British text of the Anglo-American cataloguing rules accepts serial as the super-ordinate term,[2] although he does point out the different emphasis given to the wording in the British and the American texts. Osborn especially likes Bella Shachtman's definition of serial:[3]

> Any title issued in parts, which is incomplete in a library collection.

He believes that without a large and tiresome elaboration, which would ultimately confuse, any precise attempt at definition would be doomed to failure. His addition to the already large number of synonyms and subordinates, of terms like 'continuations', 'provisional serials' and 'pseudo-serials' perhaps underlines the point.

In the principal British discussion of definitional problems, David Grenfell elects for the term periodical.[4]

> The term 'serial' is becoming unpopular and a more comprehensive interpretation is being given to the term 'periodical'.

It should be noted that Grenfell carefully covers himself by entitling his book *Periodicals and serials*! However, Grenfell was writing in 1965 and his claim that periodical was becoming an increasingly popular term has not been borne out by later events. The preference for serial of the Anglo-American cataloguing rules: British text has been noted. The British Standards Institution has wavered between the two terms. The 1970 revision of BS 4148 is entitled *Abbreviations of titles of periodicals*, but the revision of BS 2509 of the same year is *The presentation of serial publications, including periodicals*. Oddly enough the International Standards Organization's standard ISO/R 215 is for *The presentation of contributions to periodicals* and their ISO/R 8 is for *The layout of periodicals*. Even more confusing is the 1967 publication by the United States of America Standards Institute of *USA Standard for Periodicals: format and arrangement*.

Hildick[5] lists a number of terms which have been used to describe publications which are issued periodically – magazine, periodical, journal, book, review, gazette, organ. He observes that each has a slightly different meaning and his definition of periodical is neat:

Any publication which comes out periodically.

He concludes, however, that magazine is the best term to describe the whole field since it more clearly describes the contents of such publications as a store or collection of articles and stories. He is obviously taking a line from the alternative meaning of magazine as a store of arms and ammunition, which was how Edward Cave thought of his *Gentleman's Magazine* in 1731, but it is a term which is not to be taken seriously since it begs very big questions in the wider field of serial as the term is understood by Osborn.

The cause of the proponents of the term periodical has, it must be admitted, received a serious setback in the development of the International Serials Data System (ISDS) and its associated *International Standard Serials Numbers* (ISSN) programme. The ISDS Headquarters in Paris is responsible for the resolution of problems of identification and definition of material to be covered by the system but has so far published little of any consequence in the unequivocal definition of the medium. ISSNs are, however, being assigned to a large volume of material which, although issued in some kind of series, is produced irregularly and not of a nature usually described as periodical. The great convenience for the ISDS office is that being international and well supported, at least in the western world, it has a good chance to define serial in its own way as being 'anything recognized as such by the ISDS Office'!

In trying to decide whether periodical or serial is the better term to use to describe a category of publication of great and growing importance, the vulgarism 'You pays your money and you takes your choice' comes to mind. It seems more important to state a preference and stick to it, rather than to attempt to cover all problems, in the awareness that any definition of either term is bound to cause confusion. The term periodical will be used hereafter in this work, with the following as a working definition:

> Periodicals are publications issued at intervals not necessarily, but generally, regular, each issue being numbered consecutively and usually dated with no pre-determined end to the sequence of publication. A typical periodical issue consists of a number of separate items or articles from various sources or authors.

The significant sections of this definition are 'no pre-determined end', 'dated' and 'a number of separate items of information'. The claim made by some that the term serial is more inclusive than periodical can be substantiated if by no other way then certainly by the realization that a restriction to 'no pre-determined end to the sequence of publication' excludes periodical-like publications issued in weekly parts by publishers such as Purnell, which after a specified number of weeks form a complete reference work. *Golden Hands* and the *History of the Second World War* are two examples. Similarly a series of reports might fulfil the definition of a periodical by being consecutively numbered, but not being dated they are more properly serials. A series of monographs under a single general editor might fulfil some of the criteria of a periodical, even including consecutive numbering and no pre-determined end to the sequence of publication, but they would not be truly periodicals because they lack the essential quality of not being a collection of items by various hands.

The question whether newspapers are periodicals is fiercely debated in the literature. Miss P. M. Handover[6] does not regard a newspaper as a periodical, nor does the *Shorter Oxford Dictionary*. Several authorities quoted by Grenfell also argue against the inclusion of newspapers within the definition of a periodical. Kronick,[7] after devoting a great deal of space to the examination of definition problems, finds such a rejection difficult to accept:

> It is apparent that no clear distinction can be made between the periodical and the newspaper.

In the sense that newspaper files stored in libraries are used as sources of reference and information in very much the same way as periodicals there does, indeed, seem little justification for excluding them from a definition of periodicals – especially when a broad definition embracing much of the material some would term serials is being sought. Kronick suggests that the difference between periodicals and newspapers occasioning attempts at exclusive definition may be based upon the feeling that:

> The public for a newspaper has generally a geographic basis while the public for a periodical is based more on a community of interests.

This line of argument fails to convince, and newspapers are treated as part of the periodical provision problem hereafter in this work.

HOW MANY PERIODICALS ARE THERE?

Because it is so difficult to decide what periodicals are, it is naturally also difficult to count them! Undoubtedly, there are a very large number. Equally, it is clear that while many periodicals are discontinued, many more are established each year. The Library of Congress's *New serial titles* indicates that as many as 15,000 new periodicals are founded each year, but it is anybody's guess just how many exist at any one time. A number of estimates can be cited which, though now outdated, provide clues as to the method of counting. Bourne[8] gave 15,000 as the figure for 'significant journals' in 1962 and the following year Gottschalk and Desmond[9] thought 35,000 ± 10 per cent nearer the mark. Martin and Jett[10] argued cogently that 60,000 periodicals were available in 1963 but in the same year D. J. de Solla Price[11] gave 1,000,000 as the number. K. P. Barr[12] devised a formula in 1967 based upon his experiences at the British Library Lending Division (then the National Lending Library for Science and Technology) in which he argued that the best basis for making estimates of the number of periodicals available was to base them upon the size of the collections at a library like his own which had spent many years diligently seeking out the available periodical literature of the world. It is an approach with much to commend it and the 26,000 available scientific and technical periodicals which Barr estimated in 1967 would now be over 50,000, based on current British Library Lending Division stocks over the whole field of human endeavour rather than restricted, as it largely was in 1967, to science and technology.

The problem in arriving at a workable estimate of the number of periodicals available is that by reason of the obscurity of the terminology there can be no certainty that the various estimators are counting the same things. The estimators quoted above riddle their work with such qualifiers as 'significant', 'most important', 'frequently cited' and 'scientific and technological'. As Howard Rusk Long says in an introduction to a book by J. L. C. Ford:[13]

> Beyond the thousands of titles listed and cross listed in successive editions, since 1880, of the annual directories of N. W. Ayer and Son, there is an obscure non-professional journalism existing in such forms as the ship's bulletin, the club and class circular and even the handwritten family newsletter.

Even without going to such esoteric extremes as Long, church magazines, college staff and student newsletters and library bulletins add extra, uncountable, dimensions to the clearer areas of periodical activity.

Long's reminder that the directories of periodicals may provide clues to the number of periodicals available is worth following up even though Barr[12] has given reasons for treating estimates derived from such a source with caution. In 1970 the *Standard periodical directory* (New York: Oxbridge) listed 53,000 titles, whilst the 1973–4 edition of *Ulrich's international periodicals directory* listed 55,000 titles plus a further 25,000 items in the companion *Irregular serials and annuals*. The initial assignments of ISSNs made by Bowker were to some 70,000 titles (although a substantial number of them were in the irregular serials category). The *CODEN for periodical titles* system had assigned alphabetic codes to 105,000 periodical titles by February 1970 and one commentator estimated that this was 12,000–18,000 short of total coverage.[14] The same commentator added a further dimension to the discussion of the number of periodicals available by offering the estimate that since the medium began between three and three-and-a-half million periodical titles had been produced but this is an area which is, if possible, more clouded than the estimating of the numbers of currently-published titles. Estimates vary from one million titles to five million titles. Perhaps it is best simply to point out that there are large numbers of periodical titles both current and defunct and that they pose great and increasing problems to libraries, and to take the story from there.

REFERENCES

1. OSBORN, Andrew D. *Serial publications: their place and treatment in libraries.* Chicago: American Library Association, 2nd ed., 1973, pp. 3–19.
2. *Anglo-American cataloguing rules: British text.* London: Library Association, 1967. p. 268.
3. SHACHTMAN, Bella E. 'Simplification of serials record work.' *Serial Slants,* 3(6), 1962.
4. GRENFELL, David. *Periodicals and serials: their treatment in special libraries.* London: ASLIB, 2nd ed., 1965.
5. HILDICK, E. W. *A close look at magazines and comics.* London: Faber Educational, 1966.
6. HANDOVER, P. M. *Printing in London from 1476 to modern times: competitive practice and technical innovation in the trade of book and bible printing, periodical production, jobbing etc.* London: Allen and Unwin, 1960. pp. 98–9.
7. KRONICK, David. *History of scientific and technical periodicals: the origins and development of the scientific and technological press 1665–1790.* Metuchen, N. J.: Scarecrow, 2nd ed., 1975.
8. BOURNE, C. P. 'World's technical journal literature: an estimate of volume,

origin, language, field, indexing and abstracting.' *American Documentation*, 13(2) April 1963. 159–68.

9. GOTTSCHALK, C. M. *and* DESMOND, W. F. 'World-wide census of scientific and technical serials.' *American Documentation*, 14(3), July 1963. 188–94.

10. MARTIN, R. C. *and* JETT, W. *Guide to scientific and technical periodicals.* Denver: Swallow, 1963.

11. PRICE, D. J. de S. *Little science, big science.* New York: Columbia University, 1963.

12. BARR, K. P. 'Estimates of the number of currently available scientific and technical periodicals.' *Journal of Documentation*, 23(2), June 1967. 110–16.

13. FORD, J. L. C. *Magazines for the million: the story of specialised publications.* Carbondale, Ill.: Southern Illinois University Press, 1969.

14. WOODS, B. M. 'Bibliographic control of serial publications' in Allen, W. C., ed., *Serial publications in large libraries.* Urbana, Ill.: University of Illinois Graduate School of Library Science, 1970.

Part One
The history and nature of periodicals

Chapter 1
The history of periodicals

The periodical press has fractured into a much wider spread of sub-species and categories than has the newspaper press. There are a great variety of specialized applications which are dominated by two principal groups – scientific and technical periodicals, and those for leisure and recreational pursuits. The modern development of the periodical press began with the scientific periodical. Like the newspaper press, the periodical traces its antecedents in manuscript letters, newsbooks, pamphlets and recreational material such as ballads and chap-books.

Scientists, or Natural Philosophers as they would have called themselves in those days before they had any settled forms of organization such as industrial or academic communities, exchanged ideas and information by way of letters, but as McKie says:[1]

> The epistolary dissertation was not an ideal method for the communication of scientific fact and theory, even when it transcended frontiers. It was too personal. Men write to their friends and not always, or so often, to those who dispute their facts and reject their theories. Questions of priority were so easily raised; and ciphers were used for secrecy. Moreover the method could not spread new knowledge and new ideas either rapidly or widely; it was too slow and too limited within narrow personal circles.

The initial move to a form of organization designed to broaden the confines of personal acquaintance and to subject scientific work to less subjective scrutiny was with the foundation of scientific societies, first in Paris and London and then almost immediately as a tremendous vogue throughout the civilized world. The Royal Society of London and the Academy of Science in Paris began it all. The Academy of Science was established in Paris in 1666 but already, in 1665, the trend towards increased communication between scientists in France had been advanced by the publication of *Journal des Sçavans* (later *Journal des Savants*). The first issue appeared on 5 January 1665 but it was soon in difficulties with the authorities for publishing material offensive to orthodox religious opinion. (Publication was resumed later under the editorship of a cleric!) Enough had been done, however, with the thirteen issues to appear before the temporary suppression to stimulate the establishment of an English counterpart.

Members of the newly established Royal Society of London had most certainly obtained early issues of *Journal des Sçavans* and examined them carefully. As a result they decided to establish a similar periodical of their own but they decided upon monthly issues as opposed to the weekly publication of the French work. It began publication in March 1665 under the full title *Philosophical Transactions: giving some account of the present Undertakings, Studies, and Labours of the Ingenious in many considerable parts of the World*, usually shortened to *Philosophical Transactions*. It became the official organ of the Royal Society but financially it was at first the private venture of one of the joint secretaries to the Society, Henry Oldenburg. Whether this arrangement was arrived at out of the parsimony of the Fellows or through Oldenburg's own keen eye for business and his apparently chronic shortage of money is not entirely clear. Whatever it was, Oldenburg presented his first issue as 'only the gleanings of my private diversions in broken hours'.

Oldenburg was born in Bremen in 1615 but he spent the greater part of his working life in England and died in Kent in 1677. His keen interest in scientific matters was fed by contacts in Oxford, his extensive travels and his facility with languages. This led him into a voluminous correspondence with many people in a number of countries. This correspondence was the raw material of *Philosophical Transactions* and accounts for the speed with which the first issue was produced following the examination of *Journal des Sçavans*.

Oldenburg's intentions are demonstrated by his introduction to the first number:

Whereas there is nothing more necessary for promoting the improvement of Philosophical Matters, than the communicating to such, as apply their Studies and Endeavors that way, such things as are discovered or put into practice by others. It is, therefore, thought fit to employ the Press, as the most proper way to gratifie those, whose engagement in such Studies, and delight in the advancement of learning and profitable Discoveries, doth entitle them to the knowledge of what this kingdom or other parts of the World, do, from time to time, afford, as well as of the Progress of the Studies, Labors, and attempts of the Curious and Learned in things of this kind, as of their complete Discoveries and Performances; to this end, that such Productions being clearly and truly communicated, desires after solide and useful knowledge may be further entertained, ingenious Endevors and Undertakings cherished and those, addicted to and conversant with such Matters, may be invited and encouraged to search, try and find out new things, impart their knowledge to one another, and contribute what they can to the Grand Design of improving Natural knowledge, and perfecting all Philosophical Arts and Sciences. All for the glory of God, the honour and Advantage of these kingdoms, and the Universal Good of Mankind.

These curiously punctuated words almost exactly sum up the structure and function of today's scientific periodical press, of whose vastness and universality he can hardly have conceived. The circulation of *Philosophical Transactions* soon reached a figure of 1,200 copies an issue, not inconsiderable for those times, and Oldenburg was charging an annual subscription fee of £10, although he was prepared to accept £8 or even £6 in certain unspecified circumstances.

After Oldenburg's death the frequency and quality of *Philosophical Transactions* varied considerably according to the zeal and efficiency of successive Secretaries to the Royal Society. In 1750, at volume forty-seven, the Society took over full financial and editorial responsibility. The early history of *Philosophical Transactions* is the subject of an essay by R. K. Bluhm,[2] whilst the whole history of scientific journalism is chronicled by Kronick[3] who deals with the forerunners to the scientific periodical proper as well as with early attempts at their bibliographic control. Houghton[4] provides a more discursive, and readable, introduction to the subject – compared to the dense and heavily referenced writing of Kronick – and his is an explicitly British treatment.

Many imitators of *Journal des Sçavans* and *Philosophical Transactions* followed quickly from most of the intellectual centres of Europe. Before the end of the seventeenth century the scholarly periodicals, inspired by scientific societies, were joined by a more popular and vocational product with the inception of *Collection for the Improvement of Husbandry and Trade* in 1691. This branch of the medium made no significant progress until nearly a century later, when Curtis's *Botanical Magazine* (1786) set a standard for technical excellence of production and specialized approach which has rarely been bettered. The early nineteenth century was the period of expansion of technical periodicals in the United Kingdom stimulated, no doubt, by the spectacular growth of the Mechanics Institute movement.

Towards the end of the seventeenth century the first periodicals designed specifically for entertainment began to appear. *Athenian Mercury* (1690–7), published by John Dunton, and *Gentleman's Journal* (1692–4), began the process in the United Kingdom which had begun earlier in France with *Mercure Galant*, first published in 1672, which had a mixture of poetry, comment, short stories and letters to the editor, of the kind which has been the staple of many a successful recreational periodical ever since.

Virtually all of the great names of English literature have been concerned in the publication of at least one recreational periodical. Dryden wrote for *Gentleman's Journal*. Defoe, perhaps the first person who could accurately have described his profession as 'Journalist', published a periodical called *The Review* from 1704–13. Sir Richard Steele's *Tatler* (1709–11) and Joseph Addison and Richard Steele's *Spectator* (1711–12) created a style of literary essays combined with biting political satire and criticism which attracted a high circulation of 4,000 very quickly, and equally quickly brought forth official retaliation with the imposition of the Stamp Acts in 1712. These placed a relatively heavy stamp duty upon newspaper and periodical publications thus forcing up their purchase price and limiting their circulations and their economic security.

Edward Cave's *Gentleman's Magazine* (1731–1907), numbered Samuel Johnson amongst its earliest contributors. The sheer professionalism of its richly varied articles which combined many of the elements tried before in other periodicals with some new ideas, resulted in a rash of imitators. Amongst the earliest of these imitators were the *Scots Magazine*, beginning in 1739, and the *London Magazine*, which both had James Boswell as a contributor. Curiously, it was the *London Magazine* which attracted the most virulently abusive of Johnson's invective when, in the first issue for 1738 of the *Gentleman's Magazine*, he published a critique of over twenty imitators of that periodical that had commenced since 1731. At the time James Boswell was probably a sleeping partner in the *London Magazine*. By contemporary standards circulation levels were small, the *Gentleman's Magazine* was circulating 4,500 copies an issue in 1800; others rarely exceeded 3,000. Consequently the periodical market was very unstable and to an even greater extent than today periodicals tended to blossom, wither and die with bewildering rapidity.

The mechanization of printing together with significant social, political and educational reforms promoted the growth of a wide range of types and styles of publication catering for every taste. Amongst the most popular recreational periodicals in the early nineteenth century were the critical reviews, of which a large number appeared: the *Edinburgh Review* (1802) which was the model for several followers, the *Quarterly Review* (1809), the *Athenaeum* (1826), the *Westminster Review* (1824) and the still extant *Spectator* (1828). They were not, initially, the stuff of mass circulation but gradually built up a clientele as, more strongly still, did *Blackwood's Magazine* (originally *Blackwood's Edinburgh Magazine* [1817]), *Bentley's Miscellany* (1837) and, later, the *Cornhill Magazine* (1848) which laid an increasing emphasis upon fiction – especially serials. The *Cornhill Magazine*, which had Thackeray as its first editor, was the first periodical to circulate more than 100,000 copies an issue – the early issues reached more than 120,000 copies. The list of the early contributors to the *Cornhill* reads like the chapter headings for a short course in late-nineteenth-century English Literature, with George Eliot (paid £10,000 for one serial), Anthony Trollope, Mrs Gaskell, Thomas Hughes, H. Seton Merriman, Charles Reade, Wilkie Collins, Thomas Hardy and many others as prominent contributors of ten- to sixteen-part serials which were later marketed in book form by George Murray Smith of the renowned firm of Smith and Elder. The growth and times of the eighteenth- and nineteenth-century literary periodicals are painstakingly chronicled with a copious supporting bibliography by Walter Graham.[5]

Contemporary economic forces are dictating significant changes in the structure and physical presentation of periodicals. The costs of paper, post, typesetting and editorial work are all playing their part as, indeed, are changes in the habits of readers. Periodical publishers are casting around for new approaches and new formats. The *Journal of Wildlife Diseases* is the often-quoted example of the pioneer of periodical publication in microfiche. It is a format saving typesetting, proof reading and machining costs, since it is produced from the final version of the typed manuscript, and its small dimensions save on postal charges. Less radical, but aiming at similar savings, are periodicals lithographed from typescript on to flimsy paper laid out in double columns set in very small typefaces. There is also an increasing trend towards a tabloid format. Changes in reading and travelling habits are no doubt the force behind the evolution of a new breed of periodicals published on cassettes; one example is *Business Insider* (1976; 24 times a year) which is designed for the busy executive to 'read' in his car, whilst shaving, or whilst having a bath.

THE HISTORY OF THE NEWSPAPER

Although many authorities are content to regard the periodical as having emerged full grown in the middle of the seventeenth century, the relatively sophisticated presentation of the two most frequently quoted precursors of the flood which was to come, *Journal des Sçavans* and *Philosophical Transactions*, is a sure indication that the true origins were earlier. Interestingly, the origins of the periodical proper and the newspaper (which some would not acknowledge as a true periodical) are very similar.

The activity in both periodical publishing and newspaper publishing in the late seventeenth century represents more a significant stage in a continuum than a new point of departure. The history of the newspaper is an important element in the understanding of the growth of the periodical proper.

There may have been some form of regular official news bulletin in Ancient Egypt over three thousand years ago. 'If the essence of a newspaper is the regular publishing of information about recent events then something of the kind must be as old as civilisation.'[6] There was certainly a court circular established during the T'ang Dynasty in China which, though issued at irregular intervals at first, became a daily at some time in the tenth century and continued as such for a thousand years, finally closing in 1911. It was a bulletin of Government news and events which appeared in manuscript until the seventeenth century and in type thereafter. This circular, variously named during its long life, was similar in intent to an even earlier Roman bulletin, *Acta Diurna*, which was a manuscript newsheet posted in public meeting places in Rome from 59 BC onwards. It also appeared, presumably much later, in all larger townships in the Roman provinces.

In Western Europe the earliest manifestations of news gathering and disseminating, leaving aside the Roman evidence, were the manuscript newsletters produced principally at first within the big merchant houses. The *Fugger Newsletters*, from the merchant banking house of that name in Augsburg, have become particularly famous. Though only one example among many, the number of years over which they were produced and the massive organization for news gathering they required makes them an important link in a chain, ultimately leading to the modern newspaper with its network of correspondents throughout the world.

Manuscript newsletters became a significant form of news dissemination with some writers making a substantial business of a trade which was often fraught with danger in those countries, including England, where a repressive censorship of the printed word was practised and where even the manuscript could be held to be treasonable if the Sovereign or his advisers were so minded.

Newsbooks containing information about a single significant

event were another link leading ultimately to the full flowering of the newspaper and periodical press. The early evidences of this medium were occasional publications. Richard Fawkes printed *The trewe encountre* . . . in September 1513 reporting the battle of Flodden Field. One of the essential ingredients of the periodical publication, missing at first, occurred when enterprising printers began to attempt a regular, or at least frequent, publication. Before 1600 several examples of what might be termed a series of newsbooks were being issued, each carefully numbered to distinguish it from its predecessors. P. M. Handover[7] notes that a half-yearly survey of news, *Mercurius Gallobelgicus*, began to be issued in 1594. Miss Handover also ascribes to a dated newsbook, *Avisa Relation oder Zeitung*, published in Wolfenbuttel, the accolade of being the first true newspaper, dated and issued regularly although *Nieuwe Tijdinghen* may have been published as early as 1605 regularly from Antwerp. Miss Handover's definition of a periodical does indeed go no further than that it is 'distinguished from a book or a piece of jobbing work because it is dated and numbered'.

That the newsbooks, whether dated or not, became a serious force in the forming and informing of public opinion is clear from the sheer size of the collections of them made during the period of the Civil War and Commonwealth in England by George Thomason, which are now housed in the British Library Reference Division.

Cranfield[8] refers to a systematic persecution of printers in England in the sixteenth and seventeenth centuries which held back the full development of a newspaper and periodical press. He writes of a 'long stream of Star Chamber decrees, statutes, Parliamentary Ordinances and Royal Proclamations . . .' and opines that 'journalism was a dangerous profession followed only by desperate and hunted men'. Thomas Archer was one such and was imprisoned for publishing a series of 'Corantos' in early 1621 without official permission. Upon his release he joined Nathaniel Butter (who had had the foresight to procure a licence to print) and Nicholas Bourne to publish a more-or-less regular newsbook series until 1632. In that year all activity of this type was totally suppressed by the Star Chamber which was itself abolished in 1641, to bring about a brief flowering of near freedom of publishing until the end of the decade when Oliver Cromwell's Commonwealth again rigorously controlled it. Press licensing finally lapsed in 1695, having been increasingly flouted for a number of years, but before then the newspaper medium had emerged fully formed. Henry Muddiman who, besides being a printer, had made a substantial living out of the distribution of newsletters (he was charging £5 a year for his service in the 1660s) was commanded in 1665 to produce an official court circular. The *Oxford Gazette*, first published in November 1665, was the result. In 1666 when the Court returned to London following its refuge from the Plague in Oxford this became the *London Gazette* which exists to this day. It was not the signal for the growth of a strong newspaper press. The Press Licensing Acts were enforced rigorously in those troubled times. A free press might have held inconvenient opinions on a number of matters the Sovereign might not like to see aired. Large numbers of illegal presses did so air them whenever they could. When the Press Licensing Acts finally lapsed (whether by carelessness or intent is not known) printing presses multiplied in London and, as diminishing returns set in, enterprising men moved out into the provinces. The growth of the provincial newspaper industry which is so much the hallmark of the British press today had begun. Whether it began with the *Worcester Post Boy*, the *Norwich Post* or the *Bristol Post Boy* is the subject of some controversy. Totally noncontroversial is the fact that by 1702 London had a daily newspaper, the *Daily Courant*, and despite punitive taxation (the Stamp Acts 1712–) and the legal classification of any attempt to report Parliamentary proceedings as sedition, a national newspaper business based primarily upon a handful of large-circulation London-based newspapers has flourished ever since. The *Daily Universal Register*, which soon became *The Times*, began in 1785 and it was then that which it remains, an envied pioneer of technical and journalistic innovation.

The Stamp Acts had effectively strangled the ordered growth of a provincial newspaper press which did not really begin to prosper until after their final repeal, by which time the developing railway system was enabling opinion-forming mass-circulation London-based papers to compete. Despite this a provincial newspaper press thrives today, often being able to take advantage of technological developments much more readily than the London 'nationals' whose long struggle for freedom from Government interference has, seemingly, been replaced by the extreme conservatism of the Trade Unions in the printing industry when faced with technological innovation designed to increase productivity. This influence is not, perhaps, so strongly felt in the provinces.

The Stamp Acts were first imposed in 1712, at least in part to prevent the growth of a large and inconveniently-opinionated collection of newspapers and periodicals. By keeping the price of these articles artificially high it was possible to limit those which were produced to small readerships, composed mainly of the more stable elements in society who, rail though they occasionally might at the established way of doing things, had a vested interest in the status quo.

Throughout the early part of the nineteenth century *The Times* was a powerful and radical newspaper reaching, because of growing national prosperity, an increasingly wider audience. Because of the development of the railway system and postal services it was also able to extend the traditionally London-based market. It was in the hope of breaking this near monopoly that the Stamp Acts were repealed. Before 1853 there had been no morning or evening daily newspapers outside London and those in London, other than *The Times*, were few and financially unsound. From 1853 onwards newspapers sprang up all over the country. In London the twenty years after 1853 saw the establishment of a brilliant series of quality alternatives to *The Times*, beginning with the *Daily Telegraph*, which anticipated the repeal of the Stamp Acts by publishing first in 1852. Others were the *Globe*, the *Westminster Gazette* and George Smith's *Pall Mall Gazette*. *The Times* itself was hobbled in a most cunning way by the imposition of a special postal surcharge upon all newspapers weighing more than four ounces (only *The Times* did). *The Times* had a difficult decision to make. It had either to slim down and give up at least some of its established features or to maintain itself uncut. It decided to remain fat and surcharged, and quickly reverted to the role of a low-circulation 'quality' newspaper.

The story of the origins and growth of the British newspaper industry is well chronicled in a number of important sources.

Frank[9] and Dahl[10] are concerned especially with the era of corantos and newsbooks at the very beginnings of the growth of the industry. Miss Handover[11] looks in detail at one seminal source, the *London Gazette*. Cranfield[12, 13] and Wiles[14] are chiefly concerned with the growth and influence of the provincial newspaper press, whilst Page[15] provides a particularly fascinating insight by a micro-study of the history of the newspaper in one small town (Darlington) whose newspapers have had an influence entirely out of all proportion to the size of the town. *The Times*[16] has sponsored an exhaustive enumeration of all of the newspapers published in the United Kingdom over three hundred years whilst the Central Office of Information[17] has published a conveniently brief summary of the history and an appraisal of the current state of British newspapers. *Historic British Newspapers Series One*[18] is a wallet of reproductions of specimen issues of some seminal newspapers issued, including the *Daily Coranto* (1702) and the *Pall Mall Gazette* (1866). Another series of specimen copies of famous newspapers is available: *Great Newspapers*.[19] Lord Francis Williams,[20] an eminent and highly respected journalist, has written about the history of newspapers briefly, but in great detail, about their political and stylistic influences. In particular the roles of the *New York Herald* and of *The Times* are examined in his absorbing book which goes on to look critically at the nature of the press of the world, especially the former British Empire and Commonwealth, and relate it to the more recent growth of other media of mass communication.

PERIODICALS FOR WOMEN

The origins and development of periodicals produced especially for women are the subject of a re-worked Ph.D. thesis by Cynthia L. White.[21] In the course of what is a strongly sociological study, Dr White provides a detailed list of all periodicals produced in the United Kingdom since 1693 that have been exclusively or predominantly intended to interest women. The literary appraisal of early periodicals for women is attempted by Bertha M. Stearns[22] and is also dealt with by Alison Adburgham[23] and by Walter Graham.[5]

The earliest periodical produced with a female audience in

mind was John Dunton's *Ladies Mercury*, first published in 1693, as a weekly. It should be noted, however, that Dunton had in 1691 and 1692 frequently given over parts or whole issues of his *Athenian Mercury* to the 'fair sex'. This term, the 'fair sex', which sounds so gratingly condescending today, is one frequently employed during the next hundred years or more to describe aspects of editorial policy by publishers.

In the manner of its time the *Ladies Mercury* was not long-lived – it lasted only a year or so – but it did introduce to the female periodical press a feature so much thought of as a hall mark of the genre: the 'lonely hearts' page. It had another feature also found in a number of currently-published periodicals for women of being also designed for, or accidentally appealing to, male readers, with much of the correspondence seeking advice about emotional affairs coming from men.

During the eighteenth century a number of periodicals for women were published and in the early part of the century they tended to be short-lived. The *Female Tatler* (1709–10), true to its name, circulated gossip and scandal to such good effect that it attracted litigation, effectively curbing its enthusiasm and ultimately killing it off. Perhaps the most interesting of the crop produced in the early to middle eighteenth century was Miss Eliza Hayward's *Female Spectator* (1744–7) produced by women for women. Besides continuing where the *Female Tatler* left off with the gossip and scandal in prudently, if scarcely, veiled anonymity it also reflected the fashion of the time for the education of the female intellect by including material on a wide range of scientific and other topics.

Amongst the many imitators of the successful *Gentleman's Magazine* was a short-lived *Ladies Magazine* (1749–53). It is not to be confused with the later and much more enduring *Lady's Magazine* (1770–1847) which was the first periodical produced expressly for women which bears a likeness to contemporary women's-periodicals in the range and nature of its coverage. Besides news, gossip, letters to the editor and a strong leavening of fiction, fashion trends were a major feature. The resemblance was further strengthened by the provision of free inserts of sheet music and embroidery patterns.

The *Lady's Monthly Museum* (1798–1847) was constructed on a similar formula to the *Lady's Magazine* and was merged with it in 1832. In its independent years it is commended by Graham [5; p. 190] as 'the most substantial yet' of periodicals for women. These two important periodicals existed over a period when the role of the women in society changed radically. The merger in 1832 of the *Lady's Magazine* and the *Ladies Monthly Museum* was perhaps an indicator of their problems in maintaining a place as a serious minded, challenging form of journalism in an age when the message assailing women from all sides was of their essential subservience and inferiority to the male. When the periodical finally died in 1847 the new ones being established for the same type of reader were altogether lightweight and inconsequential.

Thus far the circulation levels of periodicals for women had been very low relative to today's figures. Some eighteenth-century periodicals had had circulations numbered in hundreds, the most successful of the early-nineteenth-century works had no more than several thousand. The changing social patterns in the mid nineteenth century brought into being the first women's periodical intended to generate a high circulation and to be sold at a relatively low price. This was Samuel Beeton's *Englishwoman's Domestic Magazine* which quickly reached a figure of 50,000 copies a month. Its emphasis upon home and family demonstrated two things: the rise of a middle class of great size and influence, and the confirmation of the woman's place as being in the home.

The final rescinding of the stamp duties and taxes on paper and advertising in the 1850s and 1860s cleared the way for the establishment of cheap, mass circulation periodicals to cater for the widest range of ages and tastes. One or two of the periodicals created in the 1860s bridge the years to the present day. *The Lady* (established 1885) and Samuel Beeton's other major creation, *Queen* (1861–1972), hold the record for the longest lived women's periodicals. The gradual proliferation of women's periodicals in the twentieth century makes a fascinating story culminating in a heyday of massive circulations. *Woman* (1937–   ) printed three-and-a-half million copies a week in the late 1950s and *Woman's Own* (1932–   ) two-and-a-half million copies a week in the same period. In common with the periodical industry in general it is a story also of the formation of massive integrated publishing corporations through complex mergers and purchases, killing off lively competition to the market leaders.

REFERENCES

1. McKie, D. 'The scientific periodical from 1665–1798.' *Philosophical Magazine*, 4(2), July 1948. pp. 122–32.
2. Bluhm, R. K. 'Henry Oldenburg' *in* Hartley, Sir Harold, ed., *The Royal Society: its origins and founders*. London: Royal Society, 1960. pp. 183–98.
3. Kronick, D. A. *A history of the scientific and technical periodicals: the origins and development of the scientific and technological press 1665–1790*. Metuchen, N.J.: Scarecrow, 2nd ed., 1975.
4. Houghton, B. *Scientific periodicals: their historical development, characteristics and control*. London: Bingley, 1975.
5. Graham, W. *English Literary Periodicals*. New York: Octagon, 1966.
6. Publishing, History of, *in* Encyclopedia Britannica: *Macropedia*, vol. 15. p. 235.
7. Handover, P. M. *Printing in London from 1476 to modern times*. London: Allen and Unwin, 1960. p. 109.
8. Cranfield, G. A. *The development of the provincial newspaper 1700–1760*. Oxford: Clarendon, 1967.
9. Frank, J. *The beginnings of the English Newspapers 1620–1660*. Oxford: Oxford University Press, 1961.
10. Dahl, F. *A bibliography of English corantos and periodical newsbooks 1626–1640*. London: Bibliographical Society, 1952.
11. Handover, P. M. *A history of the London Gazette 1665–1965*. London: HMSO, 1965.
12. Cranfield, G. A. *The development of the provincial newspaper 1700–1760*. Oxford: Oxford University Press, 1967.
13. Cranfield, G. A. *A handlist of English provincial newspapers 1200–1760*. Cambridge: Bowes and Bowes, 1952.
14. Wiles, R. M. *Freshest advices: early provincial newspapers in England*. Columbus, Ohio: Ohio State University Press, 1965.
15. Page, J. R. *Darlington newspapers*. Darlington: Darlington Public Library, 1972.
16. The Times. *A tercentenary handlist of English and Welsh newspapers, magazines and reviews*. London: The Times, 1920.
17. Central Office of Information, Reference Division. *The British press*. London: HMSO, 1970.
18. *A collection of historical British newspapers 1689–1866*. Brighton: Chapel House, 1972.
19. *Great Newspapers*. London: Peter Way.
20. Williams, Lord Francis. *The right to know: the rise of the world press*. London: Longman, 1969.
21. White, Cynthia L. *Women's Magazines 1693–1968*. London: Michael Joseph, 1970.
22. Stearns, Bertha M. 'Early English periodicals for ladies.' *Proceedings of the Modern Languages Association XLVIII*, 1933. pp. 38–60.
23. Adburgham, Alison. *Women in Print*. London: Allen and Unwin, 1972.

Chapter 2
The nature of periodicals

Why are periodicals of such importance that their purchase and maintenance in libraries accounts for high proportions of the available financial and labour resources? They are exceptionally difficult to handle in large numbers, require a great deal of storage space if they are to be kept for any length of time and need special, expensive and space-consuming equipment effectively to display current issues. Entered upon a library subscription list, a periodical becomes a first call upon available funds in future years and, once begun, a subscription is extremely difficult to stop; all but the least satisfactory purchases will attract their own little clientele of users who will object to their removal from the list. The bibliographic control of periodicals, although improving all of the time, is still patchy and consequently the value of retrospective files of periodicals kept by libraries is seriously reduced. In some cases the value of keeping retrospective files at all can be questioned. Many critics find the periodical medium so ineffectual that the quest for alternative methods of communication is gathering strength all the time.

So formidable a catalogue of drawbacks makes it a source of some wonder that libraries find it necessary to make large collections of current periodicals at all. That they do so and that they are also concerned to improve the quality of their exploitation indicates that, despite everything, periodicals have some properties which make them indispensable.

Periodicals provide a platform for the communication of new knowledge, the exchange of experience and the propagation of new ideas. Their regular, usually frequent, publication ensures that they publish material submitted to them relatively quickly. Certainly periodicals publish material more quickly than it could usually be produced in book form, although it will be seen later that some periodicals are increasingly being criticized for slowness in publishing. A periodical article can, in fact, allow scope for the full development of themes and subjects which would not be capable of expansion to book length, or would be of such a degree of specialization, regardless of length, as to be inappropriate for book publication. Whilst it would not be correct to say that material initially appearing as a periodical article never subsequently appears in book form, certainly much of the material published in periodicals is never subsequently re-published elsewhere. It is in recognition of this that libraries collect and store periodicals in large quantities, anticipating demand for back numbers.

Not all the material is of lasting significance (or any significance at all!). In collecting and maintaining back files of periodicals, librarians are acknowledging, if only tacitly, that in order to preserve the significant they must tolerate much that is insignificant. To be able to forecast accurately which material is likely to be called upon in future would be a great boon to the librarian and would release a great deal of storage space but it is difficult, probably impossible, to do this. There have been many attempts to produce mathematical formulae for the purpose – the work of L. Miles Raisig[1] is one example. These formulae are usually based upon calculations derived from the patterns of citations of the articles in a particular periodical in the literature. Such calculations are interesting and valuable as decision-making tools, but it is important to appreciate that the data enable forecasts to be made of material *unlikely* to be called for. It can not provide certainty that the material will never be called for but sets a level of the statistical probability that it will not be required. Librarians are often loath to take any risk at all and opt for the most comprehensive storage policy they can attain.

TYPES OF PERIODICALS

There is no really satisfactory method of categorizing periodical types into a few mutually-exclusive groups in order to undertake a detailed examination of their characteristics. However the categorization is done there are inevitably sub-groups, exceptions and unclassifiable remainders.

Categorization by main subject field is one method which may be attempted. A great deal of information exists about the nature and methods of usage of scientific and technical periodicals and they constitute the majority of periodicals published. Less fully documented are the social science periodicals but information about them is improving quickly. The humanities area is still largely uncharted territory in respect of usage patterns by scholars and there has been little formal study of the characteristics of humanities periodicals in general.

Another approach to the categorization of periodicals would be to examine the differences in editorial policy occasioned by different frequencies of publication. Daily publication almost invariably implies current news content. Weeklies are often recreational or informative in character. Monthlies can be more reflective and scholarly in their approach, with quarterlies providing the most academic and rigorous treatment of important topics. There are many other frequencies, however, and too many exceptions to any general rules – some weekly published periodicals are serious and scholarly: in this, *Nature*, recognized by Martyn and Gilchrist[2] as the most cited British periodical, is pre-eminent. Many monthlies are purely vehicles for entertainment and light relief.

Hildick[3] copes very simply with the problem by saying that there are only two types of periodical (though he calls them magazines): 'general' and 'specialist'. He does go on to provide sub-categories for each. Thus for 'general magazines' he recognizes the sub-divisions:

> news magazines
> family magazines
> women's magazines
> children's magazines

As sub-species of the genus 'specialist magazine' he has the following:

> political magazines
> fan magazines
> hobbies and pastime magazines
> trade and professional magazines
> house magazines
> literary magazines

It is a scheme which conveniently groups a range of materials to be subjected to an examination intended to satisfy the non-specialist reader and make him aware of the wide range of material available. However, it fails to provide the basis for an examination satisfactory to the needs of the librarian.

It is easier to criticize than to be constructive. In earlier versions of this work a categorization was attempted in terms of the nature of the publishing incentive behind the production of different periodicals. It produced a categorization thus:

1. Periodicals produced by learned and professional societies
2. Periodicals produced by commercial publishers in the expectation of profit
3. House journals
4. Newspapers

This was not really a happy system of categorization, and begged many large questions. The implications of category 2 are that learned societies do not expect to make profits from the publication of their periodicals and that their content and editorial approach is fundamentally and necessarily different from other periodicals. Neither statement is entirely true. It is correct to say that the majority of periodicals published by learned and professional societies are a serious financial burden to their publishers but they are not always different in kind from periodicals published commercially by speculative publishers. There is certainly no homogeneity in the periodicals produced by learned and professional societies in editorial style, frequency of publication, or financial turnover. For example the (British) Chemical Society publishes, amongst other serious research-reporting periodicals, titles designed for wider appeal (although still serious): *Chemistry in Britain* and *Education in Chemistry*, monthly and bi-monthly respectively. They could easily have come from a commercial publishing house. By the same token some serious research-reporting periodicals come from such commercial publishers as Academic Press, Pergamon Press, and Oliver and Boyd. The category 'periodicals produced by commercial publishers' is vast and amorphous, entirely different in scale to any of the other three. 'House journals' is a pretty homogeneous, but hardly very important, class compared to the first two. 'Newspapers' is also a relatively small, homogeneous and easily-recognized group but again nowhere near as significant as categories 1 and 2. The temptation is to categorize very simply into two groups 'primary periodicals' and 'the rest'. This is in recognition of the fact that librarians and others tend to write about the characteristics of a group of periodicals that publish the vast majority of the papers which report fundamentally new contributions to knowledge and to call these the primary periodicals. They then identify the rest as re-working and re-packaging that fundamental knowledge in one form or another for a variety of tastes and intellectual levels. The primary periodicals are, in fact, a very small proportion of the whole periodicals field. This also creates the possibility of the second category being enormous and gives the impression that nothing new or at any rate newsworthy appears in this category. Once again this is far from the truth but it might be convenient to make an examination based upon the divisions 'primary' and 'the rest' if only so that the special difficulties of the primary periodicals which are so urgent and pervasive can be studied first. The category 'the rest' can then be elaborated and a sub-categorization attempted purely to draw out the nature of the wide range of different styles it encompasses. It is really a description of 'periodicals produced by commercial publishers in the expectation of profit' less those few items from commercial sources which fit the designation 'primary periodicals' as that term will be elaborated here.

Because they are homogeneous groups displaying particular special characteristics it is also convenient to describe house journals and newspapers separately as special cases even if the former do, strictly speaking, form part of a non-primary publication category and the latter could be argued to form part of either the primary or the non-primary category. The categorization thus developed for use is as follows:

> primary periodicals
> non-primary periodicals
> special cases
>   a house journals
>   b newspapers

REFERENCES

1. RAISIG, L. Miles. 'Mathematical evaluation of the scientific serial.' *Science*, 131(3411), 13 May 1960. pp. 1417–19.
2. MARTYN, J. *and* GILCHRIST, A. *An evaluation of British scientific journals.* London: ASLIB, 1968. (ASLIB Occasional Publication No 1.)
3. HILDICK, E. W. *A close look at magazines and comics.* London: Faber Educational, 1966.

Chapter 3
Primary periodicals

However many periodicals there are, it is an inescapable fact that very few are of first-line significance in the transmission of newly generated knowledge carefully evaluated and thoroughly checked; this limited category is usually called the 'primary periodicals'. They have been the subject of many studies, most of them in the field of science and technology. The American Institute of Physics has devoted a great deal of time and effort to an examination of the primary periodicals in physics, of which the report by Cooper and Thayer[1] was the most important result. The primary periodicals in the biological sciences, the physical sciences and in chemistry have been studied by the Abstracting Board of the International Council of Scientific Unions.[2]

What is a primary periodical? A definition by Moore[3] supplies a brief but effective answer:

> The primary journals exist for two purposes: the dissemination and exchange of information between authors and readers and the provision of a permanent record of research findings.

Amongst the outstanding characteristics of the primary periodical as analysed by the International Council of Scientific Unions were that they are predominantly owned by learned societies and the principal language used is English (over 86 per cent of the primary periodicals in biological sciences are wholly or partly printed in English), with a monthly frequency being the most common (about one third of all periodicals examined in the three subject areas were monthlies). In stark contrast to the pattern encountered in the periodical publications of commercial publishers, the primary periodicals tend to be long lived, perhaps reflecting the sounder financial basis they enjoy as products of the learned societies. The average

age of the primary periodicals in the three fields is over fifty years, and more than half were established in the nineteenth century.

The most significant feature, perhaps, of the primary periodicals is that it is the practice of their editors to submit to a panel of referees contributions thought to be worthy of publication. A number of specialists in the subject area of the contribution will be invited to comment critically upon it. By this process it is hoped to eliminate material of less than major importance, detect flaws in the arguments of research methodologies and generally ensure the maintenance of high standards of thinking and writing. Refereeing is rarely a simple matter of accepting or rejecting. Even the most illustrious of authors may well be pleased to receive suggestions from his peers as to how his work might be improved and the referral system has valuable functions as a means of improving material which is basically acceptable. Referees are usually a permanent body of advisory editors aided, in particular cases, by invited specialists and their role is crucial to the health of the primary periodical. The criteria of what constitutes a prestigious primary periodical, and the role of the referee in the process, have been entertainingly discussed by the editor of the *New Zealand Journal of Science*.[4]

Although crucial to the standards and aspirations of the primary periodical, refereeing is subject to much criticism. Inevitably it creates delays, since a person thought to be distinguished enough in his own field to be worth consulting is likely to be busy with his own concerns. The time lost in postage, reading, reporting and returning manuscripts is sufficient in itself to cause considerable delay in publishing accepted material. There is a dilemma: it is important to a primary periodical to check carefully everything it would publish, but it is vital that it publish new research results quickly, and the two points are not really compatible.

Other criticisms of the refereeing are most often heard from disappointed authors than from commentators on the system in general. These are that referees can show bias against unconventional approaches and will play safe when confronted with work from unknown authors by recommending rejection and, further, will discriminate in favour of well-known writers by failing to impose rigorous enough standards on them. These unworthy criticisms could no doubt be sustained in a minority of cases but they are not so serious a criticism of the refereeing process compared to that of the delays it occasions. Indeed, the main complaint of rejected authors is often that the decision took a long time to reach – which is really more of a compliment than a criticism. B. K. Forscher[5] comments critically on the role of referees and their value.

The publication of material in the prestigious primary periodicals is often a matter of vital concern to academics and researchers. It is frequently a major determinant for the purposes of promotion in academic posts that the candidate is able to display the approbation of his peers as demonstrated by the papers he has prepared, arising out of research work, that have been published in periodicals known to have high standards. This 'publish or perish syndrome', as it is often called, is regarded by many as the major cause of the multiplication of periodicals and of the current pressures upon them for space.[6]

Those periodicals described as primary are a major cause for concern at the present time. There have been a number of examinations of their supposed deficiencies as transmitters of new knowledge, and of their difficulties, both economic and technical. Most examinations of the problems seem to include a rehearsal of the same proposed systems of alternatives which, it is claimed, would be more efficient as disseminators of vital material. Most of the alternative systems coexist with the primary periodicals, replacing some of them but showing not the slightest tendency to supersede them entirely. In her introduction to one of the most searching examinations of the problems and prospects of the primary periodical Helen L. Reynolds[7] says:

> . . . for a dying institution, the primary journal continues to show amazing signs of life, and even growth. New journals announce their publication and promptly attract subscribers. The primary journal is playing out a long and lively death-bed scene.

Most studies of primary periodicals deal with the scientific periodicals but there are primary periodicals in other fields.

As Walter Achtert[8] shows, they suffer from very much the same problems. The nature of these problems and proposed solutions are discussed below.

Most primary periodicals, as has been shown already, are produced by learned societies or are under Government sponsorship of some kind, and although they are only a very small section of the total number of periodicals published they have an influence out of all proportion to their numbers. Martyn and Gilchrist[9] show that if their work on British scientific periodicals is any indicator of world-wide trends, about 95 per cent of the really important material published in periodicals appears in less than 9 per cent of the periodicals published. Martyn and Gilchrist recognize this 9 per cent as the 'core' and give it as their opinion that only between 2,300 and 3,200 of the periodicals published world-wide devoted to science and technology are of front-line importance. A further most interesting finding is that if one could be content with access to only 90 per cent rather than 95 per cent of the important literature then the 'core' could be reduced by one-third.

In recent years the primary periodical has been having a hard time in terms of editorial and administrative costs to the publisher. The increased costs of paper, printing and postage have compounded an awkward situation and helped to bring about a sinister new phenomenon. Before about 1970 increased costs could be passed on to subscribers more or less with impunity. They appeared to have little or no effect upon circulation. Since that time, however, there has been a marked tendency for each increase in subscriptions to result in a rash of cancellations. At first this was counteracted by new subscriptions from developing countries, but more recently cancellations have far outstripped newly-registered subscriptions. The publishers of primary periodicals are caught in the classic economic trap. To limit their coverage or range of services could well create a further series of cancellations but with the demands upon them for space from a burgeoning population of scientists,[10] the periodicals have become ungainly and very expensive and have reached the limits of price elasticity. Koch[11] points out the startling fact that the *Physical Review* now publishes as much material in a month as it did in a whole year in the late 1930s, but even so is rejecting now as unpublishable within a reasonable period a higher proportion of submitted papers than it was in 1939. Koch stresses that the growth can in no sense be ascribed to a lower standard of editing or refereeing now as compared to before the Second World War.

Allied to the growth in size is an escalation of costs. The growth in size has, naturally, been responsible for increasing overheads considerably for subscribers already at the limit of their tolerance of price increases but unwilling to continue with a reduced service. Publishers are turning to all kinds of devices in order to limit price increases; some of these are mentioned later under 'Alternatives', but it should be noted that the massive increase in postal charges has created a trend towards the use of lighterweight papers, which create problems with binding and storage, and to printing in smaller type in double columns, which can give problems of resolution in microfilming. Many publishers have reached a crisis.

A remedy to the manifold ills of the primary periodical is desperately needed. Periodicals of this kind have rarely carried much advertising as a buffer to rising costs. Their relatively low circulation and high page costs for production make them unattractive to advertisers despite the 'select' nature of their readership. Achtert[8] found that only 38 per cent of the periodicals he surveyed had any revenue at all from advertising and in only 12 per cent of cases did advertising revenue account for more than one-tenth of production and distribution costs. It is likely, in fact, that if the publishers were successful in attracting more advertising, its introduction would render the periodicals less attractive to some purchasers, accustomed to the present practices.

The scope for cost control in the primary periodicals is very limited. Some publishers have actually introduced a system of page charges. By this process authors of articles accepted for publication are invited to make a contribution to the costs of publishing their paper. Koch[11] relates this process virtually directly to the inability of the primary periodicals to increase revenue-earning capacity through advertising. There are considerable advantages accruing to the authors of papers published in prestigious periodicals. (Enhanced reputation and even improved promotion chances have already been cited.) If authors submitting papers are asked, upon acceptance, to make a contribution towards the costs of publishing their articles they are, in effect, being asked to do no more than to invest in their own futures. In this context page charges look like an exotic form of vanity publishing! In fact the argument usually goes further to the point of showing that many papers submitted to the primary periodicals arise out of research work that has been funded by a research institution. Such funding, it is argued, carries with it the obligation to disseminate its results and also, perhaps, to promote the maintenance of as low a level of periodical subscriptions as possible to encourage the widest audience for new knowledge. The page-charge arguments are indeed sophisticated, as Koch[11] has shown; Reynolds[7] opines that they have solved no problems at all. The present turmoil in the primary periodical market undoubtedly presages massive changes in the established patterns of publication which have been basically unchanged in three hundred years.

At present, reactions to the difficulties of the primary periodical take two forms. They result in propositions for developing alternatives to traditional patterns of publication and also in attempts to reorganize the primary periodical whilst maintaining its basic form. Before considering these in detail it is convenient to summarize the disadvantages of the primary periodical as they are often presented, before indicating what steps have been taken or advocated to change the patterns of primary publication. It can then be shown that the alternatives suggested often have disadvantages greater than those of the periodical.

The principal disadvantages concern the pressures upon their space by persons seeking the prestige of publication within them. Quite apart from delay in publication of submitted material caused by refereeing, delays are also caused by this pressure. A backlog of publishable, refereed articles can be built up taking several months to include within the periodical. Instances of delays of up to a year in periodicals of monthly frequency are not uncommon. They can be even longer in the case of quarterly-published periodicals.

One method of reducing delay is for the publishers to increase the size of their periodicals so that more material can be incorporated. Publishers have tended to do this over the years until their periodicals have became large, ungainly and, perhaps, lacking in a clear focus. They may even have become variable in quality through the pursuit of comprehensiveness.

The major disadvantage of increasing the size to incorporate additional material is that it considerably increases the costs of production and therefore of subscriptions. So much is obvious, but less obvious is the way that this can significantly increase the real cost to a subscriber. It has frequently been demonstrated that the readership of any individual paper within a specific periodical issue is very much smaller than the total nominal circulation of that periodical. Out of a total nominal circulation of, say, three thousand perhaps as few as one hundred subscribers are interested in a particular paper and maybe half of them are interested in nothing else in that issue. A monthly issue of a primary periodical can cost up to £3 in these days of high subscription prices. If that issue has one hundred pages the price per page therefore is 3p. But if the article which fifty of the subscribers were interested in covered only two pages then the 'price per interesting page' to those fifty subscribers was £1·50. This argument leaves out of account any consideration of benefits which might have accrued to the fifty subscribers from browsing through the rest of the issue, and also it ignores the fact that since many subscriptions to important and expensive periodicals are taken up by librarians, total readership may exceed the nominal circulation figures many times. Nevertheless the 'price per interesting page' calculations can have a material effect upon the decision whether to continue a periodical subscription or not.

It is recognition of the fact that increased bulk creates higher costs of production that has led many periodical publishers to try to reduce size whilst increasing coverage. The resultant move to flimsier paper, smaller type sizes and double columns has already been mentioned. Another device increasingly used is the placing of arbitrary limits upon the length of articles acceptable to the publishers. The limitation usually includes severe restrictions upon the number and nature of diagrams, illustrations and supporting tables of data and references. Such reduction of length by arbitrary means can materially affect the attractiveness of a particular periodical both to would-be author and to would-be reader.

Two significant disadvantages of the primary periodical from the point of view of both the author and the reader therefore appear. For the author, publication after long delays and then only in emasculated form is likely, while the reader may find himself subscribing to a great deal of redundant material in order to obtain that which is of interest, and even then find that the parts of interest are heavily edited to the point where they constitute little more than a long abstract. The temptation to both author and reader is the same – to go elsewhere where they might obtain better service. For the reader this may mean subscribing to other periodicals which maximize their finance more effectively and improve the 'price per interesting page'. For the author it will be to cast around to find an editor and refereeing board willing to publish both quickly and without cuts.

The desire of the author to find a more hospitable place to publish is the principal cause of the phenomenon known as 'scatter'. This phenomenon was recognized by Dr S. C. Bradford.[12] It is an indicator of the inefficiency of the particular medium as a disseminator of information. It reveals that whilst the vast majority of important articles in a particular subject field will be located in a relatively small number of specialist periodicals, there will be a significant number which are distributed or 'scattered' over a large number of other periodicals. Some of them will have no obvious relationship to the subject of the article or will be relatively minor or very inaccessible periodicals which have no marked reputation for including significant material of a primary research character.

The 'scatter' phenomenon, the 'price per interesting page' concept and the sheer number of periodicals available create considerable potential for discounting the periodical as an effective means of transmitting important information.

The attempts of periodical publishers to solve the difficulties have only tended to underline some of the problems. In order to try to improve the 'price per interesting page' to subscribers whilst also attempting to widen coverage and reduce publication delays, periodicals have been split into several parts each of them covering a particular range of specializations and sometimes having a distinctive title. The hope is that the several parts will together attract a much wider list of subscribers, through being sold separately, than the previous larger whole would have done. At the same time, by offering the whole package of periodicals at a joint subscription fee considerably lower than that of the sum of the constituent parts, it is hoped that some subscribers to the previous single periodical will continue to take all of the parts, whilst the parts themselves will attract many additional subscribers in their own right. Presumably it is hoped that individuals may be persuaded to subscribe to the smaller, more sharply-focused periodicals, whilst institutions will continue to form the bulk of the subscribers to the complete package. It is a hope which has not always been fulfilled.

A different approach has been to split the periodicals into several parts, but by function rather than subject. The intention is to create one periodical devoted to the publication of serious and lengthy contributions to the literature of a particular subject, thoroughly refereed and evaluated, another devoted to short communications possibly by way of letters to the editor or summaries of results achieved and a third acting as a Society's news, notes and personal records: an 'official organ' type of publication. The aim here is usually to create circumstances in which a Society is able to relieve itself of the financial burden of supplying free to all members as part of their subscription the whole range of material previously in corporated into one periodical. Generally, the part devoted to long contributions is subject to an additional subscription.

The principal criticism of attempts of this sort to limit scope by creating several periodicals where previously only one existed, is that it frequently results in particular individuals seeing only one of the resultant parts and thus seriously reduces the benefits of browsing and the forming of ideas through accidental contact with material in other, though related, subject fields. A lesser, though not insignificant, criticism is that the larger number of periodicals thus created offers more scope for 'scatter'.

ALTERNATIVES TO THE PRIMARY PERIODICAL

The emphasis in the search for alternatives to the periodical has been on finding a means to ensure that individuals receive only material which is of immediate interest to them and that they receive it in the form and length the author intended. Most of the proposals for alternatives are based on this.

The classic review of the alternatives to the periodical is by Phelps and Herlin.[13] It is frequently cited, but it is not often pointed out that the conclusion reached by the authors is that despite its manifold inefficiencies the advantages that the alternatives present are not potent enough to offset the disadvantages, both social and economic, which are far more serious than those of the periodical. Phelps and Herlin were writing in 1960 and since then a variety of alternatives have been tried and discarded, or continue in co-existence with the periodical. A most detailed examination is the 'Record of the conference on the future of scientific and technical journals',[14] where examples of specific programmes of alternative communication forms are described and evaluated. The series of articles in *Journal of Chemical Documentation* in 1970 and 1972[7,3,15] add some methods and systems and simplify others. Line and Williams[16] provide a convenient recent summary and offer the suggestion that libraries may become agents or 'intermediate publishers' dealing with full text microforms or even computer print out.

The first alternative system to be considered is hardly an alternative at all but rather a recognition that a basic problem is the pressure upon space, as was stated earlier. This pressure has resulted in attempts to limit the length of contributions by leaving out space-consuming tables, diagrams and other supporting data. Another approach is mentioned here because, although it too attempts to limit length, it arises not out of the measures taken by editors and publishers but out of the frustrations of authors and readers and is, therefore, truly more an alternative than a publisher/editor-inspired reaction to a problem. It is also based upon the condensation of articles so that more can be put into a given, limited space; but in this instance the stylistic elegance and the verbal felicities are eliminated, whilst retaining the whole or the bulk of the supporting data. This is known as 'terse literature' and is described and advocated by Bernier[17] who has also introduced us to 'ultra-terse literature'.[18]

Terse literature is an attempt to develop a compact style of writing which embodies all the message and the conclusions of the traditional periodical article. The theory is that not only will this create the space for much more material to be published in the seminal periodicals but also that the discipline it imposes upon authors to express their thoughts concisely, compressing the maximum amount of message into the minimum of space, is itself invaluable. It is a laudable undertaking but the resultant flat, almost telegraphic, style, makes for dull reading and it is an open question whether it represents anything more than a device for drawing attention to a serious problem. If it were to be used extensively in periodicals there is no doubt that it could serve the purpose of efficiently communicating essential information to those who already know in outline the broad directions of a particular piece of work. If, however, it was intended to do more than that, to be the vehicle for conveying ideas in periodicals, which are meant to catch the interest and stimulate the imagination of casual browsers (a not insignificant role of the periodical), then the dense and daunting prose it produces surely acts as a powerful disincentive.

Preliminary communications

The delays in publication of full-length articles in properly-refereed periodicals has created a class of publications which are designed to allow for the rapid publication of research results in brief. Arising out of the practice of addressing letters to the editors of the more traditional forms of periodical, such publications are, in effect, collections of letters to the editor. *Electronics Letters* and *Chemical Communications* are two examples. Many learned societies are issuing such periodicals as a preliminary to fuller publication in due course, in their standard periodicals, of research results. The evidence is, however, that a good deal of the material published in this way does not ultimately achieve conventional periodical publication. This leads Kean and Ronayne[19] to suspect that the preliminary results/rapid notification periodicals are being abused. They claim that authors are using preliminary communications as the means of writing-up small-scale work of limited significance which would probably not merit more formal publication, or as the means of establishing priority for work the author has not yet commenced. More sinister still is their claim that authors are using this format for recording interesting by-products of their research, not related to the mainstream, which they have no intention of following up, but have published simply in order to achieve publication credit in the kinds of counts of published papers sometimes done by appointments committees in universities. Kean and Ronayne sternly enjoin that such material should not count as formal publication for this purpose and should not appear in job applications.

Omoerha[20] describes a range of services for the rapid dissemination of research results, including abstracts, preprints and reviews of forthcoming titles, which are mentioned elsewhere in this work. He notes that the norm for the publication of short communications in communication-type periodicals is between two and four weeks.

The synopsis journal

In 1975 the (British) Chemical Society issued its prospectus and a specimen copy of a new periodical of the type known as the synopsis journal. In doing so it made the observation that the primary periodical:

> . . . attempts to fulfil both a current awareness role and an archival role, and it is arguable that it does both jobs badly.

The author of the prospectus argues that the search for an alternative to the primary periodical has always been concerned principally with devising the means to separate effectively these two roles. The synopsis journal is a periodical in which summaries – or synopses – of papers accepted by the editor are published in the usual form for periodical publication with an additional service providing copies of the full texts of the papers with all of their associated data, on request and at an additional charge, and usually on microfiche. The

Chemical Society's prospectus envisages the primary periodical of the future as consisting of a synopsis journal fulfilling the current-awareness function and directed principally at the individual with a back-up service of full texts on microfiche chiefly used by libraries and institutions.

The advantages of such a system are lower printing, postage and paper costs, and faster production and distribution (principally owing to the ability to post microfiche economically by airmail). The material to be stored is also much reduced in bulk and the cost to the individual of obtaining needed papers can be reduced significantly as compared to taking whole periodicals in standard formats. In the particular field of organic chemistry, depending heavily as it does upon illustrations of structural formulae, the synopsis journal featuring such structures is eminently browsable.

Nothing is new about the system as compared to the propositions of Phelps and Herlin except, perhaps, the increased effectiveness and universality of microfiche reproduction processes. The first commercial microfiche synopsis journal to be produced was Gesellschaft Deutscher Chemiker's *Chemie-Ingenieur-Technik*. The Chemical Society had been actively investigating alternatives to the primary periodical for a number of years (Cahn[21]). A new synopsis journal, typical of its genre, is one manifestation of this concern.[22] It began publication in January 1977 and comprises microfiche versions of complete papers supported by hard copy synopses.

Separates schemes

The basis of the synopsis journal schemes is the distribution of individual articles. It is a system which has been advocated for many years as an alternative to the primary periodical under the term 'separates scheme'.

A significant number of periodical publishers operate separates schemes as an extra service to readers. Important articles are reproduced as pamphlets by 'running on' the printing of the periodical. These pamphlets are usually known as 'offprints'. An example of this is the *Bank of England Quarterly* whose annual indexes indicate with an asterisk those articles which are available as separates. Such a service enables the student, the researcher or the businessman to incorporate needed material into notes or reference files without mutilating copies of the periodical or photocopying. In addition, many such periodicals – especially the primary periodicals – give authors of articles a number of offprints of their articles for their own use, either in addition to, or in lieu of, a fee. Such offprints are frequently used by the authors as the means of keeping their colleagues, friends and official contacts informed of their activities.

This kind of offprint or separates procedure offers the clue to the manner in which advocates of an alternative to the traditional periodical developed their arguments. They pointed out how much more efficient it is to issue to interested persons copies of individual articles, rather than expecting them to purchase whole periodicals containing much material of no direct interest to them.

Peterson[23] mentions a publisher who claims that it might soon be technically possible and economically acceptable to publish periodicals individualized to the needs of the subscribers. The subscriber would be expected to specify his interests as closely as possible and would then receive his own specially-compiled periodical issue, put together automatically by a computer-controlled collating and binding system, drawing upon a bank of material selected by the editorial staff, and duly refereed as being appropriate to the needs of the full range of their subscribers. Obviously the mailing of such a periodical would also be closely controlled by computers. It is hard to imagine that potential advertisers would be enamoured of such a system.

Even more intriguing is it to speculate upon the reactions of the publishers of major indexing and abstracting services and the measures they would take to cope with the situation. Presumably they, and library and other institutional subscribers, would need to be supplied with the whole bank of material collected together to form an archival record as opposed to the consumer package. Eakins[24] describes the approach to this type of service practised by the International Research Communication System (IRCS) and termed an 'integrated publications system'. He summarizes the disadvantages of the traditional approaches to the primary periodical as does Don R. Swanson.[25] Koch and Metzner[26] present an intermediate approach, retaining much more of the semblance of the current periodical but re-packaging the current primary periodicals, which they represent as 'producer oriented', into a larger number of 'user oriented' periodicals. They create less than a comprehensive periodical, as it is traditionally known, but more than the individualized packages foreshadowed by Peterson.

Separates schemes and the carefully pre-selected and packaged periodical issues for individuals or small interest sectors have considerable disadvantages. They specialize the flow of information so much that they severely reduce the prospects of accidental discovery of useful material by browsing outside the carefully chosen field. However, when a reader is looking through a traditionally-organized periodical, ideas or data embodied in articles of little or no direct relevance to him can trigger off a helpful train of thought. Separates schemes create a very real danger of the development of tunnel vision, which itself prevents the formation of unsought links between a specialization and other associated disciplines. Some authorities argue, in fact, that a measure of browsing, and the possibility of stumbling across ideas, is essential to the health and well-being of science. They feel that scientists fed on an unrelieved diet of separates would soon become unhealthily inbred and scientific advance generally would suffer through being developed in a series of mutually exclusive channels. Scientific education and the demands of society tend to require increasing specialization, and it can be argued that it is a legitimate function of the literature to offset such channelling.

The development of a separates scheme along the lines suggested above is not a practicality. It has been overtaken by the synopsis journal plus supplementary materials system. The costs of mailing and administration separates schemes are prohibitive; in addition, storage costs, the costs of complex indexing and retrieval systems, and the overwhelming dislike of such systems manifested by libraries (who are the principal supporters of primary periodicals) effectively kills them. The most elaborate attempt to create a separates distribution scheme was begun by the American Society of Civil Engineers in 1950, but was discontinued in 1956 with the failure being ascribed to the above causes and, most particularly, to libraries cancelling subscriptions.

Other attempts to develop alternatives to the primary periodical include experiments with audio-cassette publication of preliminary research results, in a kind of news bulletin providing basic details and data on where to seek further information. The role of such a scheme is limited in a very obvious way. More adaptable and now rapidly developing are computer-readable-tape data-banks containing a large quantity of data of the preliminary communication type which can be employed, by the application of the purchaser's own computer programs, to print out data in a form and of a nature suitable to the needs of that purchaser or his clients or research workers. Such a system successfully operating is the American Institute of Physics *Searchable Physics Information Notices* (*SPIN*).

REFERENCES

1. COOPER, Marianne *and* THAYER, Candace. *Primary journal literature in Physics.* Washington: American Institute of Physics, 1969. (ID 69–4).
2. INTERNATIONAL COUNCIL OF SCIENTIFIC UNIONS. *Some characteristics of primary periodicals in the Biological Sciences/ . . . the Physical Sciences/ . . . Chemistry.* Paris: ICSU, 1967, 1966 and 1967.
3. MOORE, James A. 'An inquiry into new forms of primary publications.' *Journal of Chemical Documentation,* 12(2), May 1972. pp. 75–8.
4. GREGORY, J. Geoffrey. 'A supremely prestigious journal.' *Scholarly Publishing,* 5(3), April 1974. pp. 255–60.
5. FORSCHER, B. K. 'Rules for referees.' Science, 150(3616), 1965. pp. 319–21.
6. SEARLE, Shayle R. 'The publish or perish syndrome.' *IEEE Transactions on professional communication,* PC–16 (3), September 1973. 136–9.
7. REYNOLDS, H. L. Introduction to a symposium on the primary journal.' *Journal of Chemical Documentation,* 10(1), February 1970. p. 26.
8. ACHTERT, Walter S. 'Scholarly journals in the seventies.' *Scholarly Publishing,* 5(1), October 1973. pp. 3–11.
9. MARTYN, J. *and* GILCHRIST, A. *An evaluation of British scientific journals.* London: ASLIB, 1968. p. 7.
10. PRICE, D. J. de Solla. *Little science, big science.* New Haven, Conn.: Yale University Press, 1963.
11. KOCH, H. W. 'The role of the primary journal in physics' *in Proceedings of the Nuclear Information Symposium.* Vienna. International Atomic Energy Agency, 1970. pp. 321–34.
12. BRADFORD, S. C. *Documentation.* London: Crosby Lockwood, 2nd ed., 1953.
13. PHELPS, R. H. *and* HERLIN, J. P. 'Alternatives to the scientific periodical: a report and bibliography.' *UNESCO Bulletin for Libraries,* XIV (2) March–April 1960. pp. 61–75.

14. IEEE, 'Record of the conference on the future of scientific and technical journals.' *IEEE Transactions on professional communications*, special issue.
15. KUNEY, J. H. 'The role of microforms in journal publication.' *Journal of Chemical Documentation*, 12(2), May 1972. pp. 76–8.
16. LINE, M. B. *and* WILLIAMS, B. 'Alternatives to conventional publishing and their implications for libraries.' *ASLIB Proceedings*, 28(3), March 1976. 109–15.
17. BERNIER, Charles. 'Terse literature I: Terse conclusions.' *Journal of the American Society of Information Science*, 21(5), Sept.–Oct. 1970. pp. 316–19.
18. BERNIER, Charles. 'Terse literature II: Ultra-terse literature.' *Journal of Chemical Information and Computer Sciences*, 15(3), August 1975. pp. 189–92.
19. KEAN, P. *and* RONAYNE, J. 'Preliminary communications in Chemistry.' *Journal of Chemical Documentation*, 12(4), November 1972. pp. 218–21.
20. OMOERHA, T. 'Rapid preliminary communications in Science and Technology.' *UNESCO Bulletin for Libraries*, 27(4), July–August 1973. pp. 205–207.
21. CAHN, R. S. *Survey of Chemical publications*. London: Chemical Society, 1965.
22. THE CHEMICAL SOCIETY. *Experimental synopsis journal*. London: Chemical Society, 1975.
23. PETERSON, W. 'The bright bleak future of American magazines' *in* Allen, W. C., ed., *Serial publications in large libraries*. Urbana, Ill.: University of Illinois Graduate School of Library Science, 1970. pp. 1–10.
24. EAKINS, J. P. 'The integrated publications system: a new concept in primary publication.' *ASLIB Proceedings*, 26(1), March 1974. pp. 430–34.
25. SWANSON, D. R. 'Scientific journals and information services of the future.' *American Psychologist*, 21(3), June 1960. pp. 1005–1010.
26. KOCH, W. *and* METZNER, A. W. K. 'Primary and secondary publications in physics.' Washington: American Institute of Physics, 1970. (ID 70–4).

Chapter 4
Non-primary periodicals

The unnumbered and unnumberable mass of periodicals does not convey fundamentally original material in the sense that the relatively small number of primary periodicals does. They are much more difficult to categorize owing to the vast range of material they cover and the wide range of sources from which they emanate. In the non-primary category, periodicals are published with a variety of purposes and at a great many levels of intellectual rigour. They are produced for information, recreation, reporting current events, in order to protest and to represent highly specialized or minority views. They are published for women, for children, for the blind, for the immigrant and the racial minorities, for political parties, for religious groups. There are periodicals for the company director and the trade unionist, the contractor and public works engineer and the do-it-yourself enthusiast, the retailer and the consumer.

At one extreme are the non-primary periodicals, in intellectual content hardly or not at all different from the primary periodicals. At the other extreme are the most transient of pulp magazines or comic strip papers intended for unsophisticated tastes and yet still fulfilling all of the basic criteria of a periodical.

Many primary periodicals are published by learned societies, research associations and other official or semi-official bodies with only a small proportion produced by commercial publishers. In the non-primary sector most periodicals are published commercially in the expectation of profit. For such periodicals a major source of finance is advertising revenue. It is easy, for most purposes, to define the extreme end of the periodicals spectrum represented by transient and poorly-produced periodicals as being outside the scope of all but a very few libraries. These are the type of periodicals which appeal in the main to people who would not use libraries anyway. Periodicals produced purely for entertainment do not figure largely in the acquisition policies of libraries. Certainly the periodicals which are often called the 'pulp magazines' of the read-and-throw-away kind: the comic strip type, and publications like *True Confessions, Mad, Weekend, Reveille* and *Tit-bits*, are not likely to be found in many libraries. No doubt cogent arguments for the inclusion in libraries of this transient, entertainment literature could be advanced, indicating how they could form valuable source wells to be drawn upon for insights into social attitudes and the use of leisure in particular eras. However, it is precisely for the preservation of material for research that there is 'legal', compulsory deposit in designated libraries. It is not a valid argument for their collection and exploitation in all, or even many, libraries.

Librarians are conscious, nevertheless, that there are in the development of a selection policy a large number of borderline cases, when deciding what represents unacceptably low standards for library purposes and what falls just inside the line of acceptability.

In order to try to reduce the range of material to several groups for a closer examination, it is convenient to draw up a series of categories. It is important to appreciate, however, that the amount of material and its variety of purposes makes categorization in any exhaustive sense an enormously complex undertaking. By reducing the categories to be covered to a handful it is possible only to hint at the complexities and to suggest the range. Professor James L. C. Ford[1] has produced a detailed study of the whole field with exhaustive categorization and copious examples drawn from the American scene. At the beginning of his book Professor Ford illustrates succinctly how multifaceted we all are in our reading:

You grew up with *Humpty Dumpty* or *Jack and Jill*, then graduated in your early teens to *American Girl* or *Boys' Life*. A few years later you began reading *Hot Rod* or *Seventeen*. As an adult, your job brought you in contact with *Iron Age* and your hobby led to *Skiing*. Or, as a housewife, you subscribe to *Parents* or *Flower and Garden*.

The following categories will be considered in more detail:

current affairs
leisure, recreation and hobbies
professional, trade and technical, controlled circulation
special cases:
  a house journals
  b newspapers

CURRENT AFFAIRS

The daily newspaper reports the news with an immediacy which often defies detailed and sober analysis of the consequences of any particular event. Periodicals with their weekly, monthly or quarterly frequencies are able to devote time and space to close examinations of the issues involved in important events. Since the eighteenth century an important function of periodicals has been not simply the analysis of events but their interpretation for some specifically political or sectarian interest.

In the United Kingdom probably the most prestigious and nonsectarian current affairs periodical is the rather deceptively named *The Economist*, a periodical of enormous influence and considerable scholarship. Other well-known titles are less independent in editorial policy and include the *Spectator*, the *New Statesman*, *Tribune* and the Roman Catholic *The Tablet*; the emphasis in this type of material is largely national and political. *Private Eye*, an extremely radical commentator, bridges the national and the local with satirical comment upon national affairs, cheek by jowl with strong exposés of local scandals and ineptitudes. This approach has its echoes, indeed strong echoes, in the flurry of cheaply-produced newspapers and periodicals usually called 'alternative periodicals' or 'the underground press'. This is material published and distributed outside the normal channels of the book and periodical trade. It is usually produced in a 'home-made' way with a typewriter, transfer lettering and an offset litho machine. Indeed the development of relatively cheap high-quality reprographic processes in recent years was a considerable element in the growth of this sector of the periodical press. At its worst it represents simply the irresponsible rantings of emotionally blinkered interest groups who see good in nothing which does not directly promote those interests. At its best it provides a valuable goad and corrective to the established modes of thought of both the more formal current affairs press and the pathological secrecy of the bureaucracy, local and national. John Spiers[2] has provided a detailed bibliography of the genre in Britain together with an essay upon its development which, amongst other things, makes the point that in the early days the alternative press almost totally escaped the attention of librarians. The legal deposit regulations have been largely unsuccessful in bringing this important material into the deposit libraries. The production of the microform collection of source materials with which the Spiers bibliography is associated is a valuable service in the circumstances. John Pemberton[3] describes attempts to formalize the provision of this material, which he calls 'ephemera', noting the importance of its value as the raw material of social research.

More specialized still, and counting as current affairs material only because of their tendency to comment upon contemporary problems, are the cousins of the underground press, the 'small magazines'. Strictly speaking more a literary than an analytical group, they are usually the product of strong social or political commitment which is worked out in verse and comment in periodicals of small circulation published non-commercially and by volunteers under the guidance of an editor or publisher or proprietors who are often without hope or intention of covering their outlay. They also provide problems for the bibliographic organization and control that is provided by a continuing American bibliography[4] and supplemented, for British purposes, by two further works.[5,6] Len Fulton,[7] himself a small-press publisher, has written a perceptive critical review and evaluation of some important little magazines. *Margins* (a bi-monthly, published from 2912 North Hackett, Milwaukee, Wis., by Tom Montag) is a periodical devoted to a review of small presses and little magazines and their problems. Encompassing the whole range is a massive bibliography by Muller and the Spahns.[8] An irregular feature in *Wilson Library Bulletin*, 'Alternative periodicals', is also worth remembering.

The newsletter trade does not flourish in the United Kingdom as it does in North America, where it makes a material contribution to the dissemination of current affairs information; perhaps as many as ten thousand are produced regularly. The newsletter is truly an elaboration of the pattern of news dissemination first exploited by Henry Oldenburg, where an individual or groups with special, 'inside' information upon some seminal activity sell it in the form of a printed or duplicated broadsheet to subscribers who receive it by mail sufficiently quickly and exclusively for them to make effective use of the information. Put at its simplest, the racing tipster's envelope bought over the newsagent's counter is a 'newsletter'. More elaborate, if similar in intent, is the stockbroker's newsletter to his clients. Similarly metal and other commodity brokers issue newsletters and economic reviews regularly. Fan clubs of pop stars or even of famous authors produce newsletters to inform members of their idol's movements and habits. The newsletters which are seen to be the most significant are those produced by lobby correspondents and others with information at seats of government. In the United States the newsletters are even sometimes seen as a threat to the due processes of government through their premature and selective disclosures.

The bibliographic control of newsletters is very difficult, owing both to their numbers and to the varied nature of their publishing organizations, often totally unused to the procedures of legal deposit. The *Standard Directory on Newsletters* (New York: Oxbridge, 1972) and *Newsletter on Newsletters* (published monthly 1964–   by the Newsletter Clearinghouse, 14 East Market Street, Rhinebeck, New York 12572), are two American attempts at control.

Newsletters would often be of great value to libraries in their information function but they are rarely available to them on subscription for, naturally, the producers of these low circulation, high cost items are not interested in library subscriptions which might reduce the market for individual subscriptions. Like the controlled circulation periodicals (discussed below) newsletters will sometimes be sold to libraries only on condition that they are not shown to library users but are restricted solely to the internal needs of the library office: not a situation likely to appeal to most libraries.

LEISURE, RECREATION AND HOBBIES

Advertising revenues play a large part in the finances of this particular category of periodical. The unit costs of production, especially of the lavishly illustrated monthlies such as *Good Housekeeping* and *House & Garden*, are often three or four times the cover price. The difference, and the publishers' profit, is paid for by the advertising. The consequence for libraries of this dependence upon advertising revenues is only significant because the inability to attract advertising is the biggest cause of the demise of useful periodicals – it is, indeed, almost the only cause. Frequent and often unheralded changes might take place in editorial policy in an attempt to attract new readers. The changes might well alter the character of the periodical completely over time and this makes it essential for the librarian to exercise constant vigilance to ensure that long familiar periodicals continue to fulfil the functions for which they were originally purchased. The quest for advertising revenue and increased circulation can also result in mergers and take-overs, and changes in proprietors can create changes of emphasis and approach.

Erhard Sanders[9] tells the true story of both types of change, editorial and proprietorial, in one group of periodicals:

Once upon a time there lived a little magazine called *Television Engineering*. It was a slender thing full of useful information and beloved by many.

But along came a big bully with the pompous name of *FM Magazine and FM Radioelectronics* which had at one time been infected with the TV virus and thereafter called itself *FM-TV and Radio Communication*. Under this disguise it devoured little *Television Engineering* and ruminated it from May 1952 to December 1953. After the last big gulp, it became diet conscious and started the new 1954 quite slender, this time under the moniker of *Communication Engineering*.

But all the previous dissipation now showed its effect and after one brief issue it became so weak that it fell easy prey to another glutton, *Radio-Electronic Engineering*. This character had quite a career itself. It had entered the world as a sort of appendix to *Radio and Television News* distinguished by a lead band with the inscription *Radio-Electronic Engineering Edition of Radio and Television News*. Later it had made itself somewhat independent and gone as *Radio-Electronic Engineering Section*, and then finally eliminated the *Section*.

It can still be seen on the periodical shelves as *Radio-Electronic Engineering* but for how long?

Sanders' droll tale obviously strikes a sympathetic chord in the heart of David C. Taylor, a periodicals librarian who has founded a newsletter entitled *Title Varies: Librarians United To Fight Costly Silly Unnecessary Serial Title Changes*. LUTFCSUSTC for short. A bi-monthly since December 1973, it awards an annual prize for the worst title change of the year. Librarians' interests in stabilizing catalogue entries and publishers' in seeking sales and topicality clearly do not correspond.

Recent years have seen the demise of many periodicals of the truly recreational and leisure variety, as exemplified by *Saturday Evening Post* in the United States and *Argosy* the British short-story magazine. The general-interest recreational periodical has had a hard time since the advent of television. The once massive-circulation periodicals *Picture Post* (United Kingdom) and *Life* (United States) have folded although *Stern* (W. Germany) and *Oggi* (Italy) with a style similar to the former two, though perhaps with a harder edge, do continue. *Reader's Digest* is the highest circulation English-language general-interest periodical, although by its style, it is generally outside of the scope of libraries. So too are the lavish, expensive, pornographic periodicals; a fast growing market dealing in titillation thinly veneered with short stories and features, such as *Club International, Mayfair, Playboy* and *Penthouse*, although in a well argued paper Bill Katz[10] does not agree. A book by Katz[11] incidentally discusses the whole field of imaginative periodical literature and its relationship to library use.

Periodicals designed for women continue to dominate the market in the United Kingdom in terms of circulation size and variety of choice. *Woman* and *Woman's Own* and *Woman's Weekly* number their circulations in millions and are at the cheaper, more ephemeral end of the market not usually within the scope of libraries. More on the borderline are the more serious monthlies such as *Cosmopolitan*, but considered thoroughly acceptable, at least in public libraries anyway, are *Vogue*, *Ideal Home* and *Good Housekeeping*.

The only way to indicate the extent of the category is simply to mention pairs of periodicals, that between them comprehend vast activity areas and cater for widely varying tastes, intellectual levels and purchasing power: *Country Life* and *Amateur Gardening*; *Racing Pigeon* and *Horse and Hound*; *Racing and Football Outlook* and *Field*; *Practical Mechanics* and *New Scientist* or *Scientific American*; *Gramophone* and *New Musical Express*.

TECHNICAL, TRADE, PROFESSIONAL AND CONTROLLED-CIRCULATION PERIODICALS

Technical periodicals bear the closest relationship to the primary periodicals, for many of them have the important function of re-presenting and interpreting material which was originally published in the primary periodicals. They also purvey news and accounts of new techniques, and are a forum for the exchange of experience between subscribers. The difficulty with this group is that definition is confused by the fact that some of them carry important commissioned articles no less significant than those typically included in the primary periodicals. Examples of this group include *Engineer* (1856, weekly), *Mechanical Handling International* (1891, monthly), *Soap, Perfumery and Cosmetics* (1928, monthly).

Trade periodicals are devoted principally to the commercial aspects of a particular activity. They usually contain authoritative lists of prices for the business concerned – the *Grocer* gives retail prices, the *Builder* prices of building materials (though this particular periodical is both trade and technical in its coverage), the *Bookseller* recent book news and prices. They frequently also cover contracts and commercial opportunities offered, for example *Benn's Export News* (1973, weekly), and *Contract Journal* (1879, weekly).

Besides publishing research-level periodicals of a primary kind, many professional associations publish the equivalent of a trade periodical for their profession, or similar items are published commercially to serve the profession. They contain pass lists of professional examinations, information on the programmes and activities of branches, and short articles on aspects of professional practice or details of new legislation affecting the profession: *New Law Journal* (1822, weekly), *Accountancy Age* (1969, weekly) – the latter is also controlled-circulation as are a number of similar periodicals – *Measurement and Control* (1945, monthly), *Quantity Surveyor* (1938, monthly).

Controlled-circulation periodicals are often composed entirely of advertising matter. They represent the ultimate in advertising revenue keeping a periodical afloat financially, by dispensing with the bulk of editorial matter and, in many cases, dispensing also with subscription charges! A controlled-circulation periodical is based on the development of high quality mailing lists and on the canvassing of paid advertising on the promise of distributing the resultant periodical to that mailing list. The issues often contain pre-paid advertiser enquiry post cards so that readers may conveniently request further information.

Examples of this type of periodical are *Hospital Equipment Service* (1966, quarterly), *Applied Pneumatics* (1952, quarterly) and *Industrial Equipment News Product Information Service* (1964, three times a year). (Emery and Bottle[12] have published a bibliography of controlled-circulation periodicals in chemistry.) There are many more of this type of periodical than might sometimes be appreciated and they cause librarians problems. Some are available to libraries on request; others can be supplied to libraries but only on payment of a subscription, for example, *International Freighting Weekly* (1962, weekly); and some publishers of these periodicals will not make them available to libraries at all, since their intent is to stress to advertisers that the periodical goes directly to the desks of persons highly likely to be involved in purchase decisions. Similar stipulations are made for another category of controlled-circulation material – periodicals produced by credit control agencies noting credit, rating, debt and bankruptcy summonses to court in relation to companies and individuals. Material of this kind is obviously too sensitive to be on public display but it does raise nice ethical points which librarians must sometimes consider. If there are closed-circulation periodicals published that embody potentially damaging privileged information which the individuals under scrutiny can never see or have the chance to refute, what effect does this have upon the role of the librarian as information provider? What if it becomes known that there is some information that he is not allowed to provide, purely because of the commercial policy of private companies who are prepared to do their best to ensure that the library cannot obtain access to their publications? Is this practice simply a sensible precaution for the protection of their livelihood by such publishers or is it a sinister form of censorship?

HOUSE JOURNALS

The British Association of Industrial Editors[13] defined the house journal as:

A publication issued periodically and not primarily for profit, by an industrial undertaking, a business house a public service, or an incorporated organisation, membership of which consists mainly of people engaged in industry, business, commerce or public service.

House journals are issued chiefly as public relations, to develop customer/client contacts and staff welfare. The prime purposes of the house journal are summarized by Ford[1] as 'communication, information, persuasion'. It is as difficult to give an adequate definition of what constitutes a house journal as it is to define any other category of periodical. A major problem is deciding how wide to cast the net. In the definition above the reference to 'public service' is a reminder of the mass of material which it is possible to collect as communications enclosed with gas, electricity, telephone and water bills or with rates and tax demands. If they are issued regularly they become, in effect if not in intent, 'house journals'. In the only major study of the medium published in the United Kingdom, Hazlewood[14] points out that trades union journals, school magazines and church magazines could, perhaps, be defined as 'house journals'; they have more or less the same purpose as true house journals. Hazlewood does not actually

3

provide any reasons why they are not 'true house journals' but his use of the word 'true' indicates that he does not regard them as fully acceptable. Usually, however, the species is recognized in a more limited way than that offered by Ford and by Hazlewood, but it is still a very wide field. Ford, in common with most commentators on the house journal, is at pains to distinguish two main categories. The 'external' house journal is that kind which is intended to circulate principally outside the company publishing it, amongst clients or customers, or even competitors. By contrast the 'internal' house journal is designed to circulate within the company to personnel either in one plant or locality, or across the whole company. There is also a category, a small minority, which essays to cover both types of market in one; but these 'combinations' or 'internal/externals', as they are sometimes called, are rarely satisfactory in either role. The latter category usually exists as the only publication of its kind issued by a particular company, while it is common for the two more specialized categories to be published in pairs, so that the company staff and clients each receive a totally different periodical. Some companies, indeed, publish a number of house journals for different sectors of their clients, or for separate levels or locations of their personnel.

Ford[1] in his historical introduction recognizes the *Fugger Newsletters* of the fifteenth to seventeenth centuries as the earliest manifestation of a house journal, because of its function in the circulation of commercial intelligence to its agents, branches and selected clients. This fails entirely to convince, for Messrs Fugger were hardly attempting to engender goodwill and prestige from the free circulation of commercial intelligence, but rather to capitalize on their superior information network. They were operating the medieval equivalent of the contemporary private wire service or closed-circulation newsletter. Whatever the legitimacy of ascribing to the *Fugger Newsletters* the priority in this field, the second example Ford mentions is surely the earliest of the breed which can be recognized as tracing a direct, unbroken descent to the present. *Lowell Offering* was first published as an 'internal' house journal in 1840 by the Lowell Cotton Mills in Massachusetts. He recognizes *Harpers Monthly* from the publishing firm of that name as the first 'external' which commenced in 1850. From these beginnings the field now boasts perhaps twenty thousand examples in the United States, where it is thickest on the ground, and several thousand in each of the other larger, industrially advanced nations of the West.

EXTERNAL HOUSE JOURNALS

Possibly the most scholarly and widest distributed group of external house journals are those issued by the various banks. In terms of both size and intellectual 'weight' in the United Kingdom this group is lead by the stately *Bank of England Quarterly*. The periodical publications of the other major banking houses are not insignificant: *Barclays Bank Review* makes a feature of regular loose inserts reviewing a major economic topic of current interest, with both graphic and statistical accompaniment. *Midland Bank Review, Lloyds Bank Review* and *National Westminster Quarterly Review* all appear quarterly carrying important articles and economic news in each freely available issue. The periodical publications of banking houses are usually published in English regardless of country of origin.

Bank journals are of great value to the student, the business-man and the academic, and are frequently cited in the mass media, thus causing a demand for them, in libraries. As such they have an important current-information function but, more than that, they are also frequently given coverage in periodical indexing services and are cited in scholarly monographs and papers. They should, therefore, be available in long runs of back numbers in any large library. In the case of the *Bank of England Quarterly* a comprehensive cumulative index is issued and major articles are also made available separately as offprints on request.

A point to be very carefully watched in regard to bank journals is that their publishers regularly mount careful checks to ensure that their large and expensive mailing lists are still effective. To do this they will issue reply paid post cards which must be returned if the mailing is to be continued. It is easy to overlook such cards and, consequently, to lose several issues before the problem is revealed.

The bank journals are a relatively homogeneous group of house journals, but the mass of such material is not so easily classified. Many external house journals are, very simply, prestige-seeking, glossily printed, general-interest magazines containing several articles with little or no apparent connection with the products of the issuing company. Others are more pointed and make an obvious connection; thus the *British Airways News* contains principally travel articles of 'general interest' but with a good deal of photographs in which in one form or another British Airways is stressed. Others mix the general interest material with news of the company designed both to impress and to develop confidence in the company. Thus *The Chandelier*, the house journal of the Trust House Forte Hotels group combines articles on fashion, travel and topographical material with features about new company ventures, such as descriptions of newly built hotels. *Renault News* issued quarterly by the British distributors for Renault cars is another typical example of this type of external house journal.

A number of the largest business houses issue more than one external house journal aimed at different sectors of their clientele. The most typical addition to a basic, general journal is one of technical interest. This can take the form of serious technical papers, based on the reports of the firm's research department, for example, *G.E.C. Journal of Science and Technology*. Another type of technical journal is that developed by appropriate firms as a means of informing retailers and do-it-yourself enthusiasts of new processes and techniques: *Marley News* from the Marley Tile Company is one example. Another type is aimed at informing and motivating dealers and distributors of the company products.

The precise emphasis to place upon these periodicals in the library is difficult to determine. As already indicated, the bank journals can often be regarded as serious and invaluable items of library stock in business and academic libraries and in major public reference libraries, but elsewhere they might be used as interesting current-affairs material which is, however, quickly disposable. This is the status of most general-interest journals. External house journals are usually professionally edited and produced and the major articles are commissioned from experts. In this circumstance it is often valuable to check through any such material received in the library in case there are items which might be extracted to add to current-information files. Such journals are sometimes lavishly illustrated in colour, and it is useful to look at them with a view to extracting material for the illustrations collections or schools library project collections. This is the theme of Adeline M. Smith's article[15] which, amongst other things, provides a number of examples of the kinds of useful material for the library which might be culled from external house journals.

INTERNAL HOUSE JOURNALS

This category is intended purely for consumption within a particular firm or factory. It is thought of as a communications medium both vertically from management to employees and back again and horizontally between departments and geographically separated parts of the firm. It is a morale-boosting, newspaper-type enterprise – indeed many house journals are in newspaper format. Internal house journals are more commonly produced than externals, but firms publishing external house journals will almost invariably have at least one internal journal. An example is *Midbank Chronicle*, the internal house journal of the Midland Bank Group, which partners their external *Midland Bank Review*. Imperial Chemical Industries is one company which publishes several internal journals and Unilever is another, although in the latter case, because the subsidiaries have individual names – T. Wall and Sons, Van den Bergh, Crosfields etc. – it is less obvious.

Internal house journals are intended to be transient in nature, reporting news items such as weddings, birthdays, retirements, long service awards, presentations and inter-departmental sports activities. They are hardly the stuff of permanent archival records for the library except, perhaps, in one special sense. Internal house journals can be valuable additions to a local history collection in places where a large unit of the journal-publishing organization is situated. The information included in the journal and, perhaps, photographs and reports on people, buildings and events will constitute useful supplementary data for local history files. This rather limited local application is the only real justification for taking internal house journals in the library.

It remains only to mention – because they exist as a sub-species – those house journals whose publishers attempt to combine both types of exercise mentioned above in one periodical: the internal/external, which is not liked by the writers on the subject, both British and American. They claim that it falls between two stools doing neither job well. This is probably so but is not a problem to bother the librarian who will collect them depending upon whether or not they aid the development of reference files in one of the ways mentioned above.

Most house journals, internal and external, will be made available to libraries by their publishers. In most instances they are free but in a few, chiefly external, cases a small charge is levied. The charge is purely nominal in these cases and corresponds to that levied for its purchase by employees of the firm, since some firms argue, probably correctly, that their employees will value that which they have paid for – however little that is – more than something distributed freely. The revenue raised, incidentally, usually goes into a staff welfare fund rather than into a publications account.

NEWSPAPERS

Merrill[16] recognizes a number of categories of newspaper and grades them into very finely divided groups with primary, secondary and tertiary élites, a near élite through to a group he terms 'middle area general newspapers', and finally to the preponderant 'mass (popular) papers mainly entertainment oriented'. It is a more rigorous categorization than that commonly used in the United Kingdom – grouping into 'quality' and 'others', the others sometimes perjoratively being described as 'the Yellow Press'.

Merrill defines a quality newspaper as: 'a courageous, independent, news/views oriented journal published in an open society'. He goes on to distinguish quality from prestige by offering the following definition of a newspaper with prestige: 'A serious journal of some power élite, concerned with dogma or policy dissemination, spokesman or propagandist for some person or group and published in a close society.'

Merrill has a great deal of difficulty in the applying of his definitions to the concept of what constitutes an élite newspaper since there are, as he says, quality newspapers which have prestige and prestige newspapers which have quality, and he instances *Le Monde* (Paris) in the one case and *Pravda* (Soviet Union) in the other. In the event he allows that prestige newspapers might also have élite status despite the fact that he normally expects independence from political bias to be the true mark of an élite newspaper. His five criteria for assessing an élite newspaper are:

1. Independence, financial stability; integrity; social conscience; good writing and editing
2. Strong opinion and interpretative emphasis; world consciousness; non-sensationalism in articles and make up
3. Emphasis upon politics, international relations, economics, social welfare, cultural endeavours, education and science
4. Concern with getting, developing, and keeping a large, intelligent, well-educated, articulate, and technically proficient staff
5. Determination to serve and help expand a well-educated, intellectual readership at home and abroad; desire to appeal to, and influence, opinion leaders everywhere

Merrill's primary élite category numbers ten newspapers: *New York Times* (New York); *Neue Zurcher Zeitung* (Zurich); *Le Monde* (Paris); *Guardian* (London/Manchester); *The Times* (London); *Pravda* (Moscow); *Jen-min Jih-pao* (Peking); *Borba* (Belgrade); *Osservatore Romane* (Vatican City); *ABC* (Madrid).

It will be noted that two British daily newspapers are found in Merrill's 'Top Ten': the *Guardian* and *The Times*. *The Times*, the only British national newspaper to publish an index, albeit tardily, is found in most libraries of any size and together with the *Guardian* and *The Daily Telegraph* it forms the British 'quality' national press (although the *Telegraph* is possibly too committed politically to rate highly on the sort of scales Merrill draws up). *The Financial Times*, though more specialized, also qualifies for the epithet 'quality'. Nationally-circulated daily morning newspapers are the backbone of the British newspaper press, with some of the largest being printed simultaneously in London, Manchester, Glasgow and (occasionally) Belfast. Williams[17] traces the rise of the current group of national morning daily newspapers and shows how they have leapfrogged over each other for periods of circulation leadership. At one time or another *The Times, Daily Mail, Daily Express* and *Daily Mirror* have all been the market leaders. Whilst the quality newspapers, except perhaps *The Daily Telegraph*, are hardly competing in terms of circulation with the mass circulation press, Williams draws attention to a remarkable manifestation in the past twenty years of pressure upon what he terms the 'middle group' which has seen both the quality and tabloid newspapers increase their share at the expense of this group and forcing once powerful organs like the *Daily Sketch* and *News Chronicle* into liquidation. In the library the quality items appear as of right for their authority and news value, while the rest are judged to provide a broad basis of representation of views and also, more negatively perhaps, a means of avoiding disputes and accusations of bias.

In the United Kingdom the newspaper press splits into the following groups: national (i.e. London) morning dailies; provincial/regional morning dailies; provincial/regional (including London) evening dailies; Sunday newspapers; and provincial/regional weeklies. The United Kingdom has always had a strong tradition of high quality regional newspapers for as long as there have been national dailies in competition with them. Some of them like the *Yorkshire Post* (Leeds), the *Western Mail* (Cardiff) and the *Birmingham Post* withstand competition throughout their regions from the nationals and, indeed, manage to acquire a certain national status through the quality of their reporting of national as well as local issues. *The Scotsman* (Edinburgh) and the *Belfast Newsletter* would probably regard themselves as in a sense national for their regions. Most regional newspapers are parts of newspaper groups, for example Westminster Press, which has interests in a wide range of newspapers and, periodicals. A few, of which the *Yorkshire Post* is one example, remain sturdily independent. Most provincial regional morning daily newspapers run in tandem with evening daily newspapers which offer a good deal of material support to them after the well-known fashion of the *Manchester Evening News* and the *Guardian.* The evening newspapers, lacking competition from national sources, are often able to run up very high circulation figures usually in much more limited areas than their morning counterparts. Unlike the morning provincial regional dailies, whose attempts to merge local, national and international news and features gives them a certain potential as library material to provide balance and breadth to a collection or current display, the evening dailies have little more than parochial interest.

The pressure on the middle group noted by Williams[17] in respect of the national morning daily newspapers is even more marked in the Sunday newspapers. Except for a few examples – the *Sunday Sun*, the *Sunday Mercury*, and the *Sunday Post* – mostly with small circulations, the market is almost totally national and the polarization almost complete. Only the *Sunday Express* remains as a representative of the middle ground, five others having died out since the Second World War. At one extreme lie the quality papers attempting broad coverage of news, views, information and entertainment: *The Sunday Times*, *The Observer* and *The Sunday Telegraph.* The most self-conscious of its 'quality' is *The Observer*, and it is the most chronically short of circulation. *The Sunday Telegraph* is a late comer trying to establish itself alongside the others; it recently shifted its weekly colour supplement (an idea begun by the other two some years ago to boost advertising revenue and circulation) from the Friday issue of *The Daily Telegraph* to *The Sunday Telegraph.* An attempt to lift itself further into economic independence it must put even more pressure on the independent but suffering *Observer. The Sunday Times* has broadened its appeal in recent years to the point where it qualifies, by Williams' definition, more for 'high middle' than outright 'quality' classification. The rest – *News of the World, Sunday People, Sunday Mirror* – are useful in libraries only in the limited manner already indicated: for the researching of social history and customs. The quality Sunday newspapers themselves do not lend themselves to archival storage, after the manner of *The Times*. In public libraries they are useful for their book review sections, indicating the nature and strength of Monday-morning requests likely to arise. For all types of library their colour supplements provide occasional sources of pictorial information and feature articles to supplement current-information files but the library is rare that will want to store them permanently.

The great strength of the provincial press is in its vast number of local newspapers both daily in the evenings and, more commonly, weekly. Whereas a national morning daily feels threatened with a circulation of less than two million daily, and even a provincial/regional morning newspaper wants more than one hundred thousand and then looks to its evening stablemate for help with the overheads, the local newspapers thrive on selling as few as five thousand a week. Their backbone is local advertising supported by syndicated national efforts. Their interest in the national and international news is restricted purely to its impact upon local affairs and even then is likely to be edged off the front page by the results of the local agricultural show. The local newspaper is the very stuff of the local history collection in any library but is hardly significant for much more.

Overseas newspapers are increasingly imported into the United Kingdom as society becomes more cosmopolitan and many linguistic minorities produce their own newspapers (and, indeed, periodicals) for sale in the country. The characteristics, and an assessment, of the newspapers of the world are given both by Williams from the journalist's viewpoint and by Merrill who is both journalist and academic.

Newspapers carry enormous overheads in the form of expensive, and often under-utilized plant and with staffs often over-large for the tasks they need to perform, given the advances in technology, but kept artificially high by well organized trade unions dealing with, frequently, inept managements. Technological developments in the recent past have been such that given the means of improving industrial relations and easing trade union pressures many significant economies might be introduced into the production processes. Most notable of these is the linking of the typewriters of copywriting journalists directly to type-setting computers for subsequent printing by offset lithography at a fraction of the cost of traditional hot metal and rotary presses. It is a matter for speculation how soon the benefits of this type of development will become inevitable to the survival in its present form of the newspaper.

REFERENCES

1. FORD, J. L. C. *Magazines for millions: the story of specialised publications.* Carbondale, Ill.: Southern Illinois University Press, 1969.
2. SPIERS, John. *The underground and alternative press in Britain: a bibliographical guide with historical notes, published with a title and chronological index, as a companion to the underground/alternative press collection prepared for microform publication by Ann Sexsmith and Alastair Everett.* Hassocks, Sussex: Harvester, 1974.
3. PEMBERTON, John E. *The national provision of printed ephemera in the social sciences.* Warwick: University of Warwick, 1971.
4. FULTON, Len *and* BOYER, James, M. *International directory of little magazines and small presses.* Paradise, Ca.: Dustbooks Inc., 1964–1965–1965 – *annual.*
5. ENGLAND, G. and FINCH, V. *British directory of little magazines and small presses.* New Malden, Surrey: Dustbooks UK, 1974.
6. NOYCE, John. *Directory of alternative periodicals.* Brighton, Sussex: Smoothie Publications, 1974.
7. FULTON, Len. 'Amima rising: little magazines in the sixties.' *American Libraries,* 2(1), January 1971. pp. 25–47.
8. MULLER, Robert H., SPAHN, Theodore J. *and* SPAHN, Janet M. *From radical left to extreme right.* Metuchen, N.J.: Scarecrow, 1972. 2 vols.
9. SANDERS, E. 'The metamorphoses of a journal.' *Serial Slants,* 5(5), October 1954, p. 167.
10. KATZ, W. 'The pornography collection.' *Library Journal,* 96(22), 15 December 1971. pp. 4060–66.
11. KATZ, W. *Magazine selection; how to build a community oriented collection.* New York: Bowker, 1971.
12. EMERY, B. L. *and* BOTTLE, R. T. *Gratis controlled-circulation journals for the allied industries.* Rochester, New York, Upstate New York Chapter: Special Libraries Association, 1971.
13. BRITISH ASSOCIATION OF INDUSTRIAL EDITORS. *Why house journals?* London: B.A.I.E., n.d.
14. HAZLEWOOD, W. *House Journals.* London: Vista, 1963.
15. SMITH, A. M. 'The house organ: an index to free magazines. *R.Q.,* 10(4), Summer 1971. pp. 319–21.
16. MERRILL, John C. *The elite press; great newspapers of the world.* London: Pitman, 1968.
17. WILLIAMS, Lord Francis. *The right to know: the use of the world's press.* London: Longman, 1969.

Part Two
Bibliographic control of periodicals

Chapter 5
Bibliographic control

The bibliographic control of periodicals has two principal aspects. There is first what might be called external bibliographic control: this concerns the development of procedures, processes and bibliographical tools which provide the information by which periodicals or material contained within them can be recognized and made available for use. Secondly there is internal bibliographic control: the process of organizing and exploiting periodical material once it has been acquired by the individual library.

External bibliographic control is taken here to cover the bibliographic aids which provide information upon the existence, contents and location in libraries of periodicals which are current, have ceased but are still in demand, or are shortly to be published. It also encompasses past and current efforts to standardize the bibliographic description of periodicals and to provide agreed systems for abbreviating their titles. The elements in external bibliographic control are:

1. bibliographic description
2. bibliographies of periodicals
   including directories, union lists of periodicals (as auxiliary aids to verification), lists of periodicals indexed or abstracted appended to the various services, library holdings lists and library catalogues
3. guides to the analysis of the contents of periodicals
   including abstracting services, indexing services, contents lists, current awareness bulletins
4. guides to the location of files of periodicals in libraries
   including holdings of lists and union catalogues
5. the organization of cooperative systems for periodicals exploitation

Internal bibliographic control deals with the methods of acquiring, displaying and exploiting periodicals to the full by the individual library through cataloguing and listing, circulating periodicals or information bulletins about them to users, and recording their receipt.

Periodicals about periodicals are not common, although the problems of their organization and control is a major concern of many librarianship periodicals as a glance at any issue of *Library Literature* (New York: H. W. Wilson, 1921–) will show. As with most of the specialized aspects of the profession, the major material is American in origin. *Serial Slants* (1950–6) was published by the Serials Round Table of the American Library Association's Resources and Technical Services Division, and was a cyclostyled publication containing many practical hints for periodicals librarians. Its functions were taken over by *Library Resources and Technical Services* (1957– quarterly) published by the American Library Association's Resources and Technical Services Division and bringing together several previously separate but related topics. *Library Resources and Technical Services* has published at least one article in each issue on periodicals work and has an exceptionally valuable annual feature, 'Serials in Review 19– ', a literature review supported by lively comment from a guest editor. *R.Q.*, another American Library Association periodical (1961– quarterly, published by the Reference and Adult Services Division), also looks at periodicals and their problems for libraries but this time the emphasis is upon their exploitation rather than their acquisition and recording. Particularly worthwhile is an annual review article 'United States of America National Bibliographical and Abstracting Services and related activities in 19– ', which always gives considerable coverage to periodicals bibliography.

The *Serials Librarian* (New York: Haworth, 1976– quarterly) is a reversion to the pattern set by *Serial Slants* of a practical vehicle for the exchange of ideas and information on serials management, selection, acquisition and current awareness services.

Serials Review (Ann Arbor, Mich.: Pieran, 1975– quarterly) is the heavyweight in periodicals bibliography. It is the stable companion of their *Reference Services Review*, from which it broke away and expanded. *Serials Review* continues the 'Reference Serials' evaluation feature of the *Reference Serials Review* and updates Donald Haskell's pioneering bibliography of cumulative indexes to periodicals[1] – a very valuable function. *Serials Review* also analyses the additions and deletions of titles of periodicals covered by the major indexing and abstracting services and reviews critically new books and bibliographies on periodicals. An index to reviews of periodicals in over one hundred periodicals and monographs is another important feature.

In the United Kingdom, the most consistently periodicals-conscious librarianship periodicals have been ASLIB's two major works, *Journal of Documentation* (1945– quarterly) and *ASLIB Proceedings* (1957– monthly). *BLL Review* (previously *NLL Review*, 1971– quarterly) was, at its inception, primarily a house journal for the British Library Lending Division but it was later opened up to outside contributors. The British Library Lending Division is, of course, heavily concerned with the problems of the exploitation and management of periodicals and *BLL Review* is increasingly useful to the serials librarian.

Stechert-MacMillan Inc. produce the useful *Serials News* (monthly) which contains notes on new periodicals, continuations, major reference works and works in series. Separate editions for chemistry and medicine are also published and they also issue cards ($12 \cdot 5 \times 7 \cdot 5$ cm, 5×3 ins) with advance announcements of new periodicals.

REFERENCE

1. HASKELL, D. C. *Checklist of cumulative indexes to individual periodicals in the New York Public Library*, New York: New York Public Library, 1942.

Chapter 6
Bibliographic description

The lack of internationally agreed principles for the formulation of bibliographic citations of periodicals and of analytical entries from the contents of periodicals has bedevilled the bibliographic control and exploitation of periodicals. Wildly varying practices of abbreviating titles causes immense difficulty in the unequivocal recognition of them.

In 1967, the International Council of Scientific Unions and UNESCO commenced joint investigations into the feasibility of establishing a world-wide system for the coordination and control of scientific information. The result, in 1971, was UNISIST. Among the projects contributing to the foundation of UNISIST was one for developing an internationally standardized bibliographic description. The working party looking at this problem called for the establishment of an international register of periodicals, each assigned a unique, computer manipulable code, which was entitled *International Standard Serial Numbers* (ISSN) and which was in close correspondence with the *International Standard Book Numbers* (ISBN). The Library of Congress having been unable to accept the invitation to house the international headquarters necessary to maintain and develop the scheme, the headquarters were subsequently established, on the invitation of the French Government, in the Bibliothèque Nationale in Paris under the title *International Serials Data System* (ISDS). The system consists of a series of national and regional offices throughout the world whose functions are to encourage and facilitate the application of the system and the associated ISSNs to their own country's or region's periodicals, with modifications to suit local requirements where necessary, although not departing from the basic structure. The national centres will also forward data on new periodicals and, indeed, on all periodicals produced within their sphere of activity back to the international centre in Paris for incorporation into the central file. The national centres are also responsible for impressing upon periodical publishers the paramount importance of applying the ISSN to their publications. Koster[1] in a clear exposition of the history and development of project, adds the interesting note that to encourage publishers to use ISSNs might also help to encourage them not to make frequent and unnecessary title changes. The basic document recommending the establishment of the system was produced by Martin and Barnes,[2] and the ISDS International Centre[3] has produced a guidance document on its operation for the use of national governments and centres.

The *International Standard Serial Numbers* are assigned on an international basis, unlike *International Standard Book Numbers* which are assigned regionally or nationally. The massive growth of the periodical combined with the potential for error and failure to recognize a periodical as such from an incomplete citation, or to distinguish one periodical from another of the same or similar name, has necessitated a mechanism to ensure accurate, uniform dissemination of information about serials across political and linguistic boundaries.

A system of concise, unique and unambiguous code numbers for the identification of periodical titles has been developed. It is a seven digit number to which is added an eighth check digit. As Emery Koltay puts it in his description of ISSNs in *Ulrich's international periodicals directory*:

A unique correspondence exists between each assigned ISSN and the serial to which it is assigned. For each serial there is only one code number and for each code number there is only one serial.

The virtues of ISSNs are considerable. In the United States about 85 per cent of all library subscriptions to periodicals are entered through agents; in other countries the proportion is much smaller, but it is still substantial. By using ISSNs as the ordering medium the possibility of error is much reduced and the check digit is significant in this respect by enabling mis-transcribed numbers to be detected. ISSNs are eminently suited to computerized handling; indeed they were designed with this in mind, and for the recording of receipt of periodicals by that means. Through the intermediary of the computer, they can be used to generate lists and union lists of periodicals, by the application of the machine-readable data base developed as a sub-set of the MARC format by the ISDS Headquarters.

The procedure for obtaining an ISSN for a new periodical or for one otherwise not numbered is to forward a copy of the cover, title page and other bibliographic information from a typical issue to a national or regional centre or, where no such centre exists, to the international centre in Paris. The ISSN is assigned after careful bibliographic research to ensure that there is no duplication. In all cases of doubt and difficulty the ISDS Headquarters is the final arbiter. The chief causes of such difficulties are, of course, changed titles, mergers and the splitting of one periodical into two or more parts. In cases of title changes it is possible to alter the ISSN if necessary. A description of ISSNs with their historical background and an explanation of the application of check digits was included in *Ulrich's international press directory* (15th ed. 1973–4) pp. xxiii–xxvi. An International Standard is also available.[4]

The first assignments of ISSNs were made by the R. R. Bowker Company of New York. They were allocated ten thousand ISSNs to attach to the seventy thousand or so entries representing the output of forty-five thousand publishers in their three-volume bibliographic series comprising the two volumes of *Ulrich's international periodicals directory* (14th ed. 1971) and their *Irregular serials and annuals* (2nd ed. 1972). This was followed by the assignment of two hundred and twenty thousand ISSNs to the 1950–70 cumulation of the Library of Congress's *New serial titles*, also published by Bowker. These two processes created an immediate and substantial coverage of current and recently extinct material on a world-wide basis upon which the retrospective completion of a comprehensive register can be built.

Amendments, corrections, cancelled ISSNs and new assignments are listed in a bi-monthly *Bulletin de L'ISDS/ISDS Bulletin* (1974–) published by CIEPS, 20 Rue Bachaumont, Paris. It includes an annual cumulation.

Concurrent with the development of the ISSN was the project to develop an *International Standard Bibliographic Description for Serials* [ISBD(S)], although, in the first instance at least, it was also in danger of being unco-ordinated with the ISSNs. When, in 1971, the International Federation of Library Associations began drafting ISBD(S) they were concerned to harmonize it as far as possible with an earlier project for a standard description for monographs [ISBD(M)] in the hope that the same computer programmes might be used for periodicals as for monographs. This proved impossible because of the manifold problems of the unequivocal designation of such items as title (often subject to change in mid-publication in the periodical), publisher (subject to mergers, take overs etc. in mid-publication) and frequency changes. It also became clear that the need in the assignment of ISSNs for a clear, unambiguous title would not be served by the application of the title suggested as appropriate by the standard cataloguing codes. For the purposes of ISSNs a 'key title' was developed which departed from the strict doctrine of the codes. The result might have been a separate system of cataloguing for the national bibliography based upon an ISBD(S) slavishly following the ISBD(M), and the ISDS/ISSN system being used by the national centres of ISDS. In the event the ISBD(S) gave way and the development of the two projects was co-ordinated with the 'key title' concept being accepted for ISBD(S). Apart from this and some other fundamental differences dictated by the complexities of the periodical field, an attempt is made to follow the standard for monographs, ISBD(M), completely.

The elements suggested as appropriate for the full bibliographic description of a periodical in, say, a national bibliography using the ISBD(S) are as follows:

1. Key title
2. Parallel title, sub-titles, other titles
3. Statement of authorship
4. Place of publication
5. Publisher
6. Date of commencement and numbering practice
7. Place of printing

8. Printer
9. Illustrations
10. Size
11. Material issued as supplements to main sequence
12. Series statement
13. Notes (any additional information thought necessary)
14. ISSN and price

The full standard[5] gives very detailed prescriptions for the correct method of punctuation and presentation of the elements.

The ISBD(S) marks a fundamental departure in periodicals cataloguing and must, if strictly applied, improve bibliographic and cataloguing practice, which has never been a particularly effective area of the librarian's work. It differs considerably from the *Anglo-American cataloguing code rules*, especially in the designation of titles, and there seems to be no alternative to the alteration of the Rules.

CODEN FOR PERIODICAL TITLES

Not everybody is enthusiastic about the development of the International Standard Serial Numbers programme. In particular disagreement are the proponents of the CODEN system developed by the American Society for Testing and Materials, fully titled *CODEN for periodical titles.*[6] Donald P. Hammer[7] critically appraised the system but in the days before the development of ISSNs. It is based upon alphabetical characters rather than numbers and periodical titles are represented by five or six letter groups. Five letters describe the periodical title and a sixth can act as an optional check letter, to assist in the recognition of errors. The American Chemical Society took an early lead in the adoption of the system – the CODEN symbols for the *Journal of the American Chemical Society* are JACS-AT. The first four letters represent the title – and in this case as in many others they are instantly memorable – the fifth letter after the hyphen is a field code, used simply to extend the range of the four letter codes by a factor of 26, by the allocation of B-Z. After all possible four-letter combinations have been used they can be repeated in the field B, C, D and so on. The CODEN system was developed more than twenty years ago. It relates only to science and technology periodicals, not because of any inherent disability to encompass others but because it was conceived as a means of reducing the bulk of bibliographic records held in the data banks of major abstracting and indexing services, and these are largely science and technology based. Over one hundred thousand assignments of CODEN to periodical titles have been made but with the evolution of the ISSN there must be a question mark over their future. Batik[8] describes the CODEN system in detail and considers its future.

Andrew D. Osborn[9] leaves us in no doubt where his own sympathies lie:

> The proposed Standard Serial Number is not a coding that should be adopted; it is too easy to transpose digits and the SSN is not meaningful . . . its (i.e. CODEN's) notation is short and meaningful and can be successfully applied to either manual or computer systems.

Having advocated the CODEN system as superior for checking purposes, he goes on to deplore the evolution of the ISSN (and the earlier American system devised by the Library of Congress – Standard Serial Numbers [SSN]) as a calamity. CODEN, he says firmly, is preferable for all library operations and he dismisses ISSNs, quite wrongly, as a device generated solely for the book trade. Certainly there is justice in Osborn's case for the semi-mnemonic qualities of the CODEN system, but only in those countries where the Roman alphabet is used. The Arabic numbers employed by ISSNs have a much wider international currency and this must surely offset the presumed advantages of mnemonics in the CODEN system, while the restriction of CODEN only to science and technology periodicals is a further limitation. Provision has been made in the computer programmes associated with ISSNs for the conversion of CODEN to ISSNs and there seems little doubt that in the long term libraries heavily committed to CODEN face a considerable task in changing to ISSNs. The Chemical Abstracts Service took over the responsibility for the administration of CODEN in 1975.

ABBREVIATION OF PERIODICAL TITLES

Several attempts have been made to devise acceptable systems for the abbreviation of periodical titles. With the growth of the major abstracting services, economizing upon the amount of wordage associated with the bibliographic citation was an obvious means of keeping bulk within bounds and making savings upon production and distribution costs. If, however, such savings are made by the introduction of 'home-made' systems of abbreviation, each bearing no relation to those of other major bibliographic services, then the resultant confusion for the user would be very expensive indeed. A number of standard systems have been devised. One is the system devised for the *World list of scientific periodicals* (London: Butterworth, 4th ed., 1965, 3 vols). Another, already referred to, is the *CODEN for periodical titles* which has been used by the American Chemical Society's *Chemical Abstracts Service* for a number of years. Various national standards bodies have addressed themselves to the task of developing acceptable standards of practice. The standards devised by the British Standards Institution[10] and the American National Standards Institute[11] correspond quite closely and have had a considerable influence upon the formulation of an International Standard.[12]

REFERENCES

1. KOSTER, C. J. 'ISDS and the functions and activities of national centres.' *UNESCO Bulletin for Libraries*, 27(4), July–August 1973. pp. 199–204.
2. MARTIN, M. D. *and* BARNES, C. I. *Report on the feasibility of an International Serials Data System, prepared for UNISIST/ICSU-AB working group on bibliographic descriptions*. London: INSPEC/Institution of Electrical Engineers, 1970. (DM/CB/284).
3. UNISIST, International Serials Data System. *Guide lines for ISDS*. Paris: UNISIST, 1973. (ISDS/IC/2.2).
4. INTERNATIONAL ORGANIZATION FOR STANDARDIZATION. *Documentation-international standard serial numbering (ISSN)*. Paris: ISO/DIS 3297, 1973.
5. INTERNATIONAL FEDERATION OF LIBRARY ASSOCIATIONS, Committee on Cataloguing. *ISBD(S) International standard bibliographic description of serials . . .* London: The Committee, c/o British Library Reference Division, 1974.
6. AMERICAN SOCIETY FOR TESTING AND MATERIALS, Special Committee on Numerical Reference Data. *CODEN for periodical titles (ASTM Data Series DS 23)*. 2 vols & supplements.

7. HAMMER, Donald P. 'A review of the ASTM *CODEN for periodical titles.*' *Library Resources and Technical Services*, 12(3), Summer 1973. pp. 359–65.
8. BATIK, A. L. 'The CODEN system.' *Journal of Chemical Documentation*, 13(3), August 1973. pp. 111–113.
9. OSBORN, Andrew D. *Serial publications: their place and treatment in libraries.* Chicago: American Library Association, 2nd ed., 1973. pp. 132–4.
10. BRITISH STANDARDS INSTITUTION. *Abbreviations of titles of periodicals.* London: BSI, BSS 4148:1970.
11. AMERICAN NATIONAL STANDARDS INSTITUTE. *American standard for periodical title abbreviations* Z39.5, 1969. New York: ANSI.
12. INTERNATIONAL ORGANIZATION FOR STANDARDIZATION. *International code for the abbreviation of titles of periodicals.* Paris: ISO, 4:1972.

Chapter 7
Bibliographies of periodicals

The practice of the *British national bibliography* of including an entry in their lists of the full bibliographical details of the first issue of a new periodical, or the first issue of an established periodical after a change of name, is a considerable advance upon the practice of most current national bibliographies of books. This plus point for British bibliography has to be balanced against the fact that there is no official comprehensive current bibliography of periodicals in the United Kingdom of the kind advocated as vital for the national bibliography of a country by Knud Larsen[1] and exemplified by Supplement A to *Bibliographie de la France*, which is the official inventory of current periodicals in France.

For adequate bibliographic control, periodical publications must have their own detailed bibliographic apparatus including a list of titles published. Gray[2] and Besterman[3] have published lists of available bibliographies of periodicals, and Myatt[4] a simple checklist based upon the holdings of guides to periodical literature at the British Library Lending Division. Vesenyi[5] has analysed the problems of achieving current bibliographic control of periodicals and provided an annotated bibliography of major bibliographies on an international basis. This work can be updated by a UNESCO series[6] which deals, amongst other things, with periodical bibliographies. Fowler[7] provides a useful, although dated, subject guide to bibliographies of scientific periodicals.

Current bibliographic control is achieved by a variety of guides designed not only for use in libraries but also in publishing, bookselling and advertising. In size and coverage, the most massive bibliography is that stemming originally from the work of the Library of Congress and published under the title *New serial titles*. This began in 1951 as a cumulative bibliography issued eight times a year, cumulating quarterly and annually. It records periodical titles commencing on and after 1 January 1950. Strictly speaking this is not a bibliography at all but a union list of periodicals (see below) providing details of the location in major US libraries of new-published periodicals. In this sense it is a continuation of the five-volume *Union list of serials in the United States and Canada* (New York: H. W. Wilson, 3rd ed., 1965). It is timely to remember that union lists of periodicals are an important source of bibliographical verification, though they normally provide too little in the way of publication details to qualify as true bibliographies.

New serial titles can be considered as more than a simple union list for a variety of reasons. It is a cumulative work and provides prompt information upon newly published titles. It also has a supplementary series providing classification by subject. None of these are standard union list features. The first twenty years of *New serial titles* are now available in a four-volume work:

> *New serial titles 1950–1970: A union list of serials commencing publication after December 31st 1949* (New York: Bowker, 1974).

This is a cumulation and re-editing of the previous (seven) cumulations of the series published by the Library of Congress. It embodies details of some 220,000 periodicals providing information on commencement and cessation dates (where appropriate), Dewey class number, and data on holdings in 800 major libraries in the United States and Canada to a total of 1,700,000 locations, including 200,000 new ones added for this particular cumulation. More than 60,000 duplicate entries in the original parts had to be removed, but a further 43,000 were added, incorporating revisions and corrections, and details of new holdings. The whole work was compiled by sophisticated computer techniques, using optical character recognition to produce input to the computer from the seven individual parts, which were then edited. The four-volume work is, in effect, a visual display of a formidable computer data bank, which will play an increasingly important role in the international bibliographic control of periodicals in the future. A completely new feature of the twenty-one-year cumulation is the assignation of ISSNs to all entries. These were not, of course, included in the issues of *New serial titles* originally published by the Library of Congress.

The subject guide to *New serial titles* known as *New serial titles – classed subject arrangement* (monthly) was not cumulated at first, but there is now a companion to the main work:

New serial titles 1950–1970 : subject guide (New York: Bowker, 1975. 2 vols).

The 220,000 titles are arranged in this work under 255 subject headings and sub-arranged by 200 country designations. This arrangement is a valuable source of bibliographical information, although the small number of subject headings creates lists of five thousand or more titles under one subject heading, which is hardly conducive to easy searching, despite the large number of cross references. The *Subject guide* can not be used on its own for locations; it is necessary to refer back to the main work. Given the limitation on searching such long lists, the *Subject guide* can be used for the verification of titles suspected of being inaccurately rendered but whose subject interest is clear enough. It can be used as a checklist in the acquisition process, but again this is limited by the shortage of subject headings. Agajeenian and Keri[8] describe the way in which the work was compiled and Parr[9] provides details of its scope and intended function. Both of these articles appear in the Introduction to the work. *New serial titles 1950– 1970* will be the major international reference source for the provision of ISSN information for current and recent titles.

In terms of a true bibliography of periodicals, the most significant international title is:

Ulrich's international periodicals directory (New York: Bowker, 1932– , now published in alternate years, i.e. 15th ed. 1974; 16th ed. 1976).

The title has varied over the years and has sometimes appeared in two volumes. *Ulrich's* forms part of a series known as the *Bowker serials bibliography* of which the other elements are:

1. *Irregular serials and annuals: an international directory. A*

classified guide to current foreign and domestic serials excepting those issued more frequently than once a year (New York: Bowker, 1967– , published in alternate years). A supplement to *Bowker serials bibliography* is issued each year.

It was the *Bowker serials bibliography* series which was used as the original data base for the assignation of ISSNs, as stated earlier.

2. A new Bowker service in its first edition in 1976 is *Sources of serials* in which over nine thousand periodicals are listed under country of publication, sub-arranged alphabetically under publishers.

In all some ninety thousand titles are covered by the series, about thirty thousand of them in *Irregular serials and annuals . . .*

Ulrich's international periodicals directory provides very full bibliographical details within two hundred and fifty alphabetical subject divisions (there is a separate alphabetical index of titles). The bibliographic details provided for each entry are: title of the periodical; frequency; commencing date; publisher's name and address; subscription price; ISSN; and a specification of which of the major abstracting and indexing services cover the title. The work is international, with a bias towards North American and Latin American material. The editors take a hard line on the definition of what constitutes a periodical and the coverage is restricted to those items which have a serious informational role.

Benn's guide to newspapers and periodicals of the world: newspaper press directory (London: Benn, 1846– annual).

This work is primarily intended for the newspaper, periodical and advertising agency trade. The first main part deals with British newspapers, periodicals and directories, and also includes house journals; the second part is an international directory with notes on a wide selection of newspapers and periodicals in many countries. Further subsidiary sections provide information on television and radio in the United Kingdom, and on the press, advertising and printing trades organizations.

The British section is sub-divided into nearly twenty parts providing a series of broad categories of newspapers and periodicals, and regional groupings with subject and topographical indexes. The clear and detailed entries and the guide cards with index thumb tabs to mark sections make the Guide particularly easy to use. The nature of the listings clearly indicate that the work is basically for the advertising industry, but it is of value to the librarian both for the placement of subscriptions and for bibliographic purposes. Within its limited scope, it is a more comprehensible volume for the library user to handle than *Ulrich's*, with its over-large subject groups and obscure index.

Willings press guide (London: Skinners Directory, 1874–
annual, 102nd ed. 1976).

This is another long established British source. It gives the names of the advertising and circulation managers as well as of the editors of each title listed, indicating that this work too is more for the advertising trade than the librarian. *Willings* is principally a guide to British newspapers, periodicals and annuals (7,715 in 1976) with a selection (3,497 in 1976) from 26 European countries and the United Nations Organization and from the United States (908 in 1976). Alphabetically arranged by title within each group there is also a classified index, a topographical/regional listing of British materials, and a list of publishers' addresses. There is also a directory of press cuttings agencies and cinema newsreel producers. A typical entry is brief but bibliographically fairly complete. In the 1976 issue, house journals and free newspapers were listed for the first time.

Current bibliography on an international scale is also assisted by individual listings of the periodical holdings of particular libraries although, as in the case of *New serial titles* and similar works, the bibliographical value is largely in the verification of citations of titles as an evidence of the existence of a periodical rather than as a true bibliography. For example:

British Library Lending Division.
Current serials received September 1975. Boston Spa, the
British Library Lending Division. 1975.

This list is frequently revised: that for September 1975 carries 45,500 entries alphabetically arranged by title but carrying little else in the way of bibliographic detail. Another similar item is:

Serials keyword index. Berkeley, Ca. University of California, Library Systems Office. 1975.

This work contains 125,000 titles indexed by every significant word of the title.

Other important auxiliary aids to bibliographic control include those lists of periodicals regularly indexed or abstracted which are published as part of indexing and abstracting services or as separate items, for example:

BIOSIS list of serials: with CODEN title abbreviations, new, changed and ceased titles. Philadelphia, Pa.: Biosciences Information Service of Biological abstracts. Annual.

CAS source index (CASSI). Columbus, Ohio: Chemical Abstracts Service. Annual.

Publications indexed for engineering (PIE). New York: Engineering Index Inc. Annual.

The entries in sources such as these, as in the preliminaries to the H. W. Wilson indexes, are usually very full and provide very effective bibliographic assistance.

Periodicals news issued by the British Library Science Reference Library is one example among many of sources designed to provide information upon new titles published, cessations and title changes. Catalogues of publishers, periodical subscription agencies and microfilm and reprint-publishers are also worth remembering as auxiliary bibliographical aids. Periodicals subscription agents give news of new titles, title changes for example. Microfilming organizations that provide detailed lists of their publications in bibliographic catalogue form include:

XEROX UNIVERSITY MICROFILMS. *Serials in microform* and supplements. Ann Arbor, Mich.: Xerox University Microfilms.

MICROCARD EDITIONS. *Microfiche and microfilm 1975 publications*. Englewood, Colo.: Microcard Editions.

It is not only in microform that reprints of periodicals are made. Full sized xerographic copies from microfilm or micro-fiche stock are also produced as are photo-litho offset versions of periodicals. A bibliography of this latter is:

> WILLIAMS, S. P., *Reprints in print – serials*. Dobbs Ferry, N.Y.: Oceana.

Individual reprint publishers such as Johnson Reprint Corporation, The Kraus–Thomson Organization and H. Pordes, publish catalogues of value as bibliographic aids.

National bibliographic control is variously organized throughout the world. Neither in the United Kingdom nor in the United States is it possible to point to an officially sponsored bibliography of periodicals as is possible in many other countries. For the United Kingdom *Newspaper press directory* and *Willings press guide* provide the most comprehensive sources. *Willings*, particularly, includes items which can be called 'periodicals' and 'newspapers' only by the most generous definition as well as annuals, directories and yearbooks. More selective, though bibliographically more complete, is:

> Woodworth, David, *Guide to current British periodicals*. London: Library Association, 1970– triennial. 2 vols.

'British' in this work refers to Great Britain, Northern Ireland, the Isle of Man and the Channel Islands, and there are also some Irish Republic items. Certain categories are excluded: parish magazines, 'fan' magazines, the daily press, some children's periodicals – especially comics and student publications unless containing some serious informational material. It is arranged according to the Universal Decimal Classification, and in addition to supplying the standard bibliographic data, the entries give such useful information as whether there is a title page or index, and when and in which of the periodical indexing services the periodical is indexed. An interesting feature is that there are symbols to indicate the level of appeal of periodicals listed. In the second volume is a directory of publishers of periodicals and their addresses.

In the United States the pattern is somewhat different, much of the current bibliography being provided for the specialist use of various parts of the periodical trade, but it is also useful for libraries. For example:

N. W. Ayer and Sons directory of publications (Philadelphia, Pa.: N. W. Ayer, 1880– annual).

This is a directory of some twenty-five thousand newspapers and periodicals in the United States and Canada principally intended for the periodical, newspaper and advertising industries. Its arrangement is geographical – by States and then by individual towns and cities – with alphabetical and subject indexes. It includes details of certified circulation figures for each title listed.

For the librarian, the subject approach of publications like *Ulrich's international periodical directory* is more appropriate but its limitation to the more serious periodicals makes it less effective as a complete bibliography than:

Standard periodical directory (New York: Oxbridge, 1964– irregular).

Some 63,000 periodicals and newspapers are listed under over 200 subject headings with an alphabetical index of titles. The definition of periodical in this case is much wider and includes house journals, directories and recreational and ephemeral items.

There is a strong tradition in the United States in librarianship circles of producing selective listings of library materials for a variety of purposes in different types of library. This is typified for book publications by the H. W. Wilson Company's *Standard catalog* series which includes books selected for their value for particular types of library, for example *Junior high school library catalog*. There are a number of works of similar intent devoted to the periodical press. The most noteworthy and comprehensive is:

KATZ, Bill *and* GARGAL, Berry. *Magazines for libraries: for the general reader and public, school, junior colleges and college libraries*. New York: Bowker, 1969– every three years, with intermediate supplements.

Based upon Bill Katz's 'Magazines' column in *Library Journal*, this selective bibliography is critically and subjectively annotated and is a classified order of some 5,000 or more periodicals judged 'best' by referring to the published indexes, user surveys, and the holdings of various libraries considered

4

by the compilers to have effective periodicals collections, and by consulting a number of librarians. It covers principally United States material, although some British and other foreign periodicals are included. There are appendices for newspapers and little magazines. Notes on each entry indicate if the particular periodical is refereed and provide the date of the last issue of a particular volume. Also appended are suggested select lists for different purposes and different libraries.

Of similar intent, although for a more selective audience than *Magazines for libraries* is:

SCOTT, M. H., *Periodicals in School Libraries*. Chicago: American Library Association, 1973.

Of similar scope for the British market is:

WAITE, C. A., *Periodicals for schools: an annotated list*. London: School Library Association, 1969.

Choice, produced ten times a year by the Association of College and Research Libraries Division of the American Library Association has regular features on 'Periodicals for College Libraries' which supplements:

FARBER, E., *Classified list of periodicals for the college library*. Westwood, Mass.: F. W. Faxon, 1972.

Bibliographic control is also assisted by a vast array of subject listings. These range from attempts at comprehensive inventories of all periodicals published anywhere in the world relating to a particular subject field, to lists of periodicals in particular subject fields published in one country, or lists of the periodical holdings in a specific subject of one library. The following are examples of each category drawn at random from the large number of available listings of this sort:

ANDREWS, T. and OSLET, J. *World list of pharmacy periodicals*. Washington: American Society of Hospital Pharmacists, 1975.

DENNISON, A. T. 'Philosophy periodicals: an annotated select world list of current serials publications.' *International Library Review*, 2(3), July 1970. pp. 355–86.

JACKSON, G. and BRADLEY, O. *Mathematics and statistics*

periodicals held by the Science Reference Library. London: British Library, Science Reference Library, 1976.

MAISON DES SCIENCES DE L'HOMME. *World list of specialized periodicals in African studies*. Paris: Mouton, 1969.

NATIONAL RESEARCH COUNCIL, CANADA. *Directory of Canadian scientific and technical periodicals*. Ottawa: N.R.C., 1969.

PLUSCAUSKAS, M. *Canadian serials directory/Repertoire des publications seriées Canadiennes*. Toronto: Toronto University Press, 2nd ed., 1976.

SASSOON, G. J. *Current Japanese journals containing articles on pure chemistry*. London: British Library, Science Reference Library, 1972.

UNION OF INTERNATIONAL ASSOCIATIONS. *Directory of periodicals published by international organizations*. Brussels: U.I.A., 3rd ed., 1969.

VESENYI, P. E. *European periodical literature in the social sciences and humanities*. Metuchen, N.J.: Scarecrow, 1969.

WOODWARD, A. M. *Directory of review serials in science and technology*. London: ASLIB, 1974.

RETROSPECTIVE BIBLIOGRAPHIES OF PERIODICALS

One of the most effective ways of checking the existence of non-current periodicals and verifying correct titles is to use the major union lists. As was indicated earlier, there have been several millions of periodicals published at one time or another throughout the world which are no longer currently available. Although, obviously, none of the union lists approaches a comprehensive coverage of a fraction of them, they do have the virtue of being based upon actual inspection of titles in libraries and therefore provide reliable bibliographic data.

The more formal bibliography of periodicals is, of course, most effectively listed by the bibliographies of bibliographies mentioned earlier. The back files of copies of the current bibliographies will also give useful retrospective coverage, but such files will only be found in the major libraries. More accessible are the volumes of the various national library printed catalogues, for example:

BRITISH MUSEUM, Department of Printed Books. *Catalogue of the printed books in the Library of the British Museum: periodical publications.* London: British Museum, 1899–1900.

This bibliography lists some 25,000 titles with a title index. There is no title index to the more recent edition of the same work:

BRITISH MUSEUM, Department of Printed Books. *General Catalogue of Printed Books*, vols 184–6. 'Periodical Publications.' London: British Museum, 1963.

A four-volume series from the Bibliothèque Nationale is both a bibliography and a union list:

BIBLIOTHÈQUE NATIONALE, Départment des Périodiques. *Catalogue collectif des périodiques du début du XVIIe siècle à 1939 conservés dans les bibliothèques universitaires du départment.* Paris: Bibliothèque Nationale, 1967–9. 4 vols.

There are numerous examples of library catalogues of periodical publications and, of course, the guides to the literature in various subject fields are a source of reference to bibliographies and catalogues of periodicals and, indeed, to important examples of actual periodicals. They are often critical and evaluative. Two examples are:

MELLON, M. G. *Chemical publications: their nature and use.* New York: McGraw-Hill, 1965.

WHITFORD, R. H. *Physics literature: a reference manual.* Washington: Scarecrow, 1968.

REFERENCES

1. LARSEN, Knud, *National bibliographical services: their creation and operation.* Paris: UNESCO, 1953.
2. GRAY, R. A. *Serials bibliographies in the Humanities and Social Sciences.* Ann Arbor, Mich.: Pieran, 1969.
3. BESTERMAN, T. *Periodical publications: a bibliography of bibliographies.* Totowa, N. J.: Rowman and Littlefield., 1971. 2 vols.
4. MYATT, A. G. *Keyword index of guides to the serial literature.* Boston Spa, Yorks.: British Library Lending Division, 1974.

5. VESENYI, P. E. *An introduction to periodicals bibliography.* Ann Arbor, Mich.: Pieran, 1974.
6. UNESCO. *Bibliographical services throughout the world.* Paris: UNESCO. Annual at first, now every five years.
7. FOWLER, M. J. *Guides to scientific periodicals.* London: Library Association, 1966.
8. AGAJEENIAN, R. *and* KERI, T. 'The making of *New serial titles 1950–1970: a subject guide*' in the *Introduction* to that work and *Serials Review*, 1 (4), Oct.–Dec. 1975. pp. 89–93.
9. PARR, T. 'New dimensions in *New serial titles* . . .' in the Introduction to that work.

Chapter 8
Guides to the contents of periodicals – Abstracts

The vast numbers of periodicals published renders the prospects of reading the material contained in even a tiny fraction of them very slim. Kronick[1] notes that two hundred years ago the person who could cope with four hundred periodicals a year could be reasonably assured of keeping up to date with new developments over the whole of science and technology. Today the regular reading of four hundred periodicals would hardly ensure a comprehensive international coverage of such relatively narrow fields of knowledge as, say, bee keeping, domestic science, industrial health and welfare, or librarianship. The burgeoning of periodicals, especially in the last fifty years, has called into existence a vast array of aids to promote awareness of what is being published in periodicals so that it can be more readily located from amongst the mass. One of the major means of creating current awareness is the abstracting service. Basically, an abstracting service is an attempt to overcome the problem of trying to read a mass of periodical literature by the production of short summaries of original articles, usually, but not always, made up into periodicals in their own right. A measure of the growth of this medium is that there were almost certainly more abstracting publications in the field of science and technology published in 1976 than there were scientific periodicals published anywhere in the world in 1826.

The earliest example of abstracting is noted by Witty[2] as having occurred in Mesopotamia in the early part of the second millennium BC when clay cuneiform tablets of important documents were sealed in clay envelopes, on the outside of which was written the full text of the enclosed document, thereby proof against tampering. Alternatively the envelope bore a summary of the contents of the document. Witty goes on to describe a number of ancient and medieval activities in the abstracting and indexing field, mainly index-ing. The early history of periodical article abstracting is covered in detail by several sources notably by Kronick, Clapp[3] and, more briefly, by Woods.[4] Kronick, whilst com-menting that 'a certain amount of foolhardiness is always involved in claiming the title "first" for any . . . bibliographic event', says that it was in 1700 that the first attempts were made to produce systematic current-awareness services based upon the material being published in periodicals. Of course Oldenburg's *Philosophical Transactions* (1665) is arguably the first systematic attempt at the summarized representation of the views and ideas of various writers, as Collison[5, 6] obviously believes. This and many of the other early works noted by Kronick, Collison and by the Paslers[7] are probably more correctly defined as review literature. Abstracting services in the form we now know them probably began with the publica-tion in 1830 in Germany of *Pharmaceutisches Zentralblatt* which later became *Chemisches Zentralblatt*, covered the periodical field in pure chemistry so effectively that by the end of the nineteenth century it had begun to provide the long, in-formative abstracts to more than 120 periodicals from many countries, which were its hallmark to the end of its life (in 1969). The British *Science Abstracts* began in 1898 and still exists as *INSPEC*, as does the more stark *Chemical Abstracts* (1907–) now the most massive and most ex-pensive of all abstracting services, matched in size only by the Russian *Referativnyi Zhurnal* (1953–) and the French *Bulletin Signalétique* (1940–). By 1920, the medium with its necessary, although cumbersome, cumulative issues was fully established.

DEFINITIONS

The Expert Committee on Scientific Abstracting, convened in 1948 to do the preliminary work for the UNESCO-sponsored Conference on Science Abstracting held in June 1949, formulated some useful definitions of the basic terms:

Abstract
A summary of a publication or article accompanied by an

adequate bibliographical description to enable the publication or article to be traced.

Indicative Abstract
A short abstract written with the intention to enable the reader to decide whether he should read the original article or publication.

Informative Abstract
A summary of the principal arguments and data of the original publication or article.

Bottle[8] elaborates upon these three basic terms by defining other terms of some significance. He distinguishes four principal categories:

Title or expanded title
Today, more and more of the better scientists and editors strive to make the title as informative as possible. A good title is often sufficient to indicate, particularly to the more experienced reader, whether the paper is of interest.

The indicative abstract
This is a very short abstract written to help the reader decide whether he should refer to the original publication.

The summary or synopsis
This is similar to the indicative abstract though it is normally sufficiently long to give an outline of the whole of the work described. Many journals require authors to write a summary of their paper. These summaries are sometimes re-published in certain abstracting journals.

The informative abstract
This is the only one of the four types which can replace, to a certain extent, the original publication. Informative abstracts summarize the principal arguments and give the principal data of the original article and are thus often used in information retrieval systems, e.g. *Chemical Abstracts* and many specialized and personal indexes. Such abstracting is, of course, very time consuming and expensive . . .

Borko and Chatman[9] give even more explicit definitions in an important study supported by one hundred and thirty citations:

> The informative abstract . . . is more really a condensation of the information in the report. It contains the principal ideas, methods and data but omits excess wordage and detailed explanation . . . The indicative or descriptive abstract consists of generalized statements of the content of the article, is ordinarily shorter than the other type and is characterized primarily by the absence of qualitative and quantitive data. It is often little more than a listing of the principal subjects presented in narrative form . . .

Borko and Chatman illustrate the difference in approach of the two types of abstract with examples of each, a technique also effectively used by Bernier.[10] Bernier also presents nine reasons for the usefulness of abstracts which, in summary, are:

1. abstracts help to select documents to translate from the many languages of original publication
2. abstracts enable readers to select the most important material quickly
3. informative abstracts can be a substitute for original articles
4. abstracts save time in selecting material to include in selective bibliographies
5. abstracts are more convenient to arrange in related groups than original articles
6. indexed abstracting services greatly facilitate retrospective literature searching
7. as compared to indexes, abstracts are likely to increase accuracy in literature selection
8. abstracts are usually published in only one language thus making the task of indexing quicker than from original documents published in a variety of languages
9. abstracts facilitate the organization of articles, books, etc.; they can be photocopied, cut up and arranged in a variety of ways impossible with whole originals

Two other abstracting terms frequently encountered are 'author abstract' and 'auto abstract'. Author abstract means more or less what it says, and is an abstract which has been compiled by the author of the original article. This is a practice increasingly employed by periodical publishers who reproduce the abstract at the beginning of the article and, often, as Bottle implies (see above), they may be re-used as entries in current-awareness bulletins or abstracting services. Author abstracts are not always as effective as they might theoretically appear to be, since not many authors are also skilful abstractors and the results can often be notably uninformative about the nature of their work.

Auto abstracting, on the other hand, does not really mean what it seems to mean. Auto abstracts are not the product of magical machines which can devour a mass of complex printed material, digest it, and disgorge at great speed brilliant, succinct summaries. Rather is it a process by which the computer is programmed to recognize key words, phrases, sentences, formulae and tables, in the original articles so as to produce cryptic summaries of the originals. The human selection of material in the same way can also be termed auto abstracting. Properly done, it is a quick and reasonably effective substitute for orthodox abstracting, although the abstracts are usually not especially readable, being telegraphic in style. If the machinery is not programmed carefully they can be downright misleading. The Thomson Ramo Woolridge Corporation,[11] I.B.M. inc.,[12] Rath *et al*[13] and Push *et al,*[14] discuss several methods of auto abstracting.

NUMBERS AND NATURE OF ABSTRACTING SERVICES

Indicative abstracts are usually 50–150 words long; informative are rather longer – perhaps as many as 500 words. The typical abstract consists of two principal elements: the first is a bibliographic citation sufficiently detailed to enable the source of the original item to be unequivocally recognized; the second is the abstract itself which in the best of circumstances is signed by the abstractor – usually with initials only.

Abstracts are published in a variety of ways. First and best known are the commercially published, so-called abstracting services. Most commonly these appear in the form of periodicals in their own right and there are perhaps more than 5,000 of them currently published, most of them in science and technology. In 1962, Bourne[15] recognized 3,500 services being published in science and technology. They are published by government agencies, learned and professional societies (sometimes with government grants), research organizations, and occasionally by private industrial or commercial undertakings. In a relatively small number of instances they are produced by commercial publishers although the high cost of producing abstracting services makes them an unattractive proposition in view of the difficulties of making them economically sound. The major abstracting services are accompanied by a cumulative indexing structure of great detail (and this is where a good deal of the expense of their production is to be found): in the *Chemical Abstracts* service of the American Chemical Society there are as many as 600 words of index matter for every 1,000 words of abstract material. In recent years the major services have been surrounded by a mass of spin-off services, many deriving from re-processing the indexing data generated by computer for the basic service. Some abstracting services are produced in card form for libraries or other subscribers to arrange in whatever way they please.

In determining how many abstracting services there are, a difficulty arises in defining 'abstracting service', for besides free-standing services produced in periodical or index-card form there are a number which appear as a regular feature within periodicals principally devoted to publishing original articles. This mix of primary (original articles) and secondary material (abstracts of material originally published elsewhere) is quite common. Many examples of private circulation 'home made' abstracting services are also to be found. This type of service, normally produced for the benefit of an organization's staff, is sometimes made available either free or for a nominal subscription to outsiders.

Review journals with articles on the 'state of the art' in specific subject fields give extensive references to the recent literature: providing either long essays noting recent significant material and evaluating it on the pattern of the American Physical Society's quarterly *Reviews of Modern Physics* (1929–); or else short notices of material currently published, approximating more closely to the pattern of an abstracting service such as the American Mathematical Society's *Mathematical Reviews* (1940–). Review publications typically appear in annual publications with titles of the kind: *The Years Work in* . . . or *Advances in* . . . or *Annual Review of* . . ., as well as being regular features in periodicals. The *Chemical Abstracts* service publishes *C.A. Reviews Index* (CARI) which is a KWIC (key-word-in-context) index published twice a year, of all review articles appearing in *Chemical Abstracts*. Each volume refers to over 13,000 reviews. The Institute of Scientific Information Inc. began publishing *Index to Scientific Reviews* in 1975. The first volume, for 1974, identifies and indexes 20,000 reviews originally appearing in 2,700 periodicals. Woodward[16] has produced a guide to regular or quasi-regular publications containing critical state-of-the-art or literature reviews. Not all such works are abstracting type services; many are more akin to indexing services (see below).

What are abstracts for? There is no really satisfactory answer to such a question. Some commentators consider the abstract simply as a device for providing current awareness of what is being published. Others (more optimistically) see the abstract as a means of coping with published material in expanding areas of knowledge by supplying the means of reading more widely more quickly without needing to seek the originals. In the cliché-ridden words of the librarianship student this is invariably rendered as 'saves valuable time by providing all the information of the original without all of the unnecessary words making the reading of the original article superfluous'. Would that such sentiments were correct, but it is open to serious question whether this is so. Most authorities agree that the indicative abstract is merely a means of alerting readers to the nature of the contents of an article – in fact an elaboration of the title. Indeed, 'annotated indexing' is often employed as a synonym for indicative abstracting. The indicative abstract 'saves valuable time' simply by indicating that certain originals may not be worth the trouble of locating and retrieving.

The informative abstract is less easy to characterize. It can save valuable time in the same way as the indicative abstract, perhaps providing even more reassurance that the literary dross *is* really dross. Because informative abstracts provide material on methods and results they do, perhaps, clarify issues in less significant material sufficiently to render its reading in the original unnecessary. However, one cannot suggest that informative abstracts will serve to render the reading of all originals unnecessary. The very production of abstracts is, in a sense, the acknowledgement of defeat, indicating the literature is too large for anyone to be able to read all originals. As will be shown later, where originals are inaccessible because they are published in little known foreign languages or in periodicals not widely available, the informative abstract achieves greater significance by being better than nothing at all. This is especially so since the practice of many abstracting services is to provide fuller abstracts in such cases. Most clichés do, however, contain a grain of truth and the frequent references to 'unnecessary words' in originals, when extolling the virtues of abstracts, is a reminder of the attempts to limit the length of original articles and to construct more pointed articles. The 'terse literature' process described by Charles Bernier[10] is one example.

There are other reasons why an abstract cannot be a totally effective substitute for an original article. It relies far too much on trust in the competence of abstracters. How can one be sure that the abstracter has faithfully reflected the meaning and significance of the original? A good abstracter can, as a matter of fact, materially assist by clarifying the message of a poor writer. But just as common is the situation in which the abstracter is so good at his work that a poorly-conceived and not very significant original is made to look better than it in fact is, to the considerable annoyance of anyone who might be led thereby to seek out the original. On the other hand, poor abstracting can seriously understate the value of an original article or even distort its message out of all recognition. No matter how vigilant the editors are, variations in the quality of abstracters can never wholly be overcome. Abstracting services, it must be stressed, are secondary sources only, and it is as unwise to overstate their value (as many commentators do) as to underestimate their usefulness. Borko and Bernier[17] present what is probably the most thorough analysis of the history, nature and techniques of abstracting and of the publication of abstracting services. There is an International Standard *Abstracts and synopses* ISO/R/214.

BIBLIOGRAPHIES OF ABSTRACTING SERVICES

There are not many of these. Some of the principal bibliographies are listed by Walford[18] and Sheehy (formerly Winchell),[19] both of whom also list many individual items, thus qualifying themselves as bibliographies of abstracting services. The most convenient source is probably the 'Abstracting and Indexing Services' section in *Ulrich's*.[20] The available works can conveniently be divided into three categories:

1. comprehensive bibliographies of available abstracting services
2. lists of abstracting services held by particular libraries
3. special subject listings

Examples of each category are:

1. *Comprehensive bibliographies*

INTERNATIONAL FEDERATION FOR DOCUMENTATION. *Index bibliographicus.* The Hague: FID, 1925– irregularly revised. 2 vols.

INTERNATIONAL FEDERATION FOR DOCUMENTATION. *Abstracting services in science, technology, medicine, agriculture, social sciences, humanities.* The Hague: FID, rev. ed., 1976. 2 vols.

That there are 1,500 services given in vol. one for science and technology and only 400 in vol. two for humanities and social sciences is a clear illustration of the disparity in the bibliographic control facilities available in the two areas.

NATIONAL FEDERATION OF SCIENCE ABSTRACTING AND INDEXING SERVICES. *A guide to the world's abstracting and indexing services in science and technology.* Washington: NFSAIS, 1963.

OWEN, Dolores B. *and* HANCHEY, M.M. *Abstracts and indexes in science and technology: a descriptive guide.* Metuchen, N.J.: Scarecrow, 1974.

For each of the services listed, details are given of their arrangement, coverage, scope, nature of the abstracts and type of indexing employed.

CHICOREL, Marietta, ed. *Chicorel index to abstracting and indexing services: periodicals in humanities and the social sciences.* New York: Chicorel Library, 1974. 2 vols.

This is a rather different type of bibliographic work providing an index to the abstracting services which cover some 33,000 periodicals listed in this guide.

2. *Lists of abstracting services held in particular libraries*

BRITISH LIBRARY LENDING DIVISION. *A keyword index of guides to the serial literature.* Boston Spa, Yorks.: BLLD, 1974.

MUKHERJEE, A. K. *Abstracting and bibliographical periodicals in the Science Reference Library.* London: British Library, Science Reference Library, 1975.

3. *Special subject listings*

CORNISH, G. P. *A brief guide to abstracting and indexing services relevant to the study of religion.* Harrogate: Theological Abstracting and Bibliographical Services, 1975.

DORLING, A. R. *A guide to abstracting journals for computers and computing.* London: British Library, Science Reference Library, 1972.

FRAUENDORFER, S. V. *Survey of abstracting services and current bibliographical tools in agriculture, forestry, fisheries, nutrition, veterinary medicine and related subjects.* Munich: B.L.V. Verlagsgesellschaft, 1969.

KEENAN, Stella. '*Abstracting and indexing services in the physical sciences.*' Library Trends, 16(13), January 1968.

UNITED NATIONS, Economic Commission for Europe. *Inventory of abstracting services in the fields of applied economics in the countries of the Economic Commission for Europe.* Paris: UN, 1966.

SOME OF THE MAJOR ABSTRACTING SERVICES OF THE WORLD

When the National Federation of Science Abstracting and Indexing Services list was produced in 1963 (see above), the five countries producing the largest number of services were the United States (365), Great Britain (195), West Germany (182), France (147), the Soviet Union (117). These five countries, by the great size and scope of their services, place themselves in a category of their own when compared to the vast majority of relatively small-scale services. Some of these major services are described in detail below:

1. *Chemical Abstracts* (USA)
2. *The Biosciences Information Service of Biological Abstracts* (BIOSIS) (USA)
3. *Engineering Index* (USA)
4. *Excerpta Medica* (Netherlands and USA)
5. *Bulletin Signalétique* (France)
6. *Referativnyi Zhurnal* (USSR)
7. *INSPEC* (UK)

1. *Chemical Abstracts.* Columbus, Ohio: American Chemical Society, 1907–. This is the world's largest privately-owned abstracting service. From a modest beginning of less than 12,000 abstracts in the first year, the service has grown enormously both in terms of the basic service and of the diversity of publications which it has spawned. Statistics relating to the service are almost incomprehensible in their magnitude. Nearly 14,000 periodicals and the patent specifications of 26 countries are scanned, as are many thousands of conference proceedings and monographs in fifty languages. It is especially interesting to discover that more than half of the abstracts in the service are generated from the cover-to-cover abstracting of only 258 periodicals. Abstracts from over 8,500 periodicals appear in any one year and all 14,000 are covered in any five-year period by the abstracting of at least one paper. The growth of the service can be followed by plotting the time covered by each succeeding million abstracts if published:

GROWTH OF C.A. ABSTRACTS

Abstracts published	*Year*
1st million	1907–1937
2nd million	1937–1954
3rd million	1954–1962
4th million	1962–1968
5th million	1968–1971
6th million	1971–1974
7th million	1974–1976

The growth of the Service can also be demonstrated by reference to the increasing size of the cumulative indexes which, from the first to the fifth appeared every ten years and which have since appeared every five years:

GROWTH OF C.A. INDEXES

Years of coverage	Pages of index
1907–1916	4823
1917–1926	6591
1927–1936	8459
1937–1946	12186
1947–1956	21926
1957–1961	22864
1962–1966	41626
1967–1971	75063

More than 40 per cent of the Service's manpower and 25 per cent of its budget are devoted to indexing.

Its publication frequency has been as follows: 1907–1961, fortnightly; 1961–1966, twice weekly; 1967– weekly.

Some 8,000 abstracts are published each week in a 600-page volume (including indexes). The indexes' arrangements are such that it is possible to find the documents abstracted in 19 different ways. For each volume Author, Patent, Formula, Chemical Substance and General Subject Indexes are produced. Separate publications, each consisting of a portion of the whole, in related subject groups are available, thus: *Biochemistry sections, Organic Chemistry sections, Macromolecular sections, Applied Chemistry and Chemical Engineering sections* and *Physical and Analytical Chemistry sections.* Uncumulated indexes are included in the section subscriptions but not cumulated indexes or patent references.

The abstracts are a mixture of the indicative and the informative, with the emphasis on the informative. They are produced by a full-time staff in Columbus of 1,100 with over 2,600 volunteer abstractors in 55 countries. The abstracts prepared by the volunteers are signed but the increasing number of unsigned abstracts is a sign of growing use of author abstracts in the preparation of the work, or of abstracts prepared on behalf of the Service by organizations in the United Kingdom and Western Germany.

A massive effort to computerize the Service has taken place in the last ten years or so. This has turned the basic data into an almost infinitely-manipulable body of material to be used to produce a range of spin-off services which include both print and computer tape material, for example (this is not a complete list) :

Chemical Abstracts on Microfilm (edge coded for swift search)
Chemical Titles (hard copy and computer tape)
Chemical Biological Activities (computer tape)
Polymer Science and Technology (computer tape)
C.A. Condensates (computer tape)
Ring Index (hard copy publication)
CAS Source Index (hard copy and computer tape)

The *CAS Source Index* is particularly interesting in that it demonstrates a concern for improving access to the material publicized by the production of abstracts from it. Originating as a straightforward list of the periodicals covered by the Service, it is now a locations listing of material in 400 libraries in 28 countries, published since 1830. About 30,000 scientific and technical periodicals and conference proceedings are listed.

A brief history of the CAS system has been published[21] and the Service's regularly revised handbook is a mine of facts and figures.[22] Yagello[23] has also described the system in detail, whilst its conversion to machine production was the subject of a special report in *Chemical and Engineering News*.[24] Southampton University[25] have produced a tape-slide programme on the Service in the SCONUL series. The Service has increased its international coverage in recent years (more than 60 per cent of the sales are to non-American organizations) by the development of links with the United Kingdom and with Western Germany. In 1969 the Chemical Society, representing a group of British chemically-oriented learned societies and professional bodies, and Gesellschaft Deutscher Chemiker, the publishers of *Chemisches Zentralblatt* in Western Germany, entered into an agreement with the American Chemical Society to share in the development both of a

computerized chemical information system and of the marketing operation. The European partners have assumed responsibility for producing inputs to the main data base in specific
areas, and they hold and exploit the whole of the computerized
data bank in their regions. In 1976 Internationale Doku-
mentations gesellschaft fuer Chemie (IDC), took over the
German side of the agreement.

This agreement resulted in the demise of *Chemisches Zentralblatt*, which, with its forerunners, stretches back to 1830. The
two services had run in parallel, *Chemical Abstracts* gradually
gaining superiority. Before about 1930 *Chemisches Zentralblatt*
was definitely superior in scope and coverage, but this was
gradually eroded and with it the subscription income to the
German service, whose indexing arrangements were formidably
difficult to comprehend. The skilled *Chemisches Zentralblatt* staff
were, happily, retained under the new arrangement to operate
the computer input to the Service. Bottle[26] has compared
both services.

2. *Biological Abstracts : from the world's biological research literature.*

Philadelphia, Pa.: Biological Abstracts/Biosciences Information Service 1926–. Twice monthly, cumulating quarterly,
with annual author and subject indexes.

This produces more than a quarter of a million informative
abstracts a year from over 6,000 periodicals and some books,
reports and symposia, appearing in nearly 100 countries.
The definition of the term 'biological' is very wide and includes
such fringe areas as forestry, horticulture, physiology, public
health and agronomy. About 70 per cent of the periodicals
covered are not North American.

The advent of the computer enabled the basic service to
diversify into a wide range of specialized activities under the
generic name *Biosciences Information Service* (BIOSIS). The
computerized data base has been retrospectively completed
back to 1917 taking in *Botanical Abstracts* and *Abstracts of
Bacteriology*. The computer tapes and a microfilm edition of
the service are available on lease and appear in advance of
the printed parts, and a personalized search service with a
print out of specific groups of abstracts is available.

The specialized facilities available to subscribers either on lease or purchase include:

Bioresearch Index (monthly)
Bioresearch Today (monthly in 14 parts)
Abstracts of Entomology (monthly)
Abstracts on Health Effects of Environmental Pollutants (monthly)
Abstracts of Mycology (monthly)
Biosis Previews (magnetic tape service)
BASIC (Biological Abstracts Subjects in Context)
CROSS (Computerized Re-arrangement of Subject Specialities)

In reading the results of surveys of information requirements and resources in the biological sciences it is striking to note how often *Biological Abstracts* is preferred to more specialized services. *Biological Abstracts* has been severely criticized however; and both Voigt[27] and Bottle[28] have referred to poor indexing and occasional unevenness in quality of abstract. This is presumably the result of heavy reliance upon author abstracts by the BIOSIS Service. Parkins[29] has written what might be termed the 'official' history, and the BIOSIS Marketing Bureau produces a number of descriptive leaflets on various services including a major guide.[30]

3. *Engineering Index*. 1884–. From 1934 this has been published by Engineering Index Inc., having previously been in several different hands. From 1884–1891 it was entitled *Descriptive index of current engineering literature*. The publication and ownership patterns of the early period are confusing but the service settled down as an annual publication in 1906, with an alphabetical subject order and an author index. In 1928 a card service in 249 separately-sold weekly parts was introduced, and in October 1962 the Service became monthly cumulating into the familiar annual volumes (in four parts for 1975 in 6,300 pages). A microfilm version of the annual volume is now available and a ten-year cumulative index for the years 1965–1974 in alphabetical subject order, known as *ALPHA-DEKA Microfile*, was published in 1975, covering 650,000 abstracts. In common with other major abstracting services, computerization has developed spin-off services. COMPENDEX is the

name for the computerized version of the data base, begun in 1969, which is available for consultation upon payment of a fee, or can be leased as monthly tapes issued in advance of the monthly parts.

Engineering Index defines its coverage extremely widely and ranges well outside of the fields normally recognized as engineering, but all the references are closely aligned to the needs of engineers. In 1975 some 2,000 periodicals as well as a mass of books, reports, conference and symposium proceedings were consulted to produce 89,000 indicative and informative abstracts, with an average time-lag between original publication and abstract publication of three months. There are about 12,000 subject headings in the main sequence. Three levels of coverage are used for the material abstracted: about one third of the publications is almost totally abstracted from; another third is partially covered; and the other third is monitored to ensure that 'scatter' has not meant that something significant has appeared in an otherwise insignificant source. The length of each abstract is intended to indicate the editors' estimate of the significance of the particular material. Fifty words or less implies material of lesser value, and one hundred and fifty words more important material. Woods[31] has comprehensively described the services and their history, giving a number of references to further sources. Two million abstracts had been published up to April 1975. Creps and Carrigy[32] have discussed the role of *Engineering Index* in the development of a macro information network.

4. *Excerpta Medica*, Amsterdam: Excerpta Medica Foundation, 1947–. A family of fifty or so related abstracting and SDI (selective dissemination of information) services with the now traditional spin-off services from the computerized data base, *Excerpta Medica* began life using manual techniques and has been built up into the most comprehensive medical abstracting service in the world. It can date its firm establishment and improved efficiency and quality from the great boost to investment in scientific information services occasioned in the West by the launching of the Russian *Sputnik* in 1957. Computer processing came along in 1965.

Entries in each of the 39 abstracting sections are arranged

in classified order, and the monthly parts have annual subject and author indexes. About 3,500 periodical titles are regularly abstracted, yielding over 250,000 abstracts a year in English with an average time lag from original publication of only two months. The service now publishes from New York two computer tape services, *Drug Literature Index* and *Adverse Reactions Titles*, and also maintains selective dissemination of information (SDI) facilities for custom-designed searches for clients. Blanker[33] describes the service, and *Excerpta Medica*[34] have themselves issued an informative pamphlet.

5. *Bulletin Signalétique*. Paris: Centre National de la Recherche Scientifique, 1956–. Arising out of two earlier series entitled *Bulletin Analytique*, 1940–55.

This is a vast indicative abstracting operation published in French and, like *Excerpta Medica* and *Referativnyi Zhurnal* (see below), it is really a family of independent services under one overall director. There are fifty services available separately, in groups, or as a complete set. Most parts are issued monthly but some are quarterly, each with an author index, and there are annual author and subject indexes to each part.

Virtually the whole of human knowledge is covered and about 8,000 periodicals are regularly reviewed, although much more selectively than *Chemical Abstracts* or *Biological Abstracts*. It is useful to be able to subscribe to the parts separately since some of the areas covered by *Bulletin Signalétique* are virtually unique to this service. The coverage of humanities and social science periodicals is particularly useful. Abstracts appear very soon after the original – two months is the average time lag – but the penalty paid for such promptness is brief abstracts of very variable quality.

The services of the Centre de Documentation du Centre National de la Recherche Scientifique have been comprehensively described in a French source.[35] D'Olier,[36] in his 'official' history, draws attention to the growth of computerized services and of the most important research programme being undertaken by the Centre into establishing what they term 'lexical correspondence' of technologies, to enable a higher degree of intercommunication and exchange of data between the various documentation organizations of the world.

6. *Referativnyi Zhurnal.* 1953– Published in Moscow under the sponsorship of the Academy of Sciences.

This family of abstracting services is produced under central direction, but the individual parts are the responsibility of a variety of government agencies in the USSR. It is the largest abstracting service in the world, taken as a whole, publishing more than one million abstracts a year. It has to be appreciated, of course, that were the major abstracting services of the United States to be similarly organized – as a nationalized system – then the joint totals of *Chemical Abstracts, Biological Abstracts, Engineering Index,* etc., would greatly exceed one million.

There are 67 subject parts covering the whole of science and technology, other than clinical medicine, and over 22,000 periodicals and 150,000 patent specifications are regularly covered. The abstracts are signed unless the edited author abstract has been used in which case there is a note to that effect. The abstracts are of a high quality and informative, and appear an average of six months after the original regardless of language. English-speaking scientists able to read Russian or with access to those sections of the series which are also available in English, have a high opinion of the service, as Bedford and Van Meter[37] indicate. In the full series the abstracts are in Russian but with a full bibliographic citation in the language of the original, thus rendering the Service useful as an index, even to the non-linguist who takes the trouble to understand the pattern of arrangement. A certain amount of duplication of the material is to be found with abstracts for the same article appearing in different places, but the abstract is always slanted differently if it is repeated in another section.

Most parts appear monthly. The arrangement is by a special classification scheme with annual author and subject indexes. A separate volume is published which explains the classification and arrangement. Copley[38] has written a helpful guide to the *Referativnyi Zhurnal* series.

7. *INSPEC Services.* Published since 1898– by the Institution of Electrical Engineers.

Initially in one series, from 1903 the Service divided into

two parts: Section A, *Physics Abstracts*; Section B, *Electrical Engineering*. The Service was known as *Science Abstracts* and both parts were issued monthly with annual subject and author indexes. The participation of other organizations such as the Institute of Physics, the American Physical Society, the Physical Society and the American Institute of Electrical Engineers has been a feature of INSPEC.

With the advent of the computer came a wide range of specialized services, and the *Science Abstracts* activity became transmuted into INSPEC which initially meant the *Information Service in Physics, Electrotechnology and Control* and has since been amended, to reflect developments, to *International Information Service in Physics, Electrotechnology, Computers and Control.*

INSPEC now offers three abstract services: *Physics Abstracts* (fortnightly); *Electrical and Electronics Abstracts* (monthly); *Computer and Control Abstracts* (monthly). The three services between them cover some 2,000 periodicals, and some books, theses and conference papers, and are arranged in classified order for the fairly brief indicative abstracts. There are half yearly indexes of authors, patent specifications and reports. Spin-off services include:

Current Papers
These are in three series matching the abstracts services. They are low-cost listings of the titles of papers and full bibliographic references of all the material covered by the main services.

TABS (Tailored Abstracts)
These are abstracts grouped into fifty-five specific subject fields made up into monthly bulletins and, by their low cost, intended to be attractive to individual subscribers.

INSPEC Key Abstracts
Begun in January 1975, these are six periodicals consisting of 250 abstracts of 100–200 words each. They are *Power, Transmission and Distribution, System Theory, Communications Technology, Industrial Power and Control Systems, Electronic Circuits, Solid State Devices.*

SDI TOPICS

A service of 15 × 10 cm (6 × 4 ins) cards generated from the data base to the specification of individual subscribers, who ask for searches in particular interest fields and receive cards for every abstract falling within these fields. The service is expensive when operated to individual specifications but *TOPIC* is a cheaper form of the same thing, offering for a fixed subscription a range of cards for any one or any combination of over seventy subject fields specified by INSPEC.

In addition to these subscription services, the whole INSPEC data base can be made available to national information centres and large research organizations, who can then generate their own current awareness packages from it.

Barlow has described the Service.[39] A clear indication of the growth is given by the fact that the 16,452 abstracts published in 1957 had become 168,000 in 1976. A historical note appears in *NFAIS Newsletter*.[40]

THE NATIONAL FEDERATION OF ABSTRACTING AND INDEXING SERVICES

The Federation was established in 1958 in Washington D.C. in the United States with the following purposes and aims:

Purpose

To foster, encourage, improve and implement the documentation (abstracting, indexing and analysing) of the literature of the World, by means which shall include, but shall not be limited to, education, research and publication of lists of primary periodicals, and of other material designed to foster, encourage, improve or implement such documentation; and to foster the inter-change of information between services in the United States and foreign countries and to strive to provide for them the best possible information service.

Aims

To help members improve their services and operations, and to advance their prestige, nationally and internationally.

To undertake specific projects on behalf of members that no one single member service would undertake alone and that would broadly be useful to the majority of member services.
To achieve a compatible, decentralized information system through association and co-operation.
To act as national spokesman for the collective member services.

Membership is divided into three categories and the world wide range of the third category rather gives the lie to the term 'National' in the Federation's title:

1. Full voting members
2. Affiliate US Government services
3. Foreign affiliates

In 1976 the membership of the several categories was 24, 10 and 5 respectively, who between them produced nearly two-and-a-half million entries to their data bases.

The Federation was originally called the National Federation of Science Abstracting and Indexing Services but the 'Science' was dropped in 1972, opening the door for much broader membership. The Federation is principally concerned to standardize the construction of the various members' publications and bibliographic entries, to reduce overlap between services, improving the access to original documents, and to develop a Federation with a source list of periodicals cited modelled on *Chemical Abstracts Source Index*.

The Federation produces an information newsletter, *NFAIS Newsletter* (1958–), and many other publications including a definitive statement of aims and history.[41]

PROBLEM AREAS IN THE GROWTH OF ABSTRACTING SERVICES

Five areas can be identified:

1. Size
2. Costs and value for money
3. Time lag in production
4. Overlap
5. Seeking automated and electronic solutions to problems

Mohrhardt[42] pinpoints the most sensitive issue at least for the major services, when he says:

> Abstracts were originated to provide scholars with a convenient means for coping with increasing quantities of publications. Now abstracts themselves have become so voluminous that specialized indexes often replace the use of abstracts by those who need up-to-date and speedy access to publications.

1. *Size of abstracting services*

The literature of librarianship of the western world constantly refers to the importance of the launch of the Russian *Sputnik* in 1957. This clearly showed that Soviet technology had made far more rapid and purposeful strides than had been fully appreciated in the West. It started a boom in the support for the infrastructure of western technology – education, libraries and, especially, basic research. The 'publication flood' or 'literature explosion', already a problem, re-doubled almost overnight, and so did the means for controlling them and for revealing some at least of the mysteries of the East European literature. The abstracting services, especially, also flourished and with the application of computers to information storage and retrieval they were able to go forth, multiply, and grow fat in an attempt to keep pace with the growth of the literature. In the United States, massive inputs of resources were made to improve all bibliographical services.

The trouble is, as Mohrhardt shows, that in growing bigger they have become self-defeating. The task of scanning the weekly, monthly or quarterly parts of the major services is now so daunting to the working scientist, who must spend at least some of his time trying to apply that which he learnt from his reading, that he is faced with a dilemma: does he read extensively to keep up with other people's activities and find that it is a full-time job in itself, or does he get on with his own work and largely ignore the reports about others? For many, the services have grown so fat that they are deemed to have collapsed under their own weight; they have become too large, like the literature they mirror, to comprehend effectively.

Certainly the growth of some of the major services since 1957 has been very striking:

NUMBERS OF ABSTRACTS

	1957	*1976*
INSPEC	16,452	168,000
Biological Abstracts	40,061	240,000
Chemical Abstracts	102,525	454,600

It might be argued that nobody these days would need to read the whole of, say, *Chemical Abstracts* or *Excerpta Medica*, but when even relatively small sections of these works contain up to 25,000 abstracts a year this, in itself, takes a large bite out of anybody's time if a person has to scan so many abstracts before doing anything else.

The major abstracting services are large and cumbersome. To be used effectively they need large and cumbersome indexes. Even with the help of the wonders of the computer these indexes take time to produce; so much time in fact, that the almost inescapable conclusion is that the major services – those producing more than 100,000 abstracts a year – are no longer current awareness services but archives and retro-spective-search material. It is worth mentioning as an oddity that currently the growth in size of the abstracting services is proportionately greater than the growth of original periodical literature – a clear indicator of the way they are sacrificing selectivity for comprehensiveness.

2. Costs and value for money

This growth, coming in an age of economic inflation on a greater scale than ever before except for the time of the Weimar Republic in Germany, has produced subscription charges for the major services which are staggeringly high compared to only ten years ago. Charles Bourne[43] has produced a literative survey on cost studies of abstracting work. Woods[4] produced information on cost increases in the form of indices for the period 1959–69 (but prices at that time had hardly begun to grow in the way they have since). Some subscriptions appear to be rising in an almost geometric progression year by year and the situation has been especially awkward for British libraries with the falling value of the pound against the United States dollar. As an example – though an extreme one – of the way subscription costs have soared, the costs of *Chemical Abstracts* over the past few years may be cited.

	$
1956	80
1960	150
1966	700
1970	1,450
1976	3,800

The question arises: can libraries continue to afford to take high-cost abstracting services? Many research libraries must try to do so but as the subscription price increases, so does the need to undertake a serious appraisal of the cost and benefit of retaining the service. Some libraries have decided to cancel their own subscriptions and rely upon other adjacent libraries retaining theirs and being willing to allow access to it. At a current cost of considerably more than £2,000 for *Chemical Abstracts* one could, after all, send a number of people quite long distances by taxi to search when the need arises, and still show a profit at the end of a year! The problem for the publishers of the services is that their overheads do not decrease if subscriptions are lost due to rising costs; they must share the overheads amongst the remaining subscribers, thus increasing costs again and risking losing yet more subscribers.

Sputniks and much more awesome examples of technological advance have become the common coinage of news broadcasts; governments are less readily impressed and support grants are not so easy to attract. Little wonder that interest in co-operation and shared services is so marked a feature of the policies of many abstracting services notably, of course, the National Federation of Abstracting and Indexing Services.

3. *Time lag in production*

If an abstracting service is to be a valuable source of current awareness the individual entries must appear quickly so that attention can be called to the value of the originals. If, however, the service is to be a reliable, evaluative source, care must be taken to obtain accuracy of abstracts. The two aspects are often in conflict with each other.

Abstracting services face a peculiar quandary. They wish to be comprehensive within clearly-defined subject areas and to be international in their coverage. The major part of their work is not difficult if it is appreciated that *Chemical Abstracts* draws 80 per cent of its abstracts from 2,000 of the 12,000 periodicals it covers. From this core it is usually possible to secure high quality abstracts very quickly but from the rest it can be quite difficult.

Abstracting service publishers are sensitive about the time lag problem and tend to quote the time lag as an average: thus *Chemical Abstracts* has claimed an *average* time lag of 105 days which is, of course, very short, but the average conceals the extremes. When author abstracts are used – as increasingly they are – and lightly edited, the time lag can be very short, while to produce high quality abstracts from papers in recondite subjects in obscure languages takes time. Abstracts produced by subject experts who are also skilled abstractors and, possibly, linguists are usually called subject-authority abstracts. Subject experts of the requisite skills are obviously in short supply; they will be busy people and almost certainly not full-time employees of the abstracting service, and therefore to a certain extent the publishers are relying upon goodwill and must await the convenience of the abstractor. Unfortunately it is usually likely that the recondite and obscure is precisely the material which the person seeking current awareness of important subjects would like quickly, and this material can often take six months, a year, or more, to appear. Garfield and Sher[44] have examined the problem of time-lag in relation to four services, and Lane and Kammerer[45] provide information on the other half of the time-lag problem – the delays in publishing the original article. The production of abstracts 'in-house' at the publishers by full-time employees and the use of edited author abstracts reduces time-lag but will not secure high quality abstracts by subject authorities – which ought to be the aim of a major informative abstracting service. Woods[4] recommends the increased use of author abstracts as a means of reducing time-lags in the production of commercial services.

4. *Overlap*

This term is used to describe the case where the same paper is abstracted by two or more services independently of each other thus, perhaps, duplicating effort unnecessarily. 'Perhaps' is used advisedly, for the fact of a paper being abstracted twice does not imply total duplication of effort, since an abstract produced for, say, *Excerpta Medica* may be slanted differently from that in *Biological Abstracts*, each stressing different facets of the original.

Overlap is nevertheless a major problem. The 3,500 or so published abstracting services between them produce many more individual abstracts than there are original papers in any one year. This must mean that many of the services overlap and it cannot always be claimed that this is the inevitable product of the need to slant abstracts to suit particular readerships. Much of it is sheer duplication of effort – which is very expensive. The overlap is probably doubled if the many abstracting services produced privately 'in-house' for industrial and research organizations are taken into account. There is a great deal of interest in developing co-operation between abstracting services to eliminate unnecessary overlap and to make the services more comprehensive. The NFAIS is active in this and Wood, Flanagan and Kennedy[46] describe some phases of this initiative. Martyn[47] and Martyn and Slater[48] have examined overlap on a very wide front.

Martyn and Slater's conclusions are striking. They say that despite considerable overlap a search of all available abstracting services would not, in fact, turn up every abstract published. A significant amount of useful material is ignored by all services but, more interestingly, Martyn and Slater reveal that imperfect indexing of abstracting services makes it impossible to retrieve everything abstracted. They also discover that not all the material covered by abstracting services is readily located in libraries. They have coined the phrase 'search product' to describe 'the available portion of the indexed portion of the abstracted portion of the total relevant literature'.

5. *Seeking automated and electronic solutions to problems*

Increasing size and costs are the principal problems for abstracting services, but in the past twenty years electronic salvation has come in the form of the computer. There are two main areas for the application of automation, one is heavily used by all big abstracting services, the other is less used and still experimental. The first area is in the manipulation of the data fed into the abstracting services by human abstractors, where the computer can produce indexes to the service and especially create the necessary cumulative indexes. Indexing patterns have been considerably improved since the advent of computer manipulation and the availability of a large mass of manipulable data has created the capacity to produce indexes which have gone some way to offset the difficulties encountered with abstracting services. Subject indexes to periodical articles in various formats have come into vogue and are often of more significance in the attainment of current awareness than the abstracting services from which they are generated. Keenan[49] has edited an important collection of essays on this aspect of automation of data bases.

The second application is in attempts to replace the human intellectual effort in the generation of abstracts from originals. The aims are to increase the speed of generation of abstracts (and reduce time-lag), and to reduce or at least stabilize costs. Basically, automated generation of abstracts uses a computer to examine whole papers, which have been transferred on to machine-readable tapes. The computer sorts the words in the paper into a descending order of frequency of appearance in the text, ignoring conjunctions, articles and prepositions. The words occurring most frequently are taken to be those which represent the subject matter of greatest significance in the document. The computer then traces the sentences in which these high frequency words appear and prints them out in the form of an abstract. Automatic abstract generation is, then, basically a process of sentence selection from the original article. It is not considered by authorities to produce abstracts which are of a quality equivalent to those produced by human abstractors although the computer can find the significant parts of papers more reliably than humans. Refinements are being made all of the time. Push[14] describes efforts to improve readability and syntax, the basic process has been comprehensively described by the Ramo Woolridge Division of Thompson Ramo Woolridge,[11] and W. J. Kurmey[50] has evaluated the quality of abstracts produced automatically.

REFERENCES

1. KRONICK, D. A. *History of scientific and technical periodicals: the origins and development of the scientific and technological press 1665–1790.* Metuchen, N.J.: Scarecrow, 2nd ed., 1975.
2. WITTY, F. J. 'The beginnings of indexing and abstracting: some notes towards a history of indexing and abstracting in Antiquity and the Middle Ages.' *The Indexer*, 8(4), October 1973. pp. 193–8.
3. CLAPP, V. W. 'Indexing and abstracting services for serial literature.' *Library Trends*, 2(4), April 1954. pp. 509–21.
4. WOODS, B. M. 'Bibliographic control of serial publications.' *in* Allen, W. C., ed., *Serial publications in large libraries.* Urbana, Ill.: University of Illinois Graduate School of Library Science, 1970. pp. 161–74.
5. COLLISON, R. L. *Annals of abstracting 1665–1970.* Los Angeles: University of California Graduate School of Library Service, 1971.
6. COLLISON, R. L. *Abstracts and abstracting services.* Santa Barbara, Ca.: ABC/Clio, 1971.
7. PASLER, M. *and* PASLER, R. 'Periodical abstracting and indexing.' *R. Q.*, 10(3), Spring 1971. pp. 232–6.
8. BOTTLE, R. T. *The use of the biological literature.* London: Butterworth, 1971.
9. BORKO, H. *and* CHATMAN, S. 'Criteria for acceptable abstracts: a survey of abstracters' instructions.' *American Documentation*, 14(2), April 1963. pp. 149–60.
10. BERNIER, C. L. 'Abstracts and abstracting' *in Encyclopedia of Library and Information Science.* New York: Dekker. Vol. 1, pp. 16–38.
11. THOMPSON RAMO WOOLRIDGE CORPORATION. *Final Report on the study for automatic abstracting C107–IV12.* Rome Air Development Center, Grifiss Air Force Base, New York, 1961. RADC–TR–61–230.
12. INTERNATIONAL BUSINESS MACHINES. *An experiment in auto-abstracting.* Yorktown Heights, N.Y.: I.B.M., 1958.
13. RATH, G. J., RESNICK, A. *and* SAVAGE, T. R. 'The formation of abstracts by the selection of sentences.' *American Documentation*, 12(2), April 1961. pp. 139–43.
14. PUSH *et al.* 'Automatic abstracting and indexing: production of indicative abstracts by application of contextual inference and syntactic coherence criteria.' *Journal of the American Society of Information Science*, 22(4), July/August 1971. pp. 260–74.
15. BOURNE, C. P. 'The world's technical journal literature: an estimate of volume, origin, language, field indexing, and abstracting.' *American Documentation*, 13(2), April 1962. pp. 159–68.

5

16. WOODWARD, A. M. *Directory of review serials in science and technology, 1970–1973.* London: ASLIB, 1974.
17. BORKO, H. and BERNIER, C. L. *Abstracting concepts and methods.* New York: Academic, 1976.
18. WALFORD, A. J. *Guide to reference material.* London: Library Association. 3 vols, regularly revised.
19. SHEEHY, E. *Guide to reference books.* Chicago: American Library Association., 9th ed., 1976.
20. *Ulrich's international periodicals directory 1975–1976.* New York; R. R. Bowker and Co, 16th ed., 1976.
21. 'A brief history of the Chemical Abstracts Service' *in A century of chemistry: the role of chemists and the American Chemical Society.* Washington: American Chemical Society, 1976.
22. CHEMICAL ABSTRACTS SERVICE. *CAS Today.* Columbus, Ohio: CAS, regularly revised.
23. YAGELLO, V. 'Chemical Abstracts.' *Reference Service Review,* 2(2), April/June 1974. pp. 52–4.
24. CHEMICAL AND ENGINEERING NEWS. 'Toward a modern secondary information system for chemistry and chemical engineering.' *Chemical and Engineering News,* 54(2A), 16 June 1975. pp. 30–8.
25. SOUTHAMPTON UNIVERSITY. *A guide to Chemical Abstracts.* Southampton: Southampton University, 1974. *A tape-slide presentation.*
26. BOTTLE, R. T. *The use of the chemical literature.* London: Butterworth, 2nd ed., 1969. pp. 55 & 254–6.
27. VOIGT, M. J. *Scientists' approaches to information.* Chicago: American Library Association, 1961.
28. BOTTLE, R. T. and WYATT, H. V. *The use of the biological literature.* London: Butterworth, 2nd ed., 1971.
29. PARKINS, P. V. 'Biosciences Information Service of *Biological Abstracts*' *in Encyclopedia of Librarianship and Information Science.* New York: Dekker, 1969. Vol. 2, pp. 603–31.
30. BIOSCIENCES INFORMATION SERVICE. *Guide to Biological Abstracts, Biological Abstracts and Bioresearch Index.* Philadelphia, Pa: BIOSIS, 1972.
31. WOODS, B. M. 'Engineering Index Inc.' *in Encyclopedia of Library and Information Science.* New York: Dekker, 1972. Vol. 8, pp. 49–71.
32. CREPS, J. E. and CARRIGY, J. W. 'The engineer's worldwide, transdisciplinary information network.' *Sci-Tech News,* 26(2), Summer 1972. pp. 42–4.
33. BLANKER, R. R. 'Excerpta Medica' *in Encyclopedia of Library and Information Science.* New York: Dekker, 1972. Vol. 8, pp. 261–82.
34. EXCERPTA MEDICA. *Excerpta Medica automates storage and retrieval program of biomedical information.* Amsterdam: Excerpta Medica Foundation, 1970.
35. LE CENTRE DE DOCUMENTATION. *Science et Techniques 15.* Centre de Documentation, 1969. Supplement 9.
36. D'OLIER, J. H. 'Centre National de la Recherche Scientifique' *in Encyclopedia of Library and Information Science.* New York: Dekker, 1970. Vol. 4, pp. 396–9.
37. BEDFORD, G. M. and VAN METER, C. T. *Evaluation of the Soviet abstracting journal Referativnyi Zhurnal: Final Report.* Philadelphia, Pa.: University of Pennsylvania, 1958.
38. COPLEY, E. J. *A guide to Referativnyi Zhurnal.* London: British Library, Science Reference Library, 3rd ed., 1975.
39. BARLOW, D. H. '*INSPEC.*' *ASLIB Proceedings,* 23(10), October 1971. pp. 533–5.

40. '*INSPEC:* three milestones.' *NFAIS Newsletter,* 17(1), February 1975. pp. 12–14.
41. NATIONAL FEDERATION OF ABSTRACTING AND INDEXING SERVICES. *History and Issues 1958–73.* Philadelphia Pa.: NFAIS, 1973.
42. MOHRHARDT, F. E. *(ed.).* 'Science abstracting services – commercial, institutional and personal.' *Library Trends,* 16(2), January 1968. p. 303.
43. BOURNE, C. P. *Abstracting and indexing rates and costs: a literature review.* Washington: Department of Health Education and Welfare, 1920. ED 043–798.
44. GARFIELD, E. *and* SHER, I. H. *Article by article coverage of selected abstracting services.* Philadelphia, Pa. 1964.
45. LANE, N. *and* KAMMERER, K. L. *Writers' guide to medical journals.* Cambridge, Mass.: Ballinger, 1976.
46. WOOD, J. L., FLANAGAN, C. *and* KENNEDY, H. E. 'Overlap in the lists of journals monitored by BIOSIS, CAS, and EI.' *Journal of the American Society for Information Science.* 23(1), Jan.–Feb. 1972. pp. 36–8.
47. MARTYN, J. 'Tests on abstracting journals, coverage, overlap and indexing.' *Journal of Documentation,* 23(1), March 1967. pp. 45–70.
48. MARTYN, J. *and* SLATER, M. 'Tests on abstracts journals.' *Journal of Documentation,* 20(4), December 1964. pp. 212–35.
49. KEENAN, S. *Key papers on the use of computer-based bibliographies services.* Philadelphia Pa.: NFAIS, 1973.
50. KURMEY, W. J. *An evaluation of automatically prepared abstracts and indexes.* Chicago, Ill.: University of Chicago Graduate Library School, 1964.

Chapter 9
Guides to the contents of periodicals – Indexing services

For many years the abstracting service was regarded as the glamorous and effective aspect of current-awareness provision, outshining the indexing service, its historical antecedent. The automatic tendency to accord pride of place to the abstracting service is not so strong as it once was. Its cumbersome bulk, slowness in production – especially of the cumulative indexes – and huge cost have made it, despite great virtues, a luxury for the library and virtually beyond the means of private subscribers. In these circumstances there has been a resurgence of interest in the cheaper, quicker, although more limited, indexing services. They probably now represent the fastest growing form of current awareness provision. Their resurgence does, in fact, owe much to the automation of abstracting services, giving ease of manipulation of the data base. For example, *Current Papers in Electrical and Electronics Engineering* (INSPEC, 1964–monthly) is a classified print-out of the bibliographic citation material appearing in the *Electrical and Electronics Abstracts* but appearing significantly earlier.

Before looking at periodical indexing services in detail, it is necessary to establish some basic definitions and to examine the elementary structures of indexes to the contents of periodicals. The Expert Committee on Scientific Abstracting convened by UNESCO in 1948 formulated the following definitions of 'Index' in its several forms:

Index. A systematically arranged list giving enough information about each item to enable it to be identified and traced.

A Bibliographic Index of publications or articles contains no material descriptive of the publication or article other than the title or other bibliographical information.

An Analytical Index is a list of the specific topics contained in articles or publications, as, for instance, chemical compounds, biological organisms, processes, theoretical principles, to enable significant information to be traced.

An Annotated Index contains, in addition to the bibliographical information, information relevant to the contents, scope or importance of the publication or article.

THE CONTENTS PAGE

The most basic analysis of the contents of a particular periodical issue is the list of contents usually provided on a page close to the front of the issue. It is not always easy to find since some publishers place it amongst pages of advertising, thereby hoping to increase the exposure of the advertising. The primary periodicals (which usually carry no advertising) place a contents page very prominently at the front. Particularly effective is the placing of the contents on the front cover as, for example, is done by *Universities Quarterly*. A variation is to place the contents list on the back cover, as *Libri* does.

Elaborating upon this, some periodicals go further and supply information upon the contents of recent issues of periodicals in their own chosen subject field. *Mind* and *Philosophy* are two such examples. The evolution of separate periodicals devoted simply to the publication of copies of the title pages of a group of related periodicals was but a short step. To be able to arrange to publish them in advance of, or at least concurrently with, the periodicals they represent makes an extremely effective current-awareness service. Some periodicals notify their own subscribers two or three months in advance of the proposed contents of subsequent issues, which is also useful.

Of the separately-published contents list periodicals, those issued by the Institute of Scientific Information Inc. of Philadelphia are the best known:

Current Contents : Life Sciences
Current Contents : Physical and Chemical Sciences
Current Contents : Agriculture, Biology and Environmental Sciences

Current Contents : Social and Behavioral Sciences
Current Contents : Engineering and Technology
Current Contents : Clinical Practice

They are published weekly and between them cover about 1,000 periodicals from all parts of the world. They are mainly compiled from advance proof copies and are, consequently, up-to-date. Author, subject and periodical indexes are provided. The Institute will also supply actual copies of articles listed, on request. *Revue des Sommaires* (1975– ten times a year) and *Contents of Current Legal Periodicals* (1972– monthly) are examples from other publishers. The value of these services is limited in two ways. If they become too large they are self defeating. The multi-disciplinary nature of many periodicals tends to defy accurate classification and the provision of indexes in any case increases bulk. The second limiting factor is that the amount of information supplied is small and much depends upon the explicitness or otherwise of the actual article titles.

INDEXES TO INDIVIDUAL PERIODICALS

It is usual for the publishers of primary periodicals and other 'serious' periodicals to produce regular indexes – usual but not inevitable. Without an index the value of storing a periodical is seriously reduced. In some instances the absence of a publisher-produced index will be serious enough for the library to consider producing one itself before binding. This is especially the case with material of local interest.

Publisher-produced indexes vary considerably in quality. They are extremely expensive to compile and not all publishers have an unqualified enthusiasm for ensuring high standards. There are encouraging signs of improvement for which some credit must go to the Society of Indexers.[1] A British Standard exists[2] and Strain[3] has given some eminently practical advice. Many publishers publish their indexes in the last issue of a volume or in an early issue of the succeeding volume. In other cases only a limited quantity are printed and subscribers are invited to apply for them; in some instances there is an additional charge but usually they are free. Markus[4] mentions how few subscribers take advantage of the availability of indexes in this way. Every means of distribution has its own problems. Loosely-inserted indexes in the last issue of a volume are easily mislaid. If they are bound into the last issue of a volume that issue has to be dismembered to release them. The limitation upon the numbers printed in cases where separate application is required places the onus upon periodicals librarians to be vigilant to ensure they are claimed quickly.

The indicators against the entries in *Faxon's librarian's guide to periodicals and American subscription catalog* of the availability of indexes to the listed titles is useful. A listing produced by the Special Libraries Association is less helpful in providing indications of index availability than its title suggests, but it helps to fill in gaps.[5]

CUMULATIVE INDEXES TO INDIVIDUAL PERIODICALS

However useful the indexes to individual periodicals are, they become increasingly tiresome to search as the length of a file increases. Material can be missed as a result of fatigue during the search. In order to reduce labour and time in index searching it is desirable to have cumulative indexes. Since the cost of compiling individual indexes is sufficient to inhibit some publishers it will be appreciated that the cost of cumulative indexes is enough to inhibit most.

Cumulative indexes are relatively rare but, even so, in 1942 D. C. Haskell was able to compile a list of 6,000 examples in the New York Public Library.[6] This list is now being supplemented by entries in the quarterly *Serials Review* (Ann Arbor, Mich.: Pieran, 1974–). The *British union catalogue of periodicals* (London: Butterworth, 1955–8, 4 vols) indicates which entries in the listing have cumulative indexes available. Examples of periodicals with cumulative indexes are: *The Engineer* (1856–1956); *Notes and Queries* (every ten years); *International Associations* (1949–58). Often these cumulative indexes are difficult to use for accurate and swift searching being much abbreviated and having only the sketchiest of cross references.

PERIODICAL INDEXES COVERING A NUMBER OF TITLES

Cumulative indexes are definitely the material for retrospective searching rather than current awareness. They are also limited to one periodical and, therefore, searching a group of related periodicals for information is a considerable chore. To provide current awareness and also to enable a group of periodicals to be searched in one source, periodical indexing services are used. Traditionally these services were printed listings, frequently cumulated, providing alphabetical subject indexes to a group of related periodicals in a particular subject field, or from a specific country or both. The essence of such services is that they provide a swift, systematic notification of the contents of current periodicals. The time lag between appearance of the periodical and appearance in the indexing service is usually about three to four weeks – much shorter than for an abstract. For current awareness, frequent publication of the service is essential, and for retrospective search frequent cumulating. For both purposes the advent of the computer has enabled the publishers to improve and increase the speed of production of their services whilst containing costs. Coates[7] describes the process of computerizing one group of services.

In recent years, the computer has made possible the generation of an array of periodical-indexing activities which might initially have been regarded as useful spin-off from abstracting services, but which have come to have a major significance in their own right.

The essence of a periodical indexing service is its quickness and relative cheapness in providing current awareness to a large number of periodicals. To achieve this it is necessary to accept considerable limitations, as compared to the information provided by an abstracting service. The amount of information supplied is minimal, consisting of the bibliographical citation together with a subject heading, supplied by the editorial staff of the service. In contrast to much abstracting activity the editorial effort in indexing services is largely non-specialist and is not therefore as authoritative.

The indexing service provides basic information leaving a great deal to the user's own interpretation of the article title, periodical title and assigned subject heading. The services are usually easy to use and because they are, with only a few exceptions, compiled from a small number of periodicals, they are readily comprehensible. Sheehy[8] summarizes the main points to bear in mind in assessing the usefulness of an indexing service.

The history of periodical indexing is dealt with by Witty[9] and Kronick[10] but the contemporary process can be said to arise out of the activities of W. F. Poole, and his followers. *Poole's index to periodical literature 1802–81*: (Boston: Houghton rev. ed., 2 vols 1891, plus 5 vols of supplement 1882–1906; reprinted 1938). In 1973 Pieran Press produced a companion volume *Poole's index to periodical literature cumulative author index.* Poole indexed 479 British and American periodicals covering 590,000 articles alphabetically by subject – hence the significance of the recent 300,000 entry author index. Clapp[11] provides a summary history of *Poole's index* as well as of the history of indexing in general.

Of the works currently being produced the several indexing services of the H. W. Wilson Company of New York are, perhaps, the best known in the English-speaking world. Beginning in 1900 with the *Readers guide to periodical literature* following the successful launching of his earlier *Cumulative book index* (1898–) H. W. Wilson began to produce a large number of services; there are at present fourteen. The typical pattern is for between 100 and 300 periodicals to be indexed regularly with the emphasis chiefly upon North American published items.

The value of Wilson indexes is limited in all but the very largest non-North-American libraries. Since the Company operate their subscription policy on the basis of a rather controversial 'service basis' the subscription price is not necessarily high; the library pays a subscription in proportion to its holdings of the periodicals listed by the Company. A report form is supplied to subscribing libraries asking them to check off the periodicals they take. The Company then quotes a price to that library. Lawler[12] has written about the history of the company.

The key to the success of this dynamic organization has been its responsiveness to consumer needs and in particular its early recognition that bibliographic aids of the type they produce must have an effective and frequent cumulative pattern. Two British periodical indexing services produced in the years immediately after the Second World War – the *Cleaver Hume index* and *Index of technical articles* – soon foundered principally for lack of any cumulative pattern. They were quickly produced and were, no doubt, intended as immediate current-awareness sources. Although cheap they were not cheap enough to attract massive support from individual subscribers and their library sales were disappointing. Libraries, whilst not despising current awareness, expect to be able to employ such tools also in retrospective searching and the lack of cumulations made this impossible without much tedious searching of individual issues.

In the circumstances of these two British failures it was a venture of some daring on the part of the Library Association to publish its *British technology index* in 1962 as a monthly with annual cumulations. After a slow start it has more than justified itself. It arose out of their earlier, more general, venture *Subject index to periodicals*, which commenced in 1915 and the non-technical material indexed became *British humanities index* from the same date.

Another key to the success of a periodical indexing service is that it restricts itself to detailed coverage of a relatively small number of periodicals. Even the very broad subject coverage of H. W. Wilson's *Reader's guide to periodical literature* is based upon only 164 periodicals. However if all the periodicals indexed by services from the sources mentioned above are taken together they constitute a wide range of source material as is demonstrated by:

MARCONI, Joseph V. *Indexed periodicals*. Ann Arbor, Mich.: Pieran, 1976.

This work presents in a single volume an alphabetical listing of all of the periodicals which have ever been indexed by the various Wilson Company indexes, the Library Association's indexes, *Poole's index* . . ., *Canadian periodicals index* and *Catholic periodicals index*, in all over 11,000 items.

An indexing service produced by conventional means which does not attempt to restrict itself much in either number of periodicals covered or subjects is *Internationale Bibliographie der Zeitschriften-literatur* (Osnabrück: Dietrich, 1897– six monthly). Beginning in Leipzig *IBZ*, as the service is familiarly known, moved to Osnabrück after the Second World War. Initially it was restricted to German periodicals, but in 1911 a foreign periodicals service was instituted and the two parts were merged in 1965. Currently more than 10,000 periodicals from all subjects and languages are producing about 250,000 citations a year. The service is produced in cottage-industry fashion with the bulk of the citations being written by part-time piece workers, on slips which are then lightly edited by the very small permanent staff of this entirely privately financed venture. The editorial staff work only from the index slips received and not from the original periodicals, consequently their subject indexing is often unreliable. The work is published in three sections. Section A is an alphabetical list of periodical titles for each of which a shorthand notation is provided. This notation is the only indicator of periodical titles given in section B, which is the alphabetical arrangement of subject of citations in German with English and French cross-references. Section C is an alphabetical listing by authors. Consulting section B entails a great deal of reference back to section A.

It is remarkable that this massive work should still be produced entirely by manual means. The heavy capital inputs needed for computerization which would improve speed of publication and other aspects of production is simply not a feasible proposition. *IBZ* is an interesting, if frustrating, work. It is partly successful in its attempt to control vast numbers of periodicals but it is this which also makes it frustrating to use. It provides a little help in a lot of subjects but not much about any of them especially in the case of non-German periodicals. Its size and the extreme brevity of the entries, together with a total absence of cumulations of the parts and slowness in production, tend to make it even less popular with librarians than its undoubted disadvantages deserve. It is difficult to believe that it can continue much longer in its present form. Broadwin,[13] who has spent some time working in the *IBZ* editorial office, has given some personal impressions of the service.

Apart from these major, general services there are a very large number of specialist indexes of which the following are a small selection:

Access: the supplementary index to periodicals, 1975– quarterly
Ekistic index, 1970– quarterly

French periodical index, 1973– annual
Index to foreign legal periodicals, 1960– quarterly
Index to free periodicals, 1976– twice a year
Index to religious periodical literature, 1949– twice a year
Popular periodical index, 1973– twice a year

Many periodical indexing services exist solely as retrospective search records published annually or even less frequently, thus:

International index to film periodicals 1973– annual
Index to South African periodicals 1940– annual
Comprehensive index to English-language little magazines 1890–1970
Index to Latin American periodical literature 1929–1960 Boston, G. K. Hall, 1962.

An item of British retrospective periodical indexing, interesting though not especially effective and highly unreliable, has recently been reprinted:

COTGREAVE, A. A. *A contents–subject index to general and periodical literature.* Detroit: Gale, 1971.

There are a large number of 'home-made' indexing services currently produced by libraries and other organizations largely for internal current-awareness services. They form a mass of unco-ordinated and largely inaccessible sources, although some organizations are willing to sell or exchange copies with others.

A few indexing services are available in card form so that the recipients can create their own files and also, neatly, free the publisher of the service from the obligation of producing expensive cumulations. One example is:

INTERNATIONAL UNION OF PUBLIC TRANSPORT. *UITP Biblio-index.* Brussels: UITP, 1962– quarterly.

Grenfell[14] notes several such services.

So far the activities described have been of a traditional kind principally produced manually in volume form. The computer has been used extensively in indexing services but largely as a compiler, setting up the listings. An indexing service does not, of itself, generate spin-offs of the kind noted in abstracting services many of which are in fact periodical indexing services. However several periodical indexing services have developed almost entirely as a result of the capabilities of the computer. The most exotic of these services is, perhaps, the citation index, which is described in detail below. The genre is best introduced, however, by describing a kind of changeling which developed out of a conventional indexing activity into the massive computerized operation known as MEDLARS (Medical Literature Analysis and Retrieval System). It is produced by the US National Library of Medicine.

MEDLARS developed out of *Index medicus*, a cumulative indexing service developed in 1879 and existing continuously ever since under a variety of names. On 1 January 1964, it switched to a fully-automated system. The conventional *Index medicus* service is still produced in monthly parts from the MEDLARS tapes at very high speed, to list over 18,000 entries monthly from over 2,300 periodicals. In addition the data base thus compiled is used for making individual subject searches on demand, compiling specific bibliographies and providing current awareness listings to registered users who have specified their requirements by the use of a series of subject headings or 'keywords'. This process of selecting keywords which exactly comprehend the interests of a user are known as 'user interest profiles' and the whole system of producing personalized literature searches as 'selective dissemination of information' (SDI). SDI is a normal concomitant of most computerized storage and retrieval systems and is not restricted to the MEDLARS scheme.

A survey of the history of the SDI principle is contained in a summary of a thesis by Connor[15] who ascribes its genesis to the work of H. P. Luhn at the IBM Corporation's Advanced Systems Development Division, where it was first implemented in 1959. The personalized selections from the MEDLARS system are delivered monthly on A4 paper or cards measuring 15 × 10 cm (6 × 4ins) three weeks in advance of the publication of the monthly issue of *Index medicus*.

The computerization of the MEDLARS system allowed, as an advantage designed by its devisers, for the capacity to search the literature very thoroughly through assigning a large number of subject headings to every piece of literature dealt with. Whilst this is feasible with a manual system it does tend to produce large and cumbersome volumes which are difficult to use. It is usual with manual systems to assign only an average of two descriptors to an article; MEDLARS assigns ten (the *Chemical Abstracts* indexes assign a minimum of twelve!). The computer can deal with this large number of descriptors swiftly to produce much more precise and accurate searches.

The term used to describe the different numbers of indexing terms assigned by the various indexing services is 'indexing depth'. An index compiled from only two assigned descriptors per article would be said to have an indexing depth inferior to that of the MEDLARS index with its higher number of assigned descriptors per article. Swanson[16] and Rayward and Svenonious[17] have both evaluated the concept of indexing depth.

The MEDLARS system has been copiously written about. The National Library of Medicine has produced a number of brochures, [18, 19] and the British Library Lending Division, as the MEDLARS agents in the United Kingdom, have also issued many brochures. Their *BLL Review* frequently refers to MEDLARS.

MEDLARS is not only highly automated, it is highly expensive to use. The needs of smaller, poorer users have not been forgotten, however, and there is a smaller service for them, *Abridged index medicus* (1970– monthly) which is known by the acronym *AIM*. This publication covers about one hundred of the major English-language medical periodicals and has an annual cumulative index.

Whilst the automated MEDLARS service developed out of a traditional indexing service, as has been already mentioned, a wide range of new approaches to current awareness through periodical indexing has been generated from the data bases of abstracting services. The evolution of such services arises from the realization both that the increasing size of these services renders them unsuitable for current-awareness purposes, and that their price puts them beyond the means of individuals and of many libraries. Various forms of the re-working of the basic bibliographical data of the abstracting service have been developed to provide swifter, cheaper current-awareness for subscribers. Some of these re-presentations appear very little different in physical form from, say, *British technology index*. Those forms developed from the INSPEC services are typical

– Current Papers on Computers and Control, for instance. The American Chemical Society's *C.A. Condensates,* arranged in the same order as the *Chemical Abstracts* Service, is the major example in this category. It is produced as a computer readable file.

Unconventional services are based upon the ability of the computer to manipulate a body of knowledge, re-arranging it quickly and accurately and then producing printed versions. One group of items thus produced is listings of the periodicals regularly scanned by the abstracting services from which the computer file is generated. It is possible to generate these listings by a process known as KWIC (Keyword-in-context) indexing. The computer is instructed to 'read' all of the periodical titles stored in its files to recognize significant words ('keywords'). The same process can be used to create subject indexes of all periodical articles embodied in those periodicals, the computer printing out an alphabetical arrangement of the keywords recognized. *Chemical Titles,* produced fortnightly by the American Chemical Society, is an important example reporting more than 148,000 papers in 1976.

Services of this type can be produced with a time lag of less than three weeks from original publication. In the KWIC index the computer prints out the keyword in the centre of the page and arranges the rest of the title round it in a natural order as it appears in the original, together with a bibliographical citation. If the computer recognizes more than one keyword in a particular article then the whole of the information is repeated again at other points in the sequence according to the place of these additional keywords in the alphabetical sequence. It is a process which produces very long listings from a given series of articles. It will readily be appreciated that the effectiveness of this type of index depends very much upon the clarity of the titles of the periodicals or periodical articles being processed.

In recent years a good deal of emphasis has been placed upon the effective titling of articles by the editors of primary publications. The report of the American Institute of Biological Sciences might be cited as an example,[20] and careful instructions to would-be authors are incorporated into many primary periodicals. The importance of this concern is that besides the relatively straightforward KWIC indexing procedures, computer manipulation of the body of data is being increasingly used to present chemical reaction, taxonomic, formulae, structure and substance indexes. Opinion is divided as to whether in the absence of a fully explicit title being available from the author the editor should improve it – 'enrichment' is the term for the process. Harley and Myatt[21] discuss the question of enrichment inconclusively, although referring copiously to other papers on the topic.

The computer-generated index produced in the ways described above presents a minimum of information very quickly. Where the policy of the producers has been to allow of no enrichment or other embellishment (in the interests of speed) the material is presented with all its imperfections. Without sophisticated and expensive programs the computer is unable to recognize instances in which synonyms of terms used would be more effective as indexing terms for searching, so that like articles may become separated by unlike language in such indexes.

This type of index illustrates clearly a virtually unvarying rule in the creation of bibliographical records: speed and cheapness can be achieved only at the expense of quality and adequate clarification of listed materials.

CITATION INDEXES

This form of indexing of periodicals also owes its genesis to the capacity of the computer for swift and accurate sorting of data. It was created by Dr Eugene Garfield for the Institute of Scientific Information Inc. Garfield's own definition of the meaning of the term is intimidating:[22]

> A citation index is an ordered list of citing articles. The citing article is identified by a source citation, the cited article by a reference citation. The index is arranged by reference citations. Any source citation may subsequently become a reference citation.

The citation index is an acknowledgement of the fact that certain writers become known for their significant contribution to a particular field and are, as a consequence, frequently cited by later writers on the same topic as authorities. A very important piece of writing can trigger off a spate of other contributions to a topic and a citation index will list these chronologically by publication date, with the original paper listed as the main entry under the name of the author.

In subject indexes of the traditional kind a lack of consistency of terminology or the mis-assignment of a paper to an inexplicit subject heading causes difficulties not found in citation indexes. Nor do different usages in terminology in different countries affect the usefulness. A student familiar with a particular subject field will come to know the names of people interested in the same speciality and will, consequently, be as likely to wish to search out new writings by author as by subject. The citation index makes this very easy.

The two major citation indexes are both published by the Institute for Scientific Information Inc.: *Science citation index* and *Social science citation index*.

Science citation index (quarterly 1961–) covers books, reports, theses and other monographic items as well as 2,600 periodicals. The fourth issue of a year cumulates the other three and forms the annual volume. *Source index* and *Permuterm subject index* complete the programme of indexing of this series. *Source index* is an alphabetical listing of authors of papers that cites those papers which form the main entries in *Science citation index* with full bibliographical descriptions of their articles. The *Permuterm subject index* lists alphabetically every significant word in the titles of articles appearing in *Science citation index* and relates them to the authors using them. It is in fact an ingenious form of co-ordinate index enabling quite complex subject relationships to be recognized quickly.

The *Social science citation index* has the same array of associated indexes as *Science citation index*. It could be claimed that it is a more important work than its companion, since the bibliographical control of the social sciences generally is less effective than in the sciences and so relative to the rest of the bibliographical material it has a very high place. The value of citation indexing in providing bibliographical control over hitherto inadequately-controlled fields is mentioned by Spencer,[23] and Garfield[24] has described the means whereby it can be applied to history and the social sciences. Cawkwell[25] has discussed the practical application of *Science citation index* and Dundee University[26] have produced a tape-slide sequence on how to use it effectively. Martyn[27] has attempted an evaluation of citation indexing and a eulogy by Margolis[28] has been challenged by much more modified rapture from May and Janke[29] in separate replies.

Critics draw attention to how awkward citation indexes are to use, requiring three sequences to search for a full subject coverage and two for a complete trawl of author headings. It is true that they are more difficult to use than traditional indexes but they are fundamentally so different in concept that the direct comparison is rather unfair.

Citation indexing does beg one important question. Indexes of this kind are compiled by taking the citations attached to papers and re-distributing them as the basic raw material of the index. There can be no absolute guarantee that the citing author has thoroughly evaluated all that he cites, although the refereeing process of primary periodicals is a considerable safeguard. Cited articles may not necessarily be the most important in the opinion of the readers, they could be simply the most accessible and most heavily cited previously. May[29] believes that authors cite their friends more frequently than others and defines friends as people who cite the author's papers in return. It may be cynical to argue on these lines but the pattern has also been noted by Boyer[30] in an unrelated study. It could happen that an article assumes an undeserved significance in a citation index through being cited frequently, having once been picked up by one writer from an inaccessible source and not thoroughly checked by the rest.

Notwithstanding the objections, citation indexing has established itself as a major contribution to the bibliographic control of periodicals in particular. There is yet another way that the computer files from which they are compiled can be used to generate useful management information for librarians. The Institute of Scientific Information Inc. have been able to manipulate their data to produce a census of the number of times particular periodicals have been referred to in their indexes, and from this have generated a rank-order listing indicating which periodicals have most frequently carried important articles. They have published this information in the form of a separate periodical series.[31] Martyn and Gilchrist[32] have assembled a rank order of British periodicals using similar principles. These are interesting aids for the periodical selector to use in order to obtain one measure at least of the likely importance of a particular periodical.

REFERENCES

1. 'Standards for indexes to learned and scientific periodicals.' *The Indexer*, 2(2), Autumn 1960. pp. 63–64.
2. BRITISH STANDARDS INSTITUTE. *Recommendations for the preparation of indexes for books, periodicals and other publications.* London: BSI. British Standard 3700: 1976.
3. STRAIN, P. M. 'Indexing a periodical run.' *Sci-Tech News*, 20(4), Winter 1966. pp. 114–16.
4. MARKUS, J. 'State of the art of published indexes.' *American Documentation*, 13(1), January 1962. pp. 15–30.
5. DEVERS, C. M., KATZ, D. B. *and* REGAN, M. M. *Guide to special issues and indexes to periodicals.* New York: Special Libraries Association, 2nd ed., 1976.
6. HASKELL, D. C. *Checklist of cumulative indexes to individual periodicals in the New York Public Libraries.* New York: New York Public Library, 1942.
7. COATES, E. J. 'Computerized data processing for the *British Technology Index.*' *The Indexer*, 6(3), Spring 1969. pp. 97–101.
8. SHEEHY, E. *Guide to reference books.* Chicago: American Library Association, 9th ed., 1976.
9. WITTY, F. J. 'The beginnings of indexing and abstracting: some notes towards a history of indexing and abstracting in antiquity and the Middle Ages.' *The Indexer*, 8(4), October 1973. pp. 193–8.
10. KRONICK, D. A. *History of scientific and technical periodicals: the origins and development of the scientific and technological press 1665–1790.* Metuchen, N.J.: Scarecrow, 1976.
11. CLAPP, V. W. 'Indexing and abstracting services for serial literature.' *Library Trends*, 2(4), April 1954. pp. 509–21.
12. LAWLER, J. *The H. W. Wilson Company: half a century of bibliographical publishing.* Minneapolis, Minn.: Minneapolis University Press, 1950.
13. BROADWIN, J. A. 'An analysis of *Internationale Bibliographie der Zeitschriften-literatur.*' *Journal of Documentation*, 32(1), March 1976. pp. 26–31.
14. GRENFELL, D. *Periodicals and serials: their treatment in special libraries.* London: ASLIB, 2nd ed., 1965.
15. CONNOR, Judith Holt. 'Selective dissemination of information: a review of the literature and the issues.' *Library Quarterly*, 37(4), October 1967. pp. 373–91.
16. SWANSON, D. R. *Studies on indexing depth and retrieval effectiveness: Progress report Number 1.* Chicago: Chicago University Graduate Library School, 1966.
17. RAYWARD, W. B. *and* SVENONIUS, E. *Studies on indexing depth and retrieval effectiveness: Progress Report Number 2.* Chicago: Chicago University Graduate Library School, 1967.
18. NATIONAL LIBRARY OF MEDICINE. *The principles of MEDLARS.* Washington: Government Printing Office, n.d.

19. AUSTIN, C. J. *MEDLARS 1963–1967*. Washington: Government Printing Office, 1968.
20. AMERICAN INSTITUTE OF BIOLOGICAL SCIENCES, Biological Sciences Communications Project. *Accuracy of titles in describing content of biological sciences articles*. Washington: AIBS. 1963.
21. HARLEY, A. J. *and* MYATT, A. G. 'A contribution to the great debate.' *NLL Review*, 2(3), July 1972. pp. 77–82.
22. GARFIELD, E. '*Science citation index*- a new dimension in indexing.' *Science*, 144 (3750), 8 May 1964. p. 650.
23. SPENCER, C. C. 'Subject searching with *Science citation index* . . .' *American Documentation*, 18(2), April 1967. pp. 87–96.
24. GARFIELD, E. 'Citation indexes in sociological and historical research.' *American Documentation*, 14(4), October 1963. pp. 289–91.
25. CAWKWELL, A. E. 'The *Social sciences citation index* – description and application.' *INSPEL*, 8(3–4), July–Oct. 1973. pp. 58–63.
26. *An introduction to the Science citation index*. Dundee: Dundee University Library, 1974. *Tape slide sequence.*
27. MARTYN, J. 'An examination of citation indexes.' *ASLIB Proceedings*, 17(6), June 1965. pp. 184–96.
28. MARGOLIS, J. 'Citation indexing and evaluation of scientific papers.' *Science*, 155 (3767), 10 March 1967. p. 1213.
29. MAY, K. O. *and* JANKE, N. C. 'Abuses of citation indexing.' *Science*, 156 (3776), 4 May 1967. pp. 890–92.
30. BOYER, C. J. *The doctoral dissertation as an information source: a study of information flow*. Metuchen, N.J.: Scarecrow, 1973.
31. INSTITUTE OF SCIENTIFIC INFORMATION INC. *Journal Citation Reports*. Philadelphia, Pa.: ISI, 1974–.
32. MARTYN, J. *and* GILCHRIST, A. *An evaluation of British scientific journals*. (ASLIB Occasional Publications No 1.) London: ASLIB, 1968.

Chapter 10
Access to periodical literature

When a reference to a periodical article has been found through the use of the bibliographical apparatus already described, and when it has been established that the periodical is not available in the user's own library, recourse must be made to other libraries. This can be done either by using formal channels of inter-library co-operation or alternatively by direct application based upon personal knowledge.

The publishers of abstracting and indexing services have developed a keen interest in promoting wider access to the materials they make available. The National Federation of Abstracting and Indexing Services has a Documents Access Committee which has been investigating the problems for a number of years and which has produced a Position Statement.[1] The Committee observe that many of the services produced in the United States derive from discipline-based learned societies without major libraries of their own with the resources to provide access to the literature their services cite. The Federation point out that since 1958 their members have made seventeen-and-a-half-million citations. They believe, however, that the effectiveness of the results is not as good as it ought to be, principally because of the lack of library back-up facilities.

To British readers of the Position Statement it is a considerable boost to national pride to discover that the major abstracting and indexing services so bountifully provided by United States organizations expose a weakness in library provision in that country almost totally absent in the United Kingdom, owing to the existence of the British Library Lending Division. In the United States the growing recognition that the responsibility for the provision of access to the literature they cite rests with the publishers can be seen in the publication of such items as *Chemical Abstracts source index* (*CASSI*). This is basically a list of the periodicals monitored by the *Chemical Abstracts* Service but expanded to include a note of which major libraries the periodicals may be found in. The Federation itself is proposing the establishment of a network of depository libraries charged with the collection of designated portions of the total coverage of the member services of the Federation.

Central to the development of a depository network would be the evolution of a *CASSI*-type publication for all of the Federation's services with locations of periodicals being available on-line or off-line on computers or microfilm. The proposition is really for an articulated union list of periodicals/ co-operative inter-library loan/depository library programme. It is this kind of back-up to a bibliographical service which distinguishes bibliographic organization from bibliographic control: the latter implies simply compiling bibliographies without reference to questions of access.

The compilation and use of union lists does not normally carry with it any specific measures for developing access to periodicals, other than can be inferred from the fact that the union list is intended to draw attention to the presence of material in particular libraries. In an authoritative guide to the practice of compiling union lists, Willemin[2] provides a neat definition of what he terms union catalogues:

> A Union Catalogue is an inventory common to several libraries and containing all or some of their publications listed in one or more orders of arrangement.

A union list (or catalogue) of periodicals is a list usually, but not necessarily, arranged alphabetically by title. Notes are appended to each title to indicate the extent of the holdings of that particular title in libraries co-operating in the development of the list. The co-operating libraries are usually a predetermined group who have been approached by the editor and asked either to check their holdings against a list produced by him or else to submit to him a list of all of their holdings. The returns from the several libraries are then co-ordinated into one alphabetical sequence with notes.

Union lists of periodicals can be compiled on an international, national, or purely local basis. The periodicals covered may be general in subject matter or restricted to one particular field. As was noted before, large-scale union lists can be a significant source of auxiliary bibliography providing for the verification of the existence of particular titles, the exact title and date of commencement of a periodical and of its termination where appropriate.

Whilst the major initiatives in the establishment of union lists have tended to come from official bodies, it was an individual library which is credited with having produced the first such list in the United Kingdom. Manchester Public Libraries compiled a *List of the current scientific serial publications received by the principal public libraries in Manchester* in 1898. Another public library, Sheffield, was the base for the earliest British attempt at the co-operative provision of access to periodicals when it established the Sheffield Inter-Change Organization (SINTO). The basis of SINTO was a card file maintained in the public library of the periodical holdings of members, whence information about the availability of particular periodicals could be obtained and the necessary borrowing arranged.

The two largest union lists of periodicals in terms of the number of periodicals covered are the *British union catalogue of periodicals* and the *Union lists of serials*. Each is accompanied by a supplementary apparatus.

British union catalogue of periodicals. London : Butterworth. 1955–1958. 4 vols, with Supplement 1962.

This basic work covers periodicals in British libraries to the year 1960 if the supplement is included. For the purposes of its later supplementation it now includes an eminent union list with a considerably longer history than that of *BUCOP* itself – the *World list of scientific periodicals* (London : Butterworth 4th ed., 1965). Supplementation of both works is by means of a subsidiary series bearing the names of the two above works together with the title *New periodical titles*. This supplement appears quarterly with annual cumulations in two editions, one containing the whole of the material appearing in the quarterly parts, and the other that part of the material which creates, in effect, a supplement to *World list of scientific periodicals*. There are also five-yearly cumulations of each series.

BUCOP had a chequered early career. The initial ambitious plans to issue a master list of periodicals to be circulated to major libraries so that they could add details of their own holdings had to be ruled out on cost grounds. An alternative programme of inviting certain libraries to submit details of their periodical holdings to the editorial office was adopted. Whilst no doubt much cheaper this approach was fraught with difficulty. Different libraries had different ideas of what constituted a periodical. Some libraries submitted lists less comprehensive than the editorial committee would have wished. This results in some unevenness of coverage in the final work in which, in any case, cost considerations had again intervened to force severe restrictions upon coverage. A considerable amount of material from the lists submitted by individual libraries had to be relegated to a card file kept in the editorial office. Whilst much of this material is undoubtedly of a relatively unimportant nature it is a matter for regret that much unique material was, as a consequence, left out of the final edition. Another consequence of cost limitation was a decision to note only 'major imperfections' in the files of holdings listed.

Despite all these drawbacks the work lists 140,000 periodicals in 450 libraries (the *World list of scientific periodicals* contains 60,000 titles located in nearly 300 libraries). Entry in *BUCOP* is alphabetically by title with keywords in the title being sensibly re-arranged in many cases to enable a modicum of access by subject. The basic work was compiled manually but later supplements have been computer generated. In 1976 discussions have been under way which could well presage the end of the *BUCOP/World list* . . . series in its current form.

Union list of serials. New York: H. W. Wilson, 3rd ed., 1965. 5 vols.

This is a listing of 156,499 periodical titles in 950 libraries in the United States and Canada. Earlier editions appeared in 1927 and 1943, containing respectively 75,000 and 120,000 titles. The third edition was the final one and was intended to bring the coverage of locations of material up to the year 1950. From that point the Library of Congress *New serial titles* forms the cumulative supplement to the basic work but no measures have been taken in hand to fill pre-1950 gaps in the *Union list of serials* coverage.

The major interest in the *Union list of serials* coverage now centres upon the activities of the *New Serial titles* series of publications. Begun in 1953 as a monthly, *New serial titles* was first published under the supervision of the Joint Committee on the *Union list of serials*. The monthly parts are alphabetically arranged by titles (in their latest form) and are cumulated into annual volumes which are themselves cumulated into larger permanent volumes, the ultimate of which so far is *New serial titles 1950–1970* (New York: Bowker, 1974, 4 vols). This work, edited by Emery Koltay, contains information on 220,000 periodical titles from all over the world located in 800 United States and Canadian libraries which have reported their holdings to the Library of Congress. It supersedes all previous cumulations and, as stated earlier, was used as a data base for extending the assignment of ISSNs following the initial assignment made from the *Ulrich's international periodicals directory* and the *Irregular serials and annuals* base.

New serials titles commenced solely as an alphabetical list but it was soon complemented by a subject series, *New serial titles: classed subject arrangement* (also monthly, 1965 – but uncumulated at first). It was intended as a current selection aid for libraries. It too has been the subject of a massive cumulation exercise by the R. R. Bowker Company:

> *New serial titles 1950–1970: subject guide.* New York: Bowker, 1975. 2 vols.

The 220,000 titles in the basic alphabetical work are here arranged into 255 subject headings derived from the Dewey Decimal Classification's order of arrangement of subjects. Within each heading material is sub-divided by country and then alphabetically arranged by title. Despite about 1,200 subject cross-references the basic 255 sub-divisions are too few to prevent very large groupings under many of the headings which are not effective for their stated purpose of subject searching. Many librarians still prefer:

> *Subject index to new serial titles 1950–1965.* Ann Arbor, Mich.: Pieran, 1968.

This book indexes material in the monthly parts under some 3,000 subject headings. It costs only about one quarter the price of the Bowker set. It is not easy to see either work as absolutely essential to a library since the subject approach to periodicals is fairly adequately provided for by many other works certainly as far as current items are concerned, and most calls for discontinued items arise from citations which allow title searches to be made direct.

BUCOP and *Union list of serials/New serial titles* are the giants of this particular area but a massive range of other, lesser works exists for other countries and regions, and for general and specific subject periodicals nationally, regionally and locally. Indications of their extent and variety are given by:

LIBRARY OF CONGRESS, General Reference and Bibliography Division. *Union lists of serials: a bibliography*. New York: Gregg, 1972.

WEHEFRITZ, V. *International loan services and union catalogues*. Frankfurt/Main: Klostermann, 1974.

The second work is more limited and refers mainly to national general lists including those listing material other than periodicals. The UNESCO series *Bibliographic services throughout the world* (Paris: UNESCO, 1950–) is a regular up-dating source which notes newly published items, although with bibliographic data not adequate to enable them to be easily acquired from unfamiliar publishers in far-flung lands.

Why has so much union list material continued to thrive in the presence of the massive works mentioned earlier? A partial answer is that the large-scale works may limit their coverage in some way. They may ignore certain categories of material. The later editions of *Union list of serials*, for example, did not supply additional data on holdings for which ten locations had already been provided. Consequently more localized lists can be more extensive in several ways. They can tap the resources of a greater number of smaller local libraries than the major general listings can. They can provide more exact specifications of holdings than the major lists (*BUCOP*'s limitation of specification of holdings to express only the 'major imperfections' may be noted). More localized or more subject-specific listings can record details of unique holdings of less significant material and, by extension of the definition of periodical, trap material missing from the major listings. Apart from anything else the existence of these lesser listings helps to take pressure off the major libraries covered by the more massive listings. Most libraries will prefer to borrow locally if they can do so and their users will certainly appreciate being directed to local rather than to distant sources.

Examples of more localized listings which are general in their subject coverage are:

> *London union list of periodicals: holdings of the municipal and county libraries of Greater London.* London: Library Association, London and Home Counties Brench, 2nd ed., 1958.

Lists of a more limited subject scope exist both at the national and at local levels; examples include:

> *Union list of periodicals in the romance languages and literatures in British national university and special libraries.* London: University of London Library, 1964.
> *Union list of legal periodicals: a location guide to holdings of legal periodicals in libraries of the United Kingdom.* London: University Institute of Advanced Legal Studies, 1970.
> *Botanical periodicals in London libraries.* London: University of London Library, 1954.
> LIBRARIANS OF SCOTTISH COLLEGES OF EDUCATION. *Union list of periodicals held in the libraries of the Scottish colleges of education.* Craigie: College of Education, 3rd ed., 1973.
> *Union list of serials in the health sciences libraries in Oxford.* Oxford: Cairns Library, 1975.

INTER-LIBRARY CO-OPERATION

Union lists provide locations of material in libraries but the most significant part of the access process is the actual provision of items required. As distinct from requests for monograph sources, for which well endowed libraries will usually try to purchase materials urgently required, requests for periodicals not immediately available are usually met by borrowing copies from other libraries or by supplying photocopies.

Union lists of periodicals, on the national and international scale are rarely geared up to a comprehensive access system of the sort implied by the NFAIS programme mentioned above. At a more local level the access is frequently organized only to the extent of formal or informal agreements between libraries who have co-operated in compiling the listing to make their material available to other libraries who have contributed entries. In the United Kingdom many local associations of libraries exist that amongst their several aims seek to create a union list of periodicals and to arrange systems to interchange material and information between members. Co-operative schemes are valuable in organizing locally based resources to achieve their maximum potential and take the weight off national schemes for more common material. This is especially so when steps are also taken to rationalize acquisition policies so that important material is maintained whilst expensive and little used items are not duplicated unnecessarily.

A great deal of good work in inter-loans and sharing access to periodicals is done at the local level, but it is all overshadowed by the work of the massive British Library Lending Division (BLLD).

The National Lending Library for Science and Technology had formally come into existence in 1961 following many years of preliminary planning. Initially the National Lending Library was confined to science and technology, based on material culled from the back periodical files of the Science Museum Library. Its principal purpose was to collect and disseminate material from the Eastern Bloc countries but this role was progressively extended. It merged with the National Central Library in 1973 to form the BLLD.

The scope of the BLLD is now both world-wide and of universal subject coverage. Report literature, theses and some monographs are also included in the acquisition policy of the BLLD. The history and evolution of this most seminal of institutions has been widely reported. Houghton[3] has produced a detailed statement of history and function that is more objective than most of the material, which has usually been written by the staff of the Library. *BLL Review* (1971–) is a constant source of news and comment on the Library. A tape-slide sequence has been produced.[4]

The BLLD houses between 50,000 and 60,000 current periodicals and vast files of non-current items. Initially access to these was principally by the postal loan of actual copies. Increasingly, however, material is being made available in the form of photocopies, or microfiches of more substantial items. Very careful steps are taken to ensure that copyright regulations are not breached.

Application for material, whether photocopy or loan of actual publication, is made with loan application forms which are purchased from the Library in packs of fifty. Each form is used for one transaction, thereby contributing to the costs of photocopying, postage and administration. Special arrangements can be made for loans to be transacted by telex. Full and accurate bibliographical details must be supplied on the form by the potential borrower, which means that libraries wishing to borrow from the BLLD must have access to good sources of bibliography. From relatively humble beginnings the Library has grown to be a major source of access to periodical literature not simply for the United Kingdom but across Europe and even beyond. International loans are always effected by photocopy or microcopy which are actually non-returnable purchases of the required material. The international loans service of the BLLD has been described by Davey and Smith.[5]

The International Federation of Library Associations' Committee on International Lending and Union Catalogues has been established to encourage and improve the development of co-operation and access to materials across national boundaries. In 1975 they established an Office for International Lending and based it at the BLLD. Line[6] has described the operations of this Office, whose principal functions are:

1. to collect data on national policies on international loans and its dissemination – a guide has been produced[7]
2. to collect statistics on international loans
3. to oversee developments in inter-library loan practice in individual countries
4. to improve processes for developing universal availability of publications in accordance with IFLA policy under the Universal Bibliographic Control system

5. to collect information on barriers to international lending – customs practices and copyright regulations
6. to act as a clearing house for information and the identification of issues requiring IFLA attention and action in support of their desire to improve access internationally

An issue of extreme concern to the development of international access to literature by loan and photocopying is ensuring that costs are equitably shared amongst the various parties. Line[8] has developed some tentative ground rules identifying some major problems. Whilst acknowledging that the ideal in international lending is that each country should bear its own costs (which would, incidentally, be a useful hidden subsidy to the less developed countries) he admits that there are a number of practical objections. He lists eight such objections which, in varying strengths, lead to the conclusion that cost recovery on international transactions is impossible.

REFERENCES

1. NATIONAL FEDERATION OF ABSTRACTING AND INDEXING SERVICES, Document Access Committee. 'Position statement on document access.' *NFAIS Newsletter*, 18(3), June 1976. pp. 19–23.
2. WILLEMIN, S. 'Techniques of union catalogues : a practical guide.' *UNESCO Bulletion for Libraries*, 20(1), Jan.–Feb. 1966. pp. 2–23.
3. HOUGHTON, B. *Out of the dinosaurs*. London: Bingley, 1972.
4. *The British Library Lending Division: a tape-slide sequence.* Leeds: Leeds Polytechnic, School of Librarianship, 1975.
5. DAVEY, J. S. *and* SMITH, E. S. 'The overseas service of the British Library Lending Division.' *UNESCO Bulletin for Libraries*, 29(5), Sept.–Oct. 1975 pp. 259–67.
6. LINE, M. B. 'The functions of an IFLA Office for International Lending.' *IFLA Journal*, 2(1), 1976. pp. 34–7.
7. DIGBY, A. M. *and* THOMPSON, B. P. *A brief guide to national centres of international lending and photocopying.* Boston Spa, Yorks: British Library Lending Division, 1975.
8. LINE, M. B. 'The principles of cost recovery for international loans.' *IFLA Journal*, 2(2), 1976. pp. 81–5.

Part Three
The organization and management of periodicals

Chapter 11
Acquisition policy

Most libraries – certainly most public libraries – despite the
heavy costs of periodicals, do not appear to have an acquisition
policy which operates at a higher level than the vague feeling
that to have periodicals around the library in large quantities
is a 'good thing'. The need for care in the assembling and
maintenance of a periodicals collection can hardly be over-
stressed, given the cost of periodicals and the way their prices
have risen in the past few years far ahead of general levels of
inflation, as the regularly published indexes show.[1,2] In the
United Kingdom periodical prices showed a 27·1 per cent
increase in 1976 as compared to 1975 and on an index of
prices, where 1970 was equal to 100, they registered 264·8.
Melcher[3] is not alone in pointing out that, once entered,
subscriptions to periodicals become a standing charge on the
library accounts, for once a file has been started librarians
are loath to terminate it. Indeed they have almost invariably
expanded their collections year by year. The economic
stringency of the mid 1970s is forcing many librarians for the
first time in their lives to take a hard look at policy and to
alter the *laissez-faire* attitude of the balmy days of 'when in
doubt buy it' to ones of 'when in doubt don't buy it' or even
'unless absolutely certain don't buy it'. As Huff[4] has shown in
an important review, very few libraries have practised a
serious policy of weeding out dead stock or little-used current
material in their periodicals collection. It is a difficult and
unrewarding task in terms of the annoyance and bad feeling
they can generate by eliminating less-used periodicals.
Librarians do not like making hard and unpopular decisions
and they are, perhaps, temperamentally unsuited to the task;
in any case to assess which are the lesser-used materials ripe
for pruning is not easy. Observation of the current periodicals
display to discover the absence of any use of a particular title

over an extended period can cost far more than the saving made in cancelling the subscription. Even cancelling the subscription is never likely to be the end of the exercise for, despite all the evidence accumulated, vehement denunciations of the policy of the library will follow immediately from persons claiming to be regular users whose work will be seriously jeopardized by the removal of the particular title. When periodicals librarians meet there are even stories told of lists of periodicals being circulated, so that users can register objections to cancellations. These result in protestations of undying devotion to titles invented by the librarian for the purposes of checking the honesty of the users' responses!

Huff's study of acquisition policy in American academic libraries[4] reveals that in only 12 per cent of the libraries examined was there a formal statement of acquisitions policy. In only 6 per cent of instances was the policy actually written down. This appears to be a fairly general pattern and a small-scale survey of the practice of British Public Libraries[5] also revealed disturbing evidence of a lack of policy. In this case the researchers were sometimes left with the conviction that they were supplied with a policy statement made up on the spur of the moment for the purposes of their research. Even more startling was substantial evidence that the person or persons responsible for making the purchase decisions and authorizing payments had little or no idea of the number, nature and deployment within their system, of the periodicals taken. The only evidence of 'policy' in many public libraries in the United Kingdom is over controversial periodicals, and even then the policy is simply to refer such items to the Library Committee for a decision upon whether or not to purchase. In fact British public libraries rarely take risks on controversial materials such as the underground press or what are sometimes called 'THOSE' magazines. Oldman and Davinson[5] were unable to find even relatively 'establishment' items like *Private Eye* in any library they visited.

STUDY OF THE USAGE OF PERIODICALS

To revert to the weeding and pruning of subscription lists: this should be done on the basis of studies of use of periodicals, which is not a very highly developed or widely practised art. The most favoured method appears to be the removal of current titles from display with a view to measuring use on the basis of *when* (although in fact it should surely be *if*) an enquiry is made for the title at the counter. Despite all the obvious shortcomings of the method it is much used by librarians although, as Oldman and Davinson show, failure to see a periodical on the shelf will as often as not result in the reader leaving without making any other attempt to locate it.

For public libraries at least, use studies are few. Luckham[6] has looked at patterns in two public libraries in north-west England, principally from the sociological point of view, relating the age, sex and social status of readers to the type of material they use. Helpful though such generalizations can be in indicating the patterns to look for, it is only by carefully organized in-library investigations that the information upon which to base rational acquisitions and weeding policies can be generated. A number of limited use studies of this sort have been undertaken – the Department of Education and Science,[7] Huws,[8] Stradling.[9] Although partial and un-scientifically undertaken, these studies reveal a heavy use of periodicals for browsing and only a light use for what might be termed 'purposive study' in public libraries. This result will be further elaborated below.

In considering the application of use studies it is necessary to appreciate that they provide information only upon the use of the material supplied. More difficult and more important are studies to determine what readers want and what they need. Evidence from the Oldman and Davinson survey suggests that librarians in public libraries think that their readers want a collection of academic and scientific and technical periodicals. Perhaps that statement should read that public librarians *think* their readers *ought* to want such material and they supply it for reasons of prestige. In fact reading of periodicals as demonstrated by the survey was, in British public libraries, heavily orientated to current affairs, and popular and recreational material, material which was supplied only perfunctorily by those public libraries that had not bothered to assess the wants of readers closely.

Methods of studying use are noted and critically appraised by Oldman and Davinson who recognize the following methods:

1. removing periodicals from display shelves
2. sampling in-library use
3. observation of traffic patterns
4. self-recording techniques by placing questionnaires in periodicals
5. interviewing users to ascertain their 'wants'

If, as the result of a use study, it is discovered that a periodical is not used at all it is easy enough to argue that it should be dropped. If, however, it is discovered that use is small, how is the librarian to assess the quality of use? If it becomes important to reduce the number of periodicals in times of economic stringency, it seems only logical that those least used should be first cancelled. This might not always be the most sensible practice however if the quality of that use is high – and one measure of high quality of use might be the uniqueness of the periodical in a particular region.

An appreciable number of periodicals depend for their continuation upon library orders. There are many periodicals – especially highly specialized items – that attract almost no non-institutional subscribers. The number of studies which point to the fact that a great deal of the periodical material supplied by librarians is little used are legion. There is a widespread belief that the number of periodicals currently being published is too great. If these various factors are weighed together it is to be inferred that some at least of the responsibility for the so-called 'literature explosion' is to be placed at the door of librarians. Librarians appear unwilling, unless forced by economic circumstance, to take a hard and sober look at their periodicals acquisition policies and to endeavour to make rigorous appraisals of the material they are invited to buy. Many periodicals reach the library subscription list by a kind of negative selection policy. That is to say, by purchasing everything offered that might be remotely applicable in the good years when the funds are flowing freely, and by defending the purchases made in the bad years by squeals of outrage about the threat to standards and quality of service posed by any reduction in provision. In fact, although many librarians would disagree, a period of financial stringency is an ideal time to re-discover the art of library economy.

That 80 per cent of use is generated from 20 per cent of periodicals supplied was postulated first by Trueswell[10] who calls it the '80:20 rule'. It is a most important concept for the periodicals-acquisition librarian. Whilst it is not true to say that the proportions are always of this order, many studies of use, especially in academic libraries, have pointed to similar findings on the general point that the majority of the use of periodicals is concentrated upon a small proportion of those supplied. Oldman and Davinson discovered that this was as true of the public library as others have found it of other types of library although, as indicated above, usually for the reason that public librarians supplied the most heavily used materials less generously than the material they, the librarians, thought ought to be supplied.

In academic and research libraries the evidence of low usage of the majority of the periodicals supplied is well documented. A survey undertaken in the University of Rhode Island by Chambers and Healey[11] to determine the use made of the periodicals collection, by analysing the patterns of citations in masters theses in mathematics and education, produced some startling conclusions. A very small proportion of the periodicals supplied in the library in the relevant subject fields provided the vast majority of citations. In the survey period of 1959 to 1968, 55 per cent of all citations of periodical literature came from 0·5 per cent of the holdings and more than 75 per cent from 1·5 per cent of the holdings. Something like two-thirds of the periodicals supplied were cited less than once in ten years. One can hardly quarrel with the surveyor's conclusion that the periodicals collections are not a heavily used resource in that particular library. Surveys of a similar kind elsewhere would produce comparable results.

Trueswell's 80:20 rule appears to be less reliable as an indicator of the levels of use of large general libraries than it is of smaller specialized libraries according to Bower.[12] He is commenting upon the results of a massive survey undertaken by the British Library Lending Division for the Swedish Council for Scientific Information and Documentation.

During the first three months of 1975 a study of one-sixth of all requests for periodical literature was made by the BLLD.[13] Some 61,333 requests for 14,967 periodical titles were examined for language, age and subject of the periodical requested and for the type of organization making the request. The results correspond closely to those of similar surveys although the 'core' of periodicals heavily used is possibly smaller than that shown in any other major survey. About 10 per cent of the periodicals surveyed generated 50 per cent of all requests, and only 5 per cent of the BLLD holdings generated 80 per cent of all satisfied requests, with 83 per cent of requested material being of the scientific and technical category. A rank order of most requested periodicals resulted in *Biochimica et Biophysica Acta* showing the most requests in the three-month period.

In 1959 Urquhart and Bunn[14] provided what has become the classic statement of the case of a small core generating the majority of use. Martyn and Gilchrist[15], in a refinement of the process of studying loan requests, conclude that each 5 per cent step above 80 per cent of satisfaction of requests from a given group of periodicals requires a doubling of the supply. These various studies point to the necessity for very close examination of acquisitions policy at the individual library level to ensure that the material bought (and it is very expensive material) is fully earning its keep. The 80:20 rule seems to indicate that a good deal of periodical stock is supplied more in the spirit of providing material in case of occasional need rather than of providing only that which is heavily in demand. Every librarian likes to be able to make an immediate supply of material no matter how abstruse the request. However, the cost of providing the abstruse on demand is becoming prohibitive, and serious attention has been given to the question of when borrowing becomes more economic than owning a periodical. Gordon Williams[16] argues that less than six uses a year for a given periodical title costing more than $20 makes it more economic to borrow or obtain a photocopy, than to purchase. Williams' case is apparently scientifically constructed and obviously has value as a proposition. So many studies of this sort, however, assume that the would-be user will be prepared to wait for the material to be obtained from elsewhere. Many are not. Such studies also assume that all use of periodical literature is purposive, in the sense that the would-be user knows in advance what he requires. Whilst this is often true in the field of science and technology where the availability of abstracts, indexes and literature reviews makes material more visible, it is not a proposition which holds good for the humanities and, to a certain extent, the social sciences, where the aids and guides are less good. The BLLD seems dedicated to the proposition that all use of periodical literature follows the pattern of that in science and technology and this is simply not true. In the humanities especially there is no substitute for immediately available browsable material. To restrict access to borrowing from a central store will not work in this field as effectively as it may do in science and technology, since the current-awareness tools are not available to ensure that the necessary borrowing can take place in the absence of local supply. There will be times when, despite low usage, it will be proper to continue a subscription to a periodical. One example is when a group of libraries agrees to share resources and to maintain subscriptions to little-used periodicals co-operatively.

The development of resource-sharing activities amongst a group of local libraries is an obvious means of maintaining levels of service whilst economizing. The difficulty with centralized borrowing on the BLLD model is that although, as has already been said, it enables the person who knows what he wants to obtain material quite quickly, the person who only thinks that a certain periodical file may contain information being sought and who would like to browse through a complete file is not catered for. As in many other areas concerned with the acquisition process in libraries, resource-sharing is not attractive in the years when money is not too restricted. In the bad years, however, the impetus to co-operate and to ensure the maintenance of at least one file within a region of lesser-used material, for browsing and reference purposes, is stronger and can lead to a more general opening up of the resources of one library to the users of another, once the initial barriers have been broken through. In these circumstances resource-sharing can enhance local provision rather than restricting the service. The more enthusiastic advocates of central storage and loan collections on the BLLD model appear to see them as an alternative to the development of sound and self-sufficient local periodicals collections. This is not so. There is no effective alternative in the eyes of a library user to immediate availability of the material required. Co-operative stores and centralized inter-lending and photocopying facilities for specific items are simply the back-up – an extremely important back-up – to good local services which attempt to fulfil as much of local demand as possible. The library user will be grateful for evidences of a desire to help him by recourse to an outside source for his request but will regard it as second best. The problem for the librarian is to balance the cost of acquiring material for display and storage locally, against using the organizations. As Ward[17] puts it: 'practical decisions will require personal consultation and intuition.' Allen Kent[18] has discussed the resource sharing and co-operative storage in all its aspects including in respect of periodicals acquisition. Katz[19] provides a wide and reassuring survey of the conse-quences of acquisition policies aimed at reducing the burdens of periodical subscriptions to overstretched budgets. He cites authorities who have noted that more than 65 per cent of the 11,000 current titles in one library were not used in a twelve-month survey period and a massive 88 per cent of a 37,000 current title collection in another library failed to attract a single loan in one year; indeed, 161 titles in that library fulfilled more than 10 per cent of all use.

Periodicals collections are important to the library but the cost is enormous and the temptation simply to buy to create a large impressive collection (impressive to fellow librarians!) must be avoided. Constant weeding and relegation to central co-operative stores must be practised and the kind of arrogance noted by Huff[4] who reported a significant number of librarians who never weed their periodical subscription list on the premise that 'the selection process had been properly carried out at the time of acquisition', has no place in the periodical librarian's creed. Kraft,[20] one suspects, has a very shrewd knowledge of the psychology of the librarian when she asks:

Are we not the victims of a delusion by assuming that the

sheer existence and collection of these periodicals for which there is no demand contributes in some way to scholarship?

Oldman and Davinson constantly wondered about the librarian's capacity for self-deception when they were discovering that, despite evidence of lack of demand, British public librarians still provide large quantities of expensive scholarly periodicals.

Perhaps, however, to complain of the waste of resources in a particular library by acquiring periodicals which will be little used, is to look at the situation from too narrow a perspective? Could it be argued that the willingness of libraries to continue to purchase large numbers of prestigious periodicals which will be little used in their libraries does actually, by increasing print runs and reducing unit costs, keep them afloat financially, and therefore available to those (maybe few) libraries where they are really useful? It is an intriguing but not altogether convincing suggestion.

FINANCE FOR PERIODICALS ACQUISITION

Ward discovered that the seventeen London-based libraries he surveyed expended between 24 per cent and 90 per cent of their budgets on periodicals purchase. Presumably at the upper end of his range is a highly specialized library whilst at the lower end is a public library. If this is so, Ward selected fairly affluent public libraries; for a survey of periodical provision in all British public libraries carried out in 1971[21] revealed only an average of between 4 and 5 per cent of all total acquisition funds devoted to periodicals although even in this case London public libraries were shown to spend proportionately more. Ward shows that academic libraries spend about 40 per cent of total funds on periodicals, a proportion exactly equalling that which Huff reports for the United States. Susan Brynteson[22] offers a wry comment on that 40 per cent figure, which it is well to remember:

. . . much of their budget is already encumbered by ongoing commitments via standing orders and subscriptions, fewer monographs can be purchased. The central administration of an institution is generally unsympathetic upon learning that what it thinks is an enormously large budget has had perhaps as much as 40% plus a 13% inflation allowance already spent without the library making a single additional purchase or placing a single new order.

Brynteson also draws attention to a trend which is common to both Western Europe and North America. In 1965–6 one American academic library spent 16 per cent of its budget on periodicals, but this had risen to 33 per cent by 1970–71.

To return to the proportion of total acquisition funds spent on periodicals by public libraries, the low figures conceal a true comparison with other types of library. Periodicals in public libraries tend to be principally housed in reference libraries. The Department of Education and Science survey noted above gives the categories of periodical purchased as 2 per cent children's, 5 per cent bibliographies, 5 per cent abstracting and indexing, 41 per cent general and recreational, 47 per cent scholarly. If the non-recreational items housed in reference and information departments are considered as a proportion of total acquisition funds for such departments, then figures of between 25 per cent and 40 per cent are more usual.

Devising estimates of expenditure on periodicals

The task of calculating realistic estimates for the next year's periodicals has been made considerably easier in the past few years by the publication of annual series of price indexes mentioned earlier.[1,2] These invaluable tables analyse prices of periodicals by subject group and by total annual cost of all published periodicals; it is then possible to formulate a proposition for the increase of the previous year's fund necessary to cover existing commitments. It also provides a basis for assessing the amounts required for carrying out a programme of expansion. The only really imponderable factor in formulating estimates is this inclusion of an amount for the purchase of newly-published items. Inevitably in any year some periodicals currently subscribed will cease, and the amount saved on these will at least partially offset purchases of newly published items, but there is no means of computing in advance what will be the likely pattern of cessations.

It is doubtful if there is any real advantage in keeping the acquisition funds for periodicals separate from the rest. One reason for the practice is that several independently-itemized funds are thought to be most easily defensible than one overall fund if it is found necessary to economize. The advantages of flexibility which attend upon having one consolidated fund are considerable and far outweigh the theoretical advantages of being able to argue the case for three separate small increases for funds for periodicals, books and binding.

THE ORGANIZATION OF THE SELECTION PROCESS

Katz maintains that librarians have been collectors rather than selectors of periodicals and goes on to argue the point abrasively, cogently and in a highly entertaining fashion, especially when on his favourite hobby-horse of the controversial and the subversive periodical. Oldman and Davinson found little evidence that public librarians did anything much more than allow a modest number of new items each year to join the existing collection which, in all probability, they inherited uncritically from a predecessor. They made two general points of great significance when considering periodicals selection at least in British public libraries:

1. a lack of systematic policy is evident
2. knowledge of demand is not a particular common criterion for selection and retention decisions

These are strong criticisms but too many public library *book* selection meetings deal with periodicals as 'any other business'. Oldman and Davinson found only very few instances of any one person having responsibility for a systematic over-view of periodicals provision within a library system and able also to relate the public library provision to that of other libraries in a region or locality.

Periodical selection should be governed by the same rules as, it is to be hoped, are applied to the selection of other forms of library material. There should be a policy of regular and frequent meetings of a periodicals acquisition group. Periodical selection must not depend upon the chance of a bright cover catching the eye or be solely confined to a consideration of specimen copies of those periodicals that a publisher has been enterprising enough to send out to the library. It is advisable to use review and selection advice publication. For established titles, Bill Katz's *Magazines for libraries* (New York: Bowker) has no British parallel as indeed there are no British parallels for current reviews appearing in *Serials Review* (Ann Arbor, Mich.: Pieran, quarterly) and *Choice* (Chicago: American Library Association, 1965 – ten times a year). Nor should the selection process consider just newly published titles; it should also review, possibly subject by subject over a period of time, all of the library's holdings and offer the opportunity to give thought to entering subscriptions to established periodicals not yet taken by the library.

Meetings for periodical selection should be held quarterly at least; to hold them less frequently could result in the loss of the early issues of a required new periodical, for publishers do not like to tie up a great deal of capital and space in the storage of back numbers, and a popular new title could well go out of print in its early issues very quickly. When ordering periodicals it is, incidentally, always good policy to enter subscriptions from the beginning of a volume rather than to commence in the middle of a volume and have part volumes on hand. If financial advantage can be derived out of entering a subscription for two or three years this is worth considering; many periodicals offer a significant discount for entering subscriptions for periods longer than a year. Pergamon Press offer about 5 per cent. The cost of *Reprints from the Soviet Press* (New York: Compass, 1965 – fortnightly) is $35 for one year, for two years $65, for three $95. On the other hand, some publishers charge libraries much more than individuals – for example *Journal of Colour and Appearance* (London: Gordon-Breach, 1972 – quarterly) charges libraries twice as much as individuals. In the case of new, untried periodicals, it is probably wise not to commit the library to an initial subscription of more than a year despite attractive multi-year discounts. Some new periodicals begin in a blaze of glory with eminent names filling pages of fat early issues, but soon descend to slimmer issues with less glamorous writers, if the subscription response is disappointing. Multi-year subscriptions are best confined to established periodicals, and they do provide valuable hedges against inflation.

Meetings should be attended by the representatives of every department of the library so that co-ordination of their various requirements and equitable allocations can be made. The multi-disciplinary nature of many periodicals will raise questions about what the most useful and the most proper location for them which are best resolved in committee. In an unco-ordinated system it is not unknown for two departments to be purchasing the same periodical, in ignorance of each other.

Osborn[23] supplies fourteen 'guiding principles' for periodical selection which repay study. He rightly stresses the importance of acquiring abstracting and indexing material and using it, and of making the process not only of acquisition but of regular review of the whole list a routine.

Which are the most important periodicals?

The recognition of which periodicals are the most significant for a particular library purpose is a complex task involving a great deal of research into the nature of the periodicals available and the needs of the community. Usually, however, librarians rely upon rule of thumb either in a thoroughly straightforward fashion or surrounded by the trappings of scientific investigation.

At its simplest, the rule of thumb method consists of giving the highest priority to those periodicals which are indexed in the major commercial services, on the premise that it is these periodicals which have been carefully assessed by the editors of such services and found to be the most significant in their field. They are also the periodicals which, because they are indexed widely, are likely to be most in demand.

The more scientific rule of thumb approach is based upon an examination of the lists of references – or citations – appended to articles appearing in periodicals of established reputation and counting the frequency with which particular periodicals are mentioned. The most heavily cited items are taken to be the most significant in their field. The technique is originally credited to Gross and Gross.[24] There is some merit in its application to the task of periodical selection since it might be argued that the periodicals most likely to be called for in future are those most visible to literature searchers by virtue of their frequent citation. It is an argument with a similar intent to that of using the lists of periodicals covered by the major indexing services.

The selection of 'most frequently cited' periodicals is not the entire solution to the selection process. Brodman[25] is not alone in pointing out that what people actually use and what is most cited are often significantly at variance. Citation counting takes little account of the needs and preferences of individual communities. It has most merit in a research library where periodicals are more frequently acquired for their archival value, than in other libraries where it presupposes a level of purposiveness in reading not always appropriate. It is a method which gives rise to the risk that selection policy is based more upon what users ought to need rather than what they actually want. L. Miles Raisig[26] has described an improved method for citation analysis which, he claims, gives less prominence to the periodical which publishes many short papers and communications.

In such assessment of the merits of particular periodicals, it is reasonable to take citation patterns into account. It is even reasonable to weight a purchase decision in favour of a periodical which is found to be most cited in the literature. It would be foolish, however, to base an entire policy on this method. Martyn and Webster provide a list of the most cited British scientific periodicals in rank order, whilst Brown[27] reviews the technique of citation analysis and lists the most cited American periodicals in particular subject fields. The Institute of Scientific Information have an on-going series.[28] The BLLD/Sinfdok study indicates that another technique, based upon a rank ordering of periodicals, can be used; in this case, it is of periodicals most borrowed from a central collection. This approach is probably much more reliable in recognizing the really significant periodicals.

Vickery[29] in a very important study and literature review summarizes the various basic approaches for developing strategies to recognize the most significant periodical literature:

   a. The analysis of records compiled for other purposes, e.g. reference counts of citations at the ends of papers . . .

similar counts in bibliographies . . . analysis of library loan records . . . examination of reference questions . . . analysis of abstracts . . . and lists of journals.

b. Diaries and questionnaires to be completed by users at the actual time of reading sample items of literature.

c. Questionnaires 'recording users' opinions and estimates of their reading . . .

d. An observational study of how scientists actually spend their time . . .

REFERENCES

1. 'Prices steadier in first four months.' *Library Association Record,* 78(6), June 1976. pp. 244–6.
2. 'Price Indexes for '76. U.S. Periodicals and serials services.' *Library Journal,* 29(5), Sept.–Oct., 1975. pp. 7259–67.
3. MELCHER, D. *Melcher on acquisition.* Chicago: American Library Association, 1970.
4. HUFF, William H. 'Acquisition of serial publications.' *Library Trends,* 18(3), January 1970. pp. 294–317.
5. OLDMAN, C. M. *and* DAVINSON, D. E. *The usage of periodicals in public libraries.* Leeds: Leeds Polytechnic, Dept. of Librarianship, 1975.
6. LUCKHAM, B. 'Periodicals purchase and readership,' *Research in Librarianship,* 4(23), May 1973. pp. 141–55.
7. DEPARTMENT OF EDUCATION AND SCIENCE. *Public libraries and their use,* London: D.E.S., 1972.
8. HUWS, G. *Provision of periodicals.* Leicester: Leicester County Library, 1968.
9. STRADLING, B. *The qualitative evaluation of a public library service.* Unpublished thesis for the Fellowship of the Library Association, 1966.
10. TRUESWELL, R. L. 'Some behavioral patterns of library users: the 80:20 rule.' *Wilson Library Bulletin,* 43(5), January 1969. pp. 450–61.
11. CHAMBERS, G. R. *and* HEALEY, J. S. 'Journal citations in masters' theses: a measurement of a journal collection.' *Journal of the American Society for Information Science,* 24(5), Sept.–Oct., 1973. pp. 397–401.
12. BOWER, C. A. 'Pattern of use of serial literature at the BLLD.' *BLL Review,* 4(2), April 1976. pp. 31–6.
13. 'BLLD/SINFDOK Serial Survey 1975.' *BLL Review,* 3(4), October 1975. pp. 107–8.
14. URQUHART, D. J. *and* BUNN, R. 'A national loan policy for scientific serials.' *Journal of Documentation,* 15(1), March 1959. pp. 21–37.
15. MARTYN, J. *and* GILCHRIST, A. *An evaluation of British scientific journals,* London: ASLIB, 1968.
16. WILLIAMS, Gordon. *Library cost models: owning versus borrowing serial publications.* Washington, D.C.: National Science Foundation' 1968.
17. WARD, M. 'Observations of serials management in seventeen London libraries.' *Library Association Record,* 77(10), October 1975. p. 247.
18. KENT, Allen. (ed.). *Resource sharing in libraries.* New York. Dekker, 1974.
19. KATZ, William A. 'Serials selection' *in* Allen, W. C., ed., *Serial publications in*

large libraries, Urbana, Ill.: University of Illinois Graduate School of Library Science, 1970.

20. KRAFT, Margit. 'An argument for selectivity in the acquisition of materials for research libraries.' *Library Quarterly*, 37(3), July 1967. pp. 284–95.
21. DEPARTMENT OF EDUCATION AND SCIENCE. *The provision of newspapers and periodicals in public libraries*. London: DES, 1971. (LEC(5) LWC(5) (70)2).
22. BRYNTESON, Susan. 'Serials acquisition' *in* Speyers-Duran, P. *and* Gore, Daniel, eds, *Management problems in serials work*. Westport, Conn.: Greenwood, 1974.
23. OSBORN, Andrew D. *Serial publications: their place and treatment in libraries*. Chicago: American Library Association, 2nd ed., 1973.
24. GROSS, P. L. K. *and* GROSS, E. M. 'College libraries and chemical education.' *Science*, 66(1323), 1927, pp. 385–9.
25. BRODMAN, E. 'Choosing psychology periodicals.' *Bulletin of the Medical Library Association*, 32(4), 1944. pp. 479–83.
26. RAISIG, L. Miles. 'Mathematical evaluation of the scientific serial.' *Science*, 131(3411), 13 May 1960. pp. 1417–19.
27. BROWN, Charles Harvey. *Scientific serials: characteristics and lists of most cited publications in Mathematics, Physics, Chemistry, Geology, Physiology, Botany, Zoology, and Entomology*. Chicago: American Library Association, ACRL Monograph No 16.
28. INSTITUTE OF SCIENTIFIC INFORMATION. *ISI Journal Citation Reports*, Philadelphia, Pa.: ISI, 1973–.
29. VICKERY, B. C. 'The use of scientific literature.' *Library Association Record*, 63(8), August 1961. pp. 263–9.

Chapter 12
Acquisition, the practical considerations

When the decisions have been made about what to buy and why, the librarian must give attention to the problems of obtaining the periodicals he believes he needs. In theory there ought to be no problems. The librarian wants certain periodicals and, presumably, has the money to pay for them. Publishers of various kinds produce periodicals and hope to sell them. The periodicals librarian with money and the periodical publisher with material ought to make an ideal union of a very simple kind. Nevertheless, the vast range of problems and oddities of practice revealed by Clara D. Brown[1] demonstrates that there are many things that can, and do, go wrong. These can entail enormous amounts of miserable and often unproductive work for the librarian, when the periodicals which ought to come do not appear when they should.

Basically there are five means of supply of periodicals to libraries:

1. by purchase from a local bookshop or newsagent
2. by purchase directly from a publisher who mails copies to the library
3. by taking up membership of the learned society or professional body which is the publisher of the required material
4. by dealing with specialist library suppliers of periodicals who arrange the delivery of the required periodicals and charge a fee for the service they provide
5. by the gift or exchange of publications with publishers, libraries or other organizations

Most libraries operate their acquisitions programmes for periodicals using a combination of a number of these methods. The American Library Association[2] have produced a set of guidelines for periodicals acquisition.

1. *Purchase from local suppliers*

The meticulous attention to detail and the necessary qualities of speed, initiative, imagination and persistence which must be present in the supplier of periodicals to libraries are rarely to be found in local newsagents and booksellers. The experience to deal with a multiplicity of specialist publishers, both foreign and domestic, is acquired only by long acquaintance with the problems. Many periodicals required by libraries will be of such a nature that the supplier will be faced with the task of obtaining only a single copy, since no other member of his regular clientele will be interested in such specialist material. The profit margins on these single copies are so small (or even non-existent) that there is no incentive to give a good service, in the sense of taking time and trouble to chase missing or delayed issues.

Some local government authorities in the United Kingdom have tended to insist upon their departments placing as much of their business as possible with local suppliers. The theory is that locally levied money – in the form of rates and taxes – is returned to the local community. In many cases this is doubtful; in fact only a small commission stays in the local system, since materials must usually be ordered from national or international suppliers. The practice of local purchase is not so strong as it once was. Business obtained in this fashion by local suppliers almost as a right did not develop the necessary qualities of cherishing and carefully servicing clients. What was worse in some cases, speaking specifically of periodicals, was that a rota of booksellers and newsagents was sometimes developed, around whom the library business had to be shared year after year in turn so that no accusations of graft and corruption could be levelled at the Council and its officers. The chaos resulting from this practice can be formidable. The non-delivery of the last issues of a particular volume, being the responsibility of a supplier no longer interested in the contract, resulted in protracted argument and ultimate frustration.

Local suppliers, if they have the kind of protection mentioned above, will usually select from the library list those periodicals that are easy to supply or offer the best profit margins for little work, and throw the rest back for the library to obtain as best it may elsewhere. Worst of all possible worlds in the case of local supply, is that system in which all local suppliers are invited to tender for the supply contract. Instituted in local and central government as a guard against corruption, this system has become an incubus virtually guaranteeing sloppy service: in order to obtain the business in the first place the successful supplier will have to undercut all of his opposition, probably to such an extent that the contract is uneconomic unless he cuts corners on service. There is, of course, no guarantee of continuity, even if a successful supplier in one year proves to be efficient, he may lose the contract to a lower bid in the next year.

Local suppliers are sometimes found who will offer a small discount on the cover price of certain periodicals on condition that a certain amount of potentially lucrative book acquisition business is placed with them. To cost conscious local authorities this can be an attractive proposition. Despite the fact that the resultant discounts may amount to a substantial sum on a large contract, it is not a practice that has all of the advantages that might seem to be present. A supplier giving a poor service will waste time and energy on the part of the library far outweighing the discounts obtained. An efficient supplier aware of the problems of periodicals acquisition will rarely offer a discount, since he will realize the formidable difficulties and know that the profit margins are such that efficiency and cost cutting are incompatible.

A major source of difficulty is that local suppliers will frequently accept commissions to supply periodicals but will then make arrangements with the publishers to supply copies of their periodicals direct to the library. An arrangement of this kind is acceptable so long as the supply proceeds smoothly. The periodicals will probably arrive at the library more quickly. Difficulties arise when the periodicals do not arrive. The local supplier, although nominally responsible, is likely to disclaim all responsibility and affect ignorance of the reasons for non-supply – probably quite reasonably. The library must not, however, be trapped into the position of being expected to deal direct with the publisher. This position must be described as 'bad service' by the supplier. It is true that if the supplier has renewed the subscription on time and attended accurately to the addressing details for the direct mailing, the blame for non-supply almost certainly rests with the publisher. Labour disputes, mechanical failure, editorial delays or non-delivery of printing supplies are amongst the principal reasons preventing a publisher from delivering on time. The invitation by the supplier that the library should take up the complaint directly must be firmly resisted. The almost inevitable result of the library taking up the complaint direct will be that the publisher will claim to be unable to trace a subscription in the name of that library. His address label will show the library as a subscriber, but the central subscription record will be in the name of the supplier. Considerable correspondence will be the result. Under no circumstances must the librarian allow himself to be placed in the position that he does the supplier's job for him – a job that the supplier himself is paid to do by virtue of the discounts he receives. Not all local suppliers will adopt such tactics, but many will try it on the inexperienced librarian and it is a practice which must be watched for.

Invoices from local suppliers are usually presented monthly, one invoice covering all transactions taking place in the previous month, both for items supplied from bulk stocks received by the supplier and for subscriptions renewed during the month. In some instances differential discounts will be offered for each category.

Local suppliers are usually employed to supply material which is needed quickly and which is within their competence to supply – newspapers and weekly current affairs items such as *The Economist,* the *Spectator, New Scientist.* To have this kind of material mailed from the publisher can result in unacceptable delays.

It must be said, however, that when a local source of supply is found that is willing to accept total responsibility and has the experience to do so efficiently over the whole range of the library's needs, then this is the best possible situation. There are such local suppliers but they are rare. When local supply is badly done, as it often is, then there is nothing worse.

2. *Purchase direct from the publisher*

Almost all periodical publishers will accept subscriptions directly from a library and will mail copies at the basic subscription price, although newspapers and publications received from abroad will be subject to a higher subscription rate if they are to be mailed outside the country of publication. There are, of course, disadvantages in the practice from the library's point of view. The library must deal with a multiplicity of sources of supply and handle many separate invoices for small sums of money, perhaps in a variety of currencies. There are, nevertheless, a number of benefits to be derived from direct dealings:

1. The periodicals are delivered promptly and mistakes are few.
2. If mistakes in supply arise the lines of communication and responsibility are clearer than when third parties are involved and the chances of rectifying errors quickly are better.
3. It is possible to specify precise mailing instructions enabling material to be swiftly sorted in the library on arrival and dispatched to the relevant departments often without the need to unwrap them.
4. Economies in the form of multi-year subscriptions at reduced rate are sometimes possible. Fernald[3] indicates some of the possibilities. Academic publishers in particular often give a discount on a subscription entered for two or three years of the order of 5 per cent of the total. The American Chemical Society's *Chemical and Engineering News* cost, in 1976, overseas subscribers for a one year subscription $23 but for three years only $56. It is, of course, necessary to be careful in placing long term subscriptions to ensure that too many are not placed in any single year, so that peaks and troughs of subscriptions renewals do not distort budgets.

The most awkward problem involved in supply direct from publishers is that since most periodical subscriptions fall due for renewal in January a great many invoices need to be processed quickly in November and December, to avoid missing early issues of the new volume through the publisher's assumption that non-renewal of the subscription implies cancellation. This need to process a large number of invoices quickly causes difficulties in the flow of work at the end of a year.

3. *Membership of a learned society or professional body*

Members of learned societies and professional bodies usually have the privilege of obtaining one or more periodicals published by the organization either free or at a lower price than that charged to non-members. Other associated benefits of membership may be access to borrowing rights from the organization's library and discounts on monographs. When all of these advantages are taken into account it might well be thought appropriate for the library to take up such membership.

Many academic libraries, and those in industry, obtain a significant proportion of their periodicals as a result of such membership. Some societies, as well as offering their publications to members at lower prices, also offer personal, individual subscriptions to private members at even lower rates. It is not unknown for organizations desiring to subscribe to learned society publications to arrange to pay the membership subscriptions of individuals within their organization, on condition that they pass over the publications they receive as a result to the library. Most academic publishers offer greater reductions to individuals. Undoubtedly there are substantial financial advantages in paying the individual's rate for publications rather than that for organizations, but the ethics of the system are doubtful.

4. *Periodicals supply specialists*

Most libraries take large numbers of periodicals which provides opportunities for booksellers and other library supply specialists to establish units to deal with the periodicals needs of libraries. Such specialists or agents, as they are usually termed, are able to build up an expertise virtually impossible for the individual librarian to match. They accept the whole responsibility for the supply of periodicals to libraries from the initial placement of orders, to the renewal of subscriptions, and the payment of a multiplicity of invoices in a variety of currencies, and this represents a significant saving for librarians in staff resources. At a time when libraries are increasingly subject to cuts in their services owing to economic stringency the services of agents become of even greater significance than usual. Katz and Gellatly[4] provide guidance on how to deal most economically with agents and on the nature of their services. They also list the advantages and disadvantages of employing agents. The American Library Association[5] publishes a list of non-United States agents and both Melcher[6] and Clara Brown are in no doubt of their value to libraries.

The advantages to be derived from the creative use of agents are considerable. Where the library is taking a great many periodicals from a range of sources it can be beneficial to employ more than one agent. Some agents specialize in domestic supply, others in the supply of overseas publications and still others are expert in dealings with irregular serials and conference proceedings.

Julian Blackwell,[7] himself a specialist periodicals supply agent, lists seven points about employing agents which he considers confer important benefits to libraries:

1. The chief advantage of having an agent is the saving of time and labour. You tell the agent what you want and he does the donkey work.

2. The agent knows the manifold peculiarities of the publishers. Some will only take subscriptions by the calendar year, some by the volume, some by the current number, others have a waiting list. Some have a controlled circulation and others insist on cash with order. With one publisher there is always a two month delay, and after the order has been received we get an acknowledgement slip with a reference number saying the subscription has been entered but not when; and so we must write back and ask them in order to keep our records accurate. Most publishers' service is excellent. We were delighted when William Blackwood and Sons supplied us with a new copy from stock of *Blackwood's Magazine*, May 1821.

3. The agent will deal with foreign currency difficulties, and

many foreign publishers give a better service if subscriptions come through well known agents. This, of course, helps to cut down delay in starting new subscriptions.

4. The agent is responsible for the efficient handling of renewals, to ensure continuity, and will look after all claims.

5. The agent will provide information on new and obscure periodicals and will, of course, supply price quotations, subject lists and catalogues. Most good agents maintain an extensive collection of reference works covering periodicals.

6. You can pay for all your subscriptions with one bill once a year at any time of year you wish.

7. The agent will prevent the clash of the customer's special ordering requirements with the publishers own invoicing and ordering systems.

James Shillady,[8] the London representative of Stechert-MacMillan Inc., an old-established agency, says:

The book/periodical agent prospers and the library benefits only when any dealings are preceded by the librarian's close assessment of his or her own need and by the librarian's close questioning of the agent . . . A good account . . . is not simply one which places a large number of orders with us. Rather it is one where both we and the librarian are agreed upon those needs in the library.

Discounts are not usually forthcoming from periodicals agents. Indeed as profit margins narrow and costs rise, most agents have been obliged to levy a surcharge over and above the actual cost of subscriptions. Frank Clasquin[9] of Messrs Faxon, a noted American agency, analyses the reasons why discounts are not often possible. He says:

It is the depth and skill of expertise of the agent upon which the library client has become accustomed to rely for extended service that dictates a pricing structure which will permit the agency to continue to offer and broaden such services.

The lack of discounts and the increasing likelihood of surcharges sometimes prejudices librarians against agents. When the cost of staff time at all grades which can be tied up in servicing all the library's own requirements is calculated, however, then the use of an agent, surcharge notwithstanding, becomes more attractive.

Clasquin stresses the range of services available from agents. To stay in business and prosper agents must be able to persuade librarians that they can supply services which the library staff can not provide. Beginning modestly with furnishing often quite small lists of periodicals that they were willing to supply, the activities of agents have branched out in a number of directions designed to assist librarians maintain their period-icals collections. Even the periodicals lists themselves are, these days, often large enough to serve as useful sources of current bibliography. This is particularly the case with the massive *Librarians' handbook* produced by Ebsco Industries annually. This lists and indexes by subject over 100,000 periodicals and provides prices and frequencies also. Both Brown and the American Library Association, cited earlier, note the material available in the form of lists from agents.

Many agents also publish bulletins noting new titles or providing detailed information on supply problems for current issues of periodicals in which they deal; for example: *Stechert-MacMillan Serial News*; *Ebsco Bulletin of Serial Changes*; *Faxon's Serials Updating Service Quarterly*.

J. T. Stephens[10] writes of periodicals agents and provides detailed descriptions of the services they give. He comments on an aspect of library acquisition policy in relation to period-icals which clearly concerns him greatly and, by implication, all periodicals supply agents. He believes that the current aims at creating co-operative acquisition programmes by groups of libraries, with the intention of rationalizing selection pro-cedures amongst themselves and reducing duplication of periodical titles in their several libraries, will simply force up prices to the point at which their initial savings are negated by the reprisals of publishers protecting their investment.

5. *Gifts, donations and exchanges*

A variety of motives exist for the library and the periodical publisher, to attempt in the one case to obtain and in the other to offer periodicals as free gifts. For publishers the motive may be to place their views before the widest possible audience by obtaining free display space in libraries. They may also be attempting thereby to claim increased readership, so as to justify charging high, and lucrative, advertising rates.

For libraries the motivation is chiefly the attraction of obtaining necessary material free. It is obvious from the incidence of pro-forma solicitation letters received by any publisher of periodicals that it is the policy of many libraries always to attempt to obtain material they are interested in as a free gift from the publishers, before they will go to the lengths of issuing a purchase order. Increased costs and, especially, postage charges, are reducing the number of publishers who will offer their periodicals as gifts no matter how persuasive the solicitation. In some cases, however, periodicals needed by the library will only be obtainable by free exchange with another library willing to offer them on condition that they receive other material free in exchange also. Eastern European countries in particular, chronically short of foreign exchange as they invariably are, are keen to develop exchange arrangements with Western libraries. In the case of the scientific and technical periodical publications of Eastern European countries, often the only way to obtain them is by offering Western publications in exchange. In some instances potential exchange partners in the West will be obliged to purchase materials specifically for the purpose of achieving the desired exchange.

Brown makes the good point that although donated and exchanged material is received freely it is not without cost both in its administration and, where exchange is involved, in postage, packing and customs clearances. It is worth saying, however, that donated material and exchange items generally appear in the library with unfailing regularity, having none of the interruptions of service so often associated with subscription material which occur through communication failures in renewal payments. Library staff should be on the watch for the reply paid cards some publishers send with some of their issues to enable the updating of subscription and address lists. Failure to return the card usually results in the periodical being lost to the library; simply through overlooking the card.

Material donated to libraries is of two kinds. There is first that which the library wants and seeks out for itself, if it is not received unsolicited. Second there is the material sent to the library unsolicited and unwanted. It is not always easy to stop this material coming, even by writing to the publishers. Libraries sometimes throw it away when it arrives but occasionally a librarian will serve the purposes of the publisher by putting it on display or leaving it on tables.

Significant material obtained as gifts includes house journals, the periodicals issued by various banks, for instance – *Bank of England Quarterly*, *Midland Bank Review* are examples – and items issued by various government agencies international, national and local. It is, in fact, the practice of many international government organizations to designate certain libraries as repositories for all of their publications. Other, perhaps smaller, libraries might well be able to obtain publications of national and local government bodies free in return for display and archival storage facilities being made available. At the local level particularly, the Local History Department of a public library will use donated material as a major source of supply – school and college magazines, church magazines, company newspapers, etc.

Exchange forms the major part of the free acquisition programme of academic libraries, but it is not so important in other types of libraries, except perhaps government libraries. The sources of material are various. Many academic institutions publish a range of materials including periodicals. These will often be used as the staple to feed an exchange programme, although increasingly these days the university press will charge the university library for the material it employs in exchange schemes. In the past university presses frequently used to order run-ons of their publications specifically to provide the university library with a source of free material to exchange. Duplicate sets of periodicals can be used as the material for exchange, as can material which becomes surplus to requirements for one reason or another.

The practice of exchange of publications between libraries is well established. The massive traffic in academic theses in the eighteenth and nineteenth centuries is one evidence of this. J. A. Collins[11] in describing the activities of the

International Exchange Service of the Smithsonian Institute in Washington D.C. provides some fascinating sidelights on the history of the practice of the exchange of publications. He records that Louis XIV of France authorized the Royal Library to effect exchanges with other libraries. Collins further reveals that it was at the International Congress of Geographers in 1875 that a resolution was passed proposing the adoption of a uniform system for the exchange of scientific and literary publications between institutions both nationally and across national boundaries. This resolution was the precursor of the Brussels Convention for the international exchange of publications.

Although not all countries adopted the Brussels Convention or the later UNESCO agreements, a flourishing traffic exists in the exchange of literature. UNESCO[12] publishes a handbook of practice which enables libraries to recognize potential exchange partners. *UNESCO Bulletin for Libraries* carries regular features on exchange possibilities. Thompson[13] reviews the state of the art of exchange and donation and the organization, administration and potentialities of exchange activities in Academic Libraries is dealt with by Blake[14] and Brown summarizes the activities of various American exchange facilitating agencies.

Ford[15] reports that in the United States an analysis of the cost of instituting exchange programmes has caused many academic libraries to reduce their exchanges simply to those items which can only be acquired in this way. He argues that the costs of correspondence, record keeping and special handling arrangements often exceed the cost of regular acquisition of the same material. It is pertinent to the cost equations that whereas in the past learned societies and universities were extremely keen on exchange agreements they often now prefer the certainty and perhaps the cheaper route, taken as a whole, of direct purchase.

One of the biggest obstacles to the free interchange of materials across national barriers is the frequent insistence by administrative authorities upon the exchanges being value for value at the current rates of exchange in the two countries. This purblind bureaucratic attitude is one of the principal causes of difficulty, and indeed, of expensive book balancing exercises. Western European and North American book and periodical prices are very high indeed compared to those in many other parts of the world and using monetary exchange rates based upon the domestic subscription prices of the relevant countries it can mean that one British or American periodical equals ten Hungarian or Indonesian ones regardless of their relative intellectual merits. It can not always be said in defence of the position of the bureaucrat that the quality of the production of the relative items is invariably better in the case of the British or American press. It sometimes is, but not always. The simplest approach to soliciting material on exchange is to write to an organization with publications of interest suggesting an exchange, and indicating the nature of the exchange possibility.

Libraries frequently have surplus material – duplicates and no longer required back files of periodicals – for disposal which can be turned to good effect in arranging acquisition of needed items.

MICROFORM PUBLICATION OF PERIODICALS

There was a time when the only advantage considered about microforms of periodicals was that of compact storage of little used material – this was especially so with newspapers. It is now much more likely to be seen as a means of acquiring out of print items and as an alternative to binding recent copies that microform editions will be considered. The range of materials now available in microform is vast, with the pioneer *Journal of Wildlife Diseases* being the first of a growing number of periodicals to be originally published in microform. Xerox University Microfilms Ltd[16] produce a massive list of available microform periodicals, listing over 10,000 titles from all over the world. It is the largest amongst a number of periodicals in microform coming from publishers at the present time. For completing broken files, extending files retrospectively, and for collection building for new and growing libraries, microforms show considerable cost savings as compared to acquiring bound volumes of the same material. In many cases the cost of acquiring the microform will be less than the cost of binding material already held in parts. When used in association with a reader–printer through the medium of which full sized copies of the microforms can be reproduced, much of the reader resistance to microforms might be dispersed.

REFERENCES

1. BROWN, C. D. *Serials acquisition and maintenance.* Birmingham, Al.: EBSCO Industries, 1972.
2. AMERICAN LIBRARY ASSOCIATION, Resources and Technical Services Division, Book Dealer-Library Relations Committee. *Guidelines for handling library orders for serials and periodicals.* Chicago: American Library Association, 1975.
3. FERNALD, E. R. 'Cutting periodicals costs through long term subscriptions.' *Wilson Library Bulletin,* 36(4), December 1961. pp. 297–9.
4. KATZ, W. A. and GELLATLY, P. *Guide to magazine and serial agents.* Ann Arbor, Mich.: Bowker, 1975.
5. AMERICAN LIBRARY ASSOCIATION, Resources and Technical Services Division. *International subscription agents.* Chicago: American Library Association, 1969.
6. MELCHER, D. *Melcher on acquisitions.* Chicago.: American Library Association, 1971.
7. BLACKWELL, J. 'Some problems of bookselling.' *ASLIB Proceedings,* 14(3), March 1962. pp. 57–66.
8. SHILLADY, James. *Private communication,* 13 September 1976.
9. CLASQUIN, F. 'Jobber's side: cost of acquiring periodicals.' *R. Q.,* 10(4), Summer 1971. pp. 328–30.
10. STEPHENS, J. T. 'Subscription services to libraries.' *Serials Review,* 1(4), Oct.–Dec. 1975. pp. 9–10.
11. COLLINS, J. A. 'The international exchange service.' *Library Resources and Technical Services,* 10(3), Summer 1961. pp. 337–41.
12. UNESCO. *Handbook on the International Exchange of Publications* Paris: UNESCO, regularly revised.
13. THOMPSON, D. E. 'Gifts and exchanges' *in* Shaw, R. R., *The state of the library art.* New Brunswick, N.J.: Graduate School of Library Service, The State University, Rutgers, 1961. Vol 1, parts 4 & 5.
14. BLAKE, F. M. 'Expanding exchange services.' *College and Research Libraries,* 24(1), January 1963. pp. 53–56.
15. FORD, S. *The acquisition of library materials.* Chicago: American Library Association, 1973.
16. XEROX UNIVERSITY MICROFILMS. *Serials in Microform.* Ann Arbor, Mich./ High Wycombe, Bucks.: X.U.M. 1941–.

Chapter 13
Recording periodical acquisitions

It is necessary to make a careful note of the arrival in the library of every issue of all periodicals subscribed to and of any special issues, indexes, volume title-pages or other matter regularly accompanying them. This is most important, for such notes are the evidence against which the library will be able to check suppliers' invoices before payment to ensure that all parts charged have been received. More critical even than that, will be the regular checking of the notes – or records as they will be called here – to ensure that periodical parts are being received as soon as published. It is a function of the record to alert the library staff to the possibility of errors of mailing, of the need to enter subscriptions at the publishers or, more usually, of a delay in printing. Where the record produces evidence of unaccountable delay in receipt of issues, the library staff responsible for the maintenance of the periodicals collections must immediately follow up these delays to discover the cause. It will often be found that the missing part is not yet published, but it will sometimes be that the part has been lost in transit. In these cases early follow up is essential since publishers rarely print very many more copies than they know they will need and delay in applying for replacements could result in discovering the part is 'out of print at the publishers'. This leaves a gap in the file and probably creates discontent amongst library users who are regular readers of the periodical. Adequate records are of course necessary for precisely the purpose suggested by impli- cation in the last sentence – that of keeping library users informed of the missing parts of current periodicals and the reasons for it. A clear and accurate system of records is required for the purpose of preparing parts for binding, and for in- dicating the location and extent of back files held, and the method and place of display of current parts. A clear and comprehensive record will considerably aid the production of lists of periodical holdings.

Periodicals records must, therefore, be able to serve a variety of purposes and it is a good plan to try to centralize all functions which call for a periodicals record in one place. Not all libraries will be large enough to contemplate the establishment of a permanent staff to run a periodicals record system but, nevertheless, an attempt should be made to give the responsibility for their receipt and the related duties – dispatch to departments, subscription control, storage, binding, etc. – to one or two people as a regular task even if only on a part-time basis. The special problems associated with periodicals require careful, knowledgeable attention and are too important to be left to anyone with an idle moment.

RECORDING SYSTEMS

There are a considerable variety of systems in use for the recording of periodicals in various sizes and types of library. It is a matter of great importance to the library to choose a system appropriate to its needs; perhaps the most important consideration is the number of periodicals taken. To install a complex and expensive system to deal with a small number of periodicals will, in all probability, be a waste of both money and staff time. On the other hand to install an over-simple system incapable of easy expansion to adapt to a large and growing collection is equally time-consuming and expensive. It is always best to assume that a periodicals collection will grow – or at any rate show significant changes over time – and to select a system which can expand or adapt without strain or much re-writing of the whole record.

The systems for recording periodicals can be summarized as follows:

1. book records
   a bound
   b loose-leaf
2. card records
   a blind
   b visible
3. automated recording systems

1a *Bound book records*

The book may be a specially prepared, carefully bound volume
with pages already ruled and titled for their purpose or simply
a notebook or small ledger with plain pages ruled out in ink
or pencil as required by the library staff. For any collection of
periodicals other than a small and fairly static number this
method is most cumbersome. The only way to accommodate
new or changed titles in the alphabetical sequence is to leave
spaces between each title written into the book so that the
new material may be intercalated between existing titles in
the sequence. New titles could be accommodated by entering
them at the end of the sequence, of course, but such a method
places a premium on the good memory of the recording
assistant. In either case a great deal of re-writing of the book
to reorganize it will be inevitable.

1b *Loose-leaf book records*

To overcome the disadvantage inherent in the bound book
method, whereby a great deal of transcription and re-writing
needs to be done regularly, a loose-leaf volume might be used.
At its simplest this may be a collection of pages similarly ruled
to those of a bound book but secured not by a permanent
stitched binding but by a clamp of some sort with prongs
onto which the pages are slotted by means of holes punched
in their inner margins. A refinement of the basic loose-leaf
form is a patent binder which has prongs all along the spine
onto which slips or cards punched on one edge are slotted
from the bottom upwards, in such a way that about 1 cm
($\frac{1}{2}$ inch) of each slip is left visible until at the top, of course,
the whole of the last slip is visible. The binder will usually
hold about twenty-five slips at each opening and, by inserting
dividing cards, further series of slips can be built up, several
hundreds to a volume.

The purpose of loose-leaf arrangements of both kinds is to
obviate re-writing the whole sequence and to enable easy
re-arrangement and intercalation. The first method enables
the permanent information about each title to be written on
one sheet with a second, narrower sheet (so that it does not

7

obscure the permanent information) providing space to record receipts and other notes. The permanent information in this case will be title of the periodical, frequency, publisher, price, location, binding and storage information. A number of titles might be recorded on each page with the possibility of dividing the titles listed over two sheets when amendments have to be made. The amount of re-writing necessary in this case is therefore limited.

Suppliers of binders to hold the second type of loose-leaf slips will arrange for the slips to be printed in any desired manner. It is usual for the titles of periodicals to be written or typed on the leading edge of the slips and for the rest to be ruled to record the necessary management information and for several years' issues of the periodical to be checked off on receipt. The leading edge of the slip might be adapted to enable some kind of coloured signalling devices to be used.

2a   *Blind cards*

This is the familiar system of housing cards in filing drawers. They are termed 'blind' simply because cards must be withdrawn from the sequence, at least partially, for any of the information contained upon them to be seen. Cards of 15 × 10 cm (6 × 8 ins) or 20 × 12·5 cm (8 × 5 ins) are best for this system. The body of the card is ruled so that the periodical title that each card in the record represents is written along the top edge with the rest of the significant information being accommodated below together with space for recording the receipt of issues as received.

This is a cheap system to adopt requiring no special equipment. It has the great advantage over the systems so far mentioned that the records can be quickly re-arranged or can be added to in sequence. The principal disadvantage is that cards must be sought in the file, withdrawn from sequence to enable notes to be made, and then returned. Not only is this a relatively slow process but it is also susceptible to error in the refiling of items.

There are several possibilities for the arrangement of cards. They might be arranged alphabetically by title in one sequence.

Alternatively they might be segregated into several alphabetical sequences according to the various frequencies of issue of the periodicals. This method has no particular advantage over the first and requires those using it to be familiar with frequencies of issue. A third method is to arrange periodicals record cards broadly by dates of expected delivery. For example at the beginning of the year all cards representing monthly periodicals are filed behind a guide card marked 'January'. As periodical receipts are checked off the cards are moved behind a 'February' guide card. It can then easily be seen that cards remaining behind the January marker are overdue and need to be investigated. Other frequencies can be organized in a similar way – week by week, day by day, quarter by quarter. A great deal of arranging and re-arranging is necessary using this method but it is an extremely effective means of arranging blind cards to give warning of overdue items. Other arrangements necessitate individual inspection of cards to discover overdue items.

The major disadvantage of blind cards – that they are not visible and must be withdrawn from the sequence for marking – is overcome by mounting the cards on rotating drums fitted with clips round the edge. Whilst this is expensive it enables both sides of the cards to be used without withdrawal from a sequence; it obviates subsequent misfiling; and at the same time ensures that required cards can be speedily located. Suitable drums or wheels, as they are sometimes called, can be seen in the catalogues of any good office equipment supplier.

2b   *Visible records*

Many libraries have discovered that the installation of a visible record system has either allowed the existing periodicals control staff significantly to increase the number of periodicals dealt with compared to systems described earlier, or has at least enabled them to improve accuracy and efficiency in dealing with a static number of items.

The cards used are basically similar to those employed as blind cards. They are housed in trays, each card being held by a metal holder or wire retainer which engages under flanges on the sides of the trays. This holder allows the cards to hinge so that both sides may be consulted whilst at the same time ensuring that the cards are arranged in such a way that each displays only about ½ cm (¼ inch) of its outer edge underneath the card next above it. The trays house about sixty cards each and are fitted into cabinets. An important feature of these cabinets is that the trays do not need to be completely withdrawn in order to consult the cards. Within the trays the cards can be removed or interpolated at will by disengaging a simple locking device and such interpolation does not affect the amount of leading edge shown by each card. It simply means that the cards at the bottom of a tray must be moved to the next to maintain the sequence and not overfill a tray. The control information – that is, the periodical title for which the card is a record – is written on the leading edge which may then be protected by a plastic sleeve which also contains any control signals.

The arrival of new issues is noted on the body of the card. The signals under the plastic sleeves can be used to provide a visual indication of the arrival if the card edge is zoned in months or weeks of the year and the signal moved along the edge from one zone to the next. In an ideal situation all signals for periodicals of, say, monthly frequency will appear in a straight, vertical line on the tray of cards indicating that all have arrived on time. A swift visual check on the position of signals will indicate if any periodicals are late in arriving. Different coloured cards can be used to represent different sources of supply, different coloured signals the various frequencies of periodicals. A second signal at one extreme edge might represent departmental locations within the library. Lakhanpal[1] describes a system for using visible card records.

3   *Automated recording systems*

The highly routine nature of much of the process of controlling periodicals makes it a suitable candidate for computerization. The question is to decide at what point this is likely to prove economical. If it is necessary to buy a computer especially for the purpose the answer is 'never'. However the parent bodies of most libraries own, or have access to, computers and they are usually keen to see them fully employed in view of their high cost. Herein lies a grave risk. It is tempting to computerize library operations – including periodicals recording – simply to employ the computer and justify its existence, regardless of the real costs and benefits of the particular operation. The suspicion is that many automated library processes are undertaken more because the computer was there than because greater efficiency resulted from using it.

Osborn[2] has referred to a number of computerized recording projects in American libraries and Massil[3] has made a comprehensive review of the literature. The pioneer system is that at the University of San Diego, California (UCSD), described by Voigt[4] who states that:

1. Serials processing is laborious and costly.
2. The resulting records, using traditional means, are difficult to use and are not accessible to library users except through a staff member (in contrast to monographs which are accessible directly through a card catalogue).
3. Serials are the most important library materials in the sciences and, with the present emphasis on science at UCSD, were most in need of immediate improvements in records.
4. The repetitive nature of successive up-datings of serials records provides an appropriate application of mechanization.

Voigt makes the further point that unlike all other recording systems costs do not rise in direct proportion to numbers of items recorded – a very significant factor for the fast growing UCSD Library's collection of periodicals. The generation of peripheral records – binding lists, claims lists, lists of complete or selected holdings, and lists of the expiration dates of subscription – is also mentioned by Voigt and is believed by Ward[5] to be the most effective use of computers, since he thinks computerized records are 'not so useful for entering and claiming'.

Automated aid for periodical recording in medium sized libraries (holding between 1,000 and 2,500 periodicals) is the subject of a number of studies. Wall[6] has listed the desiderata for such a system in the Loughborough University of Technology, whilst Livingston[7] describes a system which uses cheap batch-processing methods of applying the computer to the problem.

REFERENCES

1. LAKHANPAL, S. K. *A manual for recording serial publications in Kardex.* Saskatoon: Murray Memorial Library, University of Saskatchewan, rev. ed., 1971.
2. OSBORN, Andrew D. *Serial publications: their place and treatment in libraries.* Chicago: American Library Association, 2nd ed. rev., 1973.
3. MASSIL, Stephen W. 'Mechanization of serials records: a literature review.' *Program*, 4(4), October 1970. pp. 156–68.
4. VOIGT, M. J. 'The costs of data processing in university libraries: in serials handling.' *College and Research Libraries*, 24(6), November 1963. pp. 489–91.
5. WARD, M. 'Observations of serials management in seventeen London libraries.' *Library Association Record*, 77(10), October 1975, p. 247.
6. WALL, R. A. 'A proposed experiment in automated serials accessioning.' *Program*, 5(3), July 1971. pp. 141–51.
7. LIVINGSTON, Frances G. 'A semi-automated journal check-in and binding system: or variations on a common theme.' *Bulletin of the Medical Library Association*, 55(3), July 1967. pp. 316–20.

Chapter 14
Storage of periodicals

The housing of periodicals and other library materials involves many more costs than simply binding the items and building the stores to put them in, formidable though those costs are. In addition there is also the expense of heating, lighting, cleaning and maintenance. If stores are large, inconveniently planned or relatively inaccessible from the service area there will be high costs associated with the retrieval and return of items in terms of staff time. Close study of storage charges and the capital costs of building new stores or extensions will frequently reveal the fact that the storage policies of many libraries need serious rethinking. Wootton[1] in an examination of storage costs shows that between 1960 and 1974 they rose four-and-a-half times, and in recent years have been rising by thirteen per cent every year.

Leaving aside the potential of microforms as a method of storage until later, it has to be said that periodicals are bulky, awkward to handle and difficult to keep clean when in store. Current files grow at an alarming rate and due consideration for the growth of holdings must be made in planning the acquisition process. Especially in the early years of the life of a periodicals store, the space is not used economically because of the need to make allowance for growth. In a very real sense a periodical store is uneconomic until it is full and there is the need for more expenditure on additional space. It is when it is realized that new buildings are likely to be needed that it is time to re-examine policy. The requirement for more storage space almost certainly arises out of a policy which has not been re-examined for many years and may well be out of date or otherwise inappropriate. The policy may in fact consist of no more than that everything bought has been stored regardless of subsequent use. Chambers and Healy[2] note, rather wryly, that three major libraries in the Rhode Island area were all found during their survey to be binding and permanently storing *Reader's Digest*. In their survey of usage in the University of Rhode Island, *Reader's Digest* was cited by thesis writers only once in ten years and yet there was a bound set of the periodical over thirty-three years on the shelves in the library store. The surveyors ask 'what decisions have been made to bind, process and store a thirty-three-year run of this title?' They answer their own question: 'what probably occurred was that once the title was purchased, no one ever thought to question its inclusion in a research collection.' Inertial storage, as this tendency might be termed, unfortunately accounts for a good deal of the storage of periodicals, because no one has bothered to make a positive decision not to store. A 'more voluminous than thou' complex, as Line[3] has described it, in which a librarian tries to build up a massive collection for prestige reasons is another unfortunate manifestation which causes the storage of little-used material for no useful purpose. In this case a positive decision has been made, but it is not one which bears the needs of the reader in mind.

Storage policies may have been formulated before the introduction and widespread use of microforms as a means of recording periodicals or the instigation of comprehensive inter-library loan facilities – and in the United Kingdom especially, the growth of the British Library Lending Division. At an even more simplistic level present storage areas may be uneconomically used because of inappropriate arrangement and furnishing – a lack of compact shelving of the 'rolling stack' type, for example. Gawrecki[4] has discussed compact library shelving, its economics and advantages, at some length.

All of the above points should at least be examined before any decision is made about the need for increased storage space. Indeed even before that time comes – as it eventually does to all libraries – constant monitoring of costs and use must be the rule. It was an area of public library activity which Oldman and Davinson[5] found very unsatisfactory and which is at the heart of the University Grants Committee's unhappiness[6] in relation to academic libraries in the United Kingdom at the present time.

The mere fact of needing to make allowances for the growth

of specific files in the early years of a store can lead to trouble. Unless the allowances are accurately forecast a great deal of tiresome moving of large quantities of bound material is the inevitable result. Such moving is not only unpopular with staff and expensive in terms of their time but seriously increases the risks of damage to materials. Speyers-Duran[7] has produced a useful guide to the techniques of moving library materials which is relevant in this context if it must be done, and provides useful lists of further references. Heintze[8] describes the various types of library shelving used for storage areas. The special problems of the BLLD in relation to the bulk handling of periodical materials have resulted in a great deal of research being carried out there, and have produced many specially designed devices and systems described by Smith.[9]

USE FACTORS OF STORED PERIODICALS

Various estimates of the expected pattern of use of periodicals as compared to their age have been made, chiefly for scientific and technical periodicals. It is possible to compute the length of time a periodical earns its keep in stores, relative to its frequency of use, mathematically. The presence of the BLLD's valuable loan and photocopy service for periodicals enables librarians, if they are so minded, to set their own limits upon their retention policy for little-used material by deciding that below a certain frequency of use they would rather borrow from the British Library than retain the materials themselves at great cost. Unfortunately too few have been so minded in the past, largely because they have failed to keep a check on use and the costs of storage. In almost any library the logic of borrowing, rather than retaining in store, little-used science and technology material is quite as irrefutable as it is ignored.

R. M. Strain[10] refers to a quotation attributed to a critic of the British Museum Library (as it then was) and states, 'half of the books in the British Museum could be burned without anyone to the end of time knowing it.' The first Lord Leverhulme apparently made much the same remark in relation to the effectiveness of his organization's advertising but concluded that the waste of the half must be cheerfully borne since he had no means of knowing in advance which was likely to be the effective half. It is the same with books – and periodicals. Strain provides statistical evidence to show that fifty per cent of the periodicals in libraries she studied could be discarded without much risk of their absence ever being noticed, but, like Leverhulme, she admits she was unable to state which fifty per cent should go.

Attempts to answer the 'which half' question are made in several ways by researchers. The most usual is to plot the use made of periodicals, compared to their age. Another method is to study the patterns of citations in the literature. This latter approach argues that the heavy incidence of citation to a periodical will result in more frequent calls being made upon it by readers as a result of the increase in its visibility. A more crude, rule of thumb method involves the examination of lists of periodicals indexed and abstracted in the major services. The assumption is that those periodicals most often covered by such services will at a later date be most in demand owing again to their increased visibility, as compared to those periodicals less in evidence in the abstracting and indexing services.

It must be stressed that only in the fields of science and technology and *perhaps* some fields within the social sciences is it possible to make any attempts to solve the 'which half' question statistically. In other fields almost nothing is known about the patterns of use of periodical material, nor is it very well covered bibliographically. Many writers attempt to argue that the literature of the humanities will conform to much the same rules as that for science and technology – perhaps most notably the pundits of the BLLD – and it just is not possible to say whether it does or does not. There is no evidence, but it almost certainly does not.

Amongst the available studies of literature use in relation to storage needs are those of Cole,[11] Wilson[12] and Burton and Kebler.[13] Central to many of the studies is the concept of 'half-life'. This is a term used to mean the period of time over which half of the expected total use of a periodical will have occurred. Sandison[14] elaborates the half-life concept and reviews the literature critically, and concludes that it is not a useful term, although he commends a study of Line's thoughts.[15]

However suspect to the purists the concept may be, half-life does provide the hard pressed librarian with some data with which to make rough and ready decisions. Those periodicals with a long half-life or, more accurately, the subject fields they represent, might be bound in a durable binding whilst those in areas where the rate of obsolescence of knowledge is high might not be bound at all.

REQUIREMENTS OF PERIODICAL STORES

The principal requirements fall into two groups: the equipment and maintenance of the store; and its location in relation to the needs of users.

Equipment and maintenance

All library stores must be kept dust free. This statement has special force in respect of periodical stores where the weight and bulk of material would make the task of manual dusting, in the absence of dust control equipment, expensive and difficult. A free flow of air is important to a periodical store but it should always be filtered first.

Temperature and humidity controls are very important factors to bear in mind. They are largely complementary and without a correct balance of the two much harm can come to the stored material. Too much heat and too low a humidity causes drying-out of bindings – especially leather (but buckram cracks and tears easily when dry). Too much humidity, especially in the presence of too much heat, encourages mould growth and, in some countries, insect attack is more likely in higher temperatures. If stores are too cold dampness results, causing problems with paper – especially the 'imitation art' types which are commonly used in periodical production.

The question of the correct temperature for storage areas is be-devilled by considerations of whether the store is 'open' or 'closed', that is, whether for public use or staff use only. In 'closed' stores it is possible to stipulate a temperature of not more than 13°C (55°F). 'Open' stores pose more of a problem. Their temperature levels must be higher if people are to be able to spend a good deal of time browsing or even sitting to study. Humidity controls should allow for a moisture content of not more than 10 per cent or less than 7½ per cent. The massive monograph by Keyes D. Metcalf[16] provides detail on the technical points.

Shelving for storage can be cheaper and less 'photogenic' than for public areas of the library. Steel is usually a cheaper material for the purpose than wood and more functional, being less likely to warp and easier to erect. Shelf lengths should be kept to a maximum of one metre to reduce the risks of deformation under load. The layout of the shelving runs should be so planned that every part of them can be served by trolleys. A certain amount of moving of material is inevitable, even in well planned stores, and it must be possible to use mechanical aids in view of the weight and bulk of material involved.

The likelihood of movement raises the question of whether all shelves should be adjusted to a common pitch large enough to take the majority of the collection, or whether they should be individually adjusted to the heights of the various periodicals they are meant to accommodate. The latter solution undoubtedly saves considerable space, since it is often possible to insert one or two additional shelves into a tier holding small periodicals. Where movement of material takes place, it is a solution involving much readjustment of shelf heights. This means at least that the shelving used must be of a type to enable rapid readjustments. When all factors have been considered, unless space is really at a premium it is usually good practice to standardize the pitch of the shelves as far as possible so that movements can take place freely and quickly. The standard pitch could be of the order of 33 cm (13 ins) which will comfortably accommodate the majority of bound periodicals. A separate sequence will be needed for larger periodicals and, of course, newspapers, which have a bigger pitch from top to bottom and are also wider from front to rear. It is wise to think in terms of these oversized, heavy items being placed as close as possible to the points at which they will be used. It is also good planning to dispose them on shelves in such a way that none are placed above shoulder height. This implies only two rows of shelves per tier. A flat-topped trolley for their transport should always be provided.

The location of storage areas

Whilst many libraries are obliged to operate in conditions in which stores are physically separate from the main service areas, every effort must be made to store materials close to the points where they will be used. Colley[17] has written interestingly about the methods of organizing and planning the most effective arrangement of stored material. Bearing in mind that the highest incidence of use occurs within the first few years of a periodical's life, the organization of stores on a zonal basis might be considered, by placing the preceding five years' issues in an area adjacent to the service point. Earlier volumes could then be placed somewhere more remote, on the grounds that they are less likely to be called for. This division may well cause inconvenience when volumes from both sequences are called for by the same reader, but it has the virtue of being simple to understand and remember. An alternative method is to keep together at a point adjacent to service areas complete sequences of those periodicals which studies of use or citation have shown to be frequently called for. To zone stores on this basis implies the creation of two or more sequences, less easy to remember but having the virtue of keeping runs of individual periodicals together, whilst attempting to create conditions in which heavily used material has the least distance to travel.

For the most part, however, periodical stores are arranged in alphabetical order by title. This gives rise to the problem of what to do with the many items which have changed their titles. One solution is to file periodicals by their cover titles, thus splitting the run of a periodical into parts. This system has the virtue of filing periodicals according to those titles by which users of bibliographies and abstracts will tend to call for them. The relevant volume can be retrieved in these circumstances without needing to know the current title of the periodical. In most cases, periodicals in store are filed according to their latest title with earlier volumes published under different titles being treated as if the latest title is the only one. In either case some form of guidance by way of reference from unused or latest titles must be provided on the shelves to guide staff or reader searchers efficiently. Storing under most recent titles does, of course, imply considerable movements around the store when titles change.

Classified arrangements for periodicals in store are seen most clearly in those circumstances where periodicals are split according to subject between a number of subject departments. Classified arrangements do not seem to have much to recommend them for periodicals in store, since citations from periodical articles, bibliographies etc., tend to be given by title rather than subject field or classification symbols. The test of whether to classify a periodicals collection is, therefore, whether or not a librarian believes that it will therefore be possible to supply readers' needs more quickly. Borden[18] and Pierson[19] both examine the issue of classification of periodicals in store.

NEWSPAPERS

Bound or unbound newspapers are not easy to store. Not least of the problems is the low quality and short store life of newsprint paper. Where it is intended to store newspapers indefinitely there is no alternative to a programme of microcopying, if the ravages of physical decay are to be guarded against.

Newspapers which are to be stored in their original form must always be bound. They should be shelved flat if at all possible, in individual pigeon holes. If they must be shelved vertically, owing to space considerations, then it is essential that frequent vertical divisions are provided to prevent damage, both from warping as a result of large numbers of heavy volumes leaning against each other and from the physical effort involved in removing and replacing volumes in sequence. Three or four volumes to a rigid division of shelving is a maximum, and they should be shelved fairly tightly for mutual support but not so tightly that damage might be caused when removing or replacing them. When items must be taken out for use, a wooden chock should be inserted into the vacant space to prevent the remaining volumes from falling sideways. The shelving for newspaper volumes must be of adequate width to support them over their whole length. The sheer bulk of this material and its high storage cost make more imperative than with periodicals really informed decisions as to whether it is needed at all or whether bulk-reducing micro-copying is not a sensible alternative.

BINDING PERIODICALS

Whether periodicals should be bound or not is a difficult question to answer. Binding is very expensive indeed and, since it also implies that the material bound is intended to be kept for a long period, to the costs of binding must be added the costs of long term storage which are, themselves, formidable, as an article by Clough reveals.[20]

An immediate problem in determining what to bind is that unless binding is done without delay, periodical parts can be lost, damaged or stolen. As Macbeth had it, ' 'twere well it were done quickly', but unfortunately in the case of periodicals their period of greatest usefulness is in the two or three years after their publication. To dispatch periodicals to a commercial bindery (where they may rest for anything up to four months) is to lose access to them at a time when they are most in demand. It is a difficult problem.

There are some powerful advantages in binding periodicals if they are to be kept for any length of time in store. Unbound parts are bulky, difficult to handle and easily misplaced and damaged. If aesthetic considerations have any part in the policy of a particular library, then unbound parts of periodicals inevitably look messy and untidy. Bound volumes are easier to move round the library, they are less bulky and they can be titled and shelf marked on their spines for ease of accurate replacement in sequence. They are easier to refer to and there is no risk of losing the index if it is bound into the volume.

There are disadvantages, of course, of which the already mentioned point of high binding cost is not least. Bound volumes of periodicals and especially newspapers are themselves very heavy and bulky. They are very expensive to post in cases of interlibrary loan and, of course, if a whole volume is loaned, it is effectively lost to other potential users for the period of the loan – which was probably necessitated by a requirement for one issue only. It would be possible to overcome these disadvantages by binding individual parts separately, but the costs would be prohibitive and the resultant file would be very space-consuming. Another potential source of difficulty is that tightly bound periodicals are difficult to photocopy, and if photocopying of specific articles is to be an alternative to postage of whole volumes or whole issues, as it increasingly is, then this is an argument for the serious review of policies on binding, with the intention of cutting it down.

The fact is that most libraries keep most of their periodicals for too long and do not co-ordinate their policies with other local libraries, who probably keep the same periodicals also for too long in view of the use that is made of them. If periodicals are to be kept for a long time – say, more than ten years – then they should be bound, but it must be questioned whether many periodicals in most libraries, aside from the great research collections and major academic libraries, need to be kept for more than ten years. Even when binding is considered essential, then it must be further questioned whether for most purposes it is necessary to choose any but the cheapest forms of binding material. Some libraries have a long-standing policy of binding too much and binding it in quarter leather, when simple cloth would do just as well, simply because they have always done it that way and anyway it looks nicer!

Once binding has been decided upon, then it has next to be noted that a good deal of the non-primary periodical at least is composed of advertising material. The question of whether advertising should be removed from periodicals before binding has been a source of inconclusive argument in librarianship circles for many years. It is often pointed out that the advertising sections of old periodicals are valuable sources for social and economic historians. This is true, but it is no justification for the elaboration of the argument that, therefore, all libraries should retain advertising material. This is the task of the great research libraries and anyone wishing to study periodicals for that purpose must expect to have to travel to such libraries. Most libraries should discard advertising material in the interests of reducing bulk and making the volumes easier to consult. For any librarian retaining vestigial ambitions of developing scholarly research, the compromise of retaining the advertising sections of two or three issues in each volume might be adopted.

For most purposes an acceptable durable binding is provided by cloth covered boards. Cheaper and still durable are uncovered boards with a cloth spine – with the addition of protective corners at the outer edges of the boards. This is an acceptable method for binding newspapers.

For most periodicals which are to be kept for only a few years the library should examine alternatives to binding such as storage in pamphlet boxes, a method enthusiastically advocated by Ward.[21] Taping volumes of little-used periodicals together inside card or hardboard is another possibility. Obviously these are expedients but in the prevailing climate of spiralling binding costs, they must be seriously examined.

MICROFORMS

Katz[22] notes that most periodicals of any significance are, these days, available in microform both for current and retrospective volumes. Purchasing microform copies of periodical volumes must be very seriously considered as an alternative to binding for two main reasons. Firstly, they cost very little, if at all more to purchase than a volume of a periodical costs to bind, and secondly, they take up far less space in store – about twenty times less than a bound volume. Not surprisingly University Microfilms Ltd,[23] one of the principal suppliers of microform editions of periodicals, waxes very enthusiastic about the economics of microform as an alternative to binding. Conversely the University Grants Committee Report[6] at Appendix F argues that microform storage of periodicals is no cheaper than the storage of bound volumes, especially when the need to reproduce full-sized copies of articles from the microforms for home reading is taken into account. This paper, and another from the BLLD by Parsons[24] which is supported by considerable cost analyses, argues the case from a standpoint which may not be entirely fair. The assumptions made to arrive at the conclusion of lack of economic justification for conversion to microform are that the library will need to produce the microform itself at commercial prices for that operation. For the great mass of periodicals this is not true, as the University Microfilms statement makes clear and as an examination of their catalogues and those of other major producers will show. Some publishers are, themselves, producing microform editions of their periodicals at reasonable prices, for example Wiley and Pergamon Press. Were costings of periodical storage on microform to be done, purely on the basis of the retention of existing files in libraries in bound form and the continuance of them on microform as an alternative to binding (thus offsetting the cost of binding against the cost of acquiring the microform), and then costings of the value of space saved by this change of policy, the results could well be very different and much more favourable to the microform than the studies by the University Grants Committee and by Parsons show. The trouble is that they, and indeed the University Microfilms studies, are concerned to show up a particular standpoint, neither of them totally disinterested. The one has purely commercial motives and the other is attempting to show the efficacy of a particular library system. In fact, the authors of Appendix F were the BLLD! The whole field is beset by special pleading and there is no alternative for an individual librarian wishing to examine the possibilities than to do it himself against the background of his own particular problems. It could be that the result of doing the sums would be to abandon entirely the idea of keeping periodicals for more than two or three years at all.

A NOTE ON PHOTOCOPYING AND COPYRIGHT PROBLEMS

Many librarians undertake the production of multiple copies of articles or excerpts from material stored in their libraries, including periodicals. In so doing they are in clear breach of the copyright regulations as they are presently framed. The law states at present that only single copies can be made from copyright material with the express permission of the copyright holder, and even then the receiver must sign a declaration that the copy is purely for the purposes of private study, saving him the labour of transcribing notes from it manually. A check of the notes of almost any student in any academic institution anywhere in the world would reveal at least one example of copyright material in his possession which had been supplied to his whole class in breach of the copyright regulations. Many academic publishers find it necessary to print warnings about the nature of the offence committed by untrammelled photocopying, others simply seek to forbid it by injunction. Thus in Pergamon Press periodicals appear the following:

No part of this publication may be reproduced, stored in a retrieval system, or transmitted in any form or by any means – electronic, electrostatic, magnetic tape, mechanical photocopying, recording or otherwise – without permission in writing from the Publishers. Such permission will not be unreasonably withheld.

The difficulty is the ubiquity of the photocopying machine. There is not the slightest chance of being able to enforce the law as it is at present framed. The Council for Educational Technology[25] have produced a statement outlining the rights and privileges of all parties in the copyright question, as far as it applies to educational activity. In the United Kingdom, a Government Committee of Inquiry under the Chairmanship of Mr Justice Whitford was set up to determine what changes were necessary to the law of copyright to take account of recent developments. It published its Report in 1977.

REFERENCES

1. WOOTTON, C. B. 'The growth of the literature and its implications for library storage. 2: Serials.' *BLL Review*, 4(2), 1976. pp. 41–5.
2. CHAMBERS, G. R. *and* HEALEY, J. S. 'Journal citations in masters theses: one measurement of a journal collection.' *Journal of the American Society for Information Science*, 24(5), Sept.–Oct. 1973. pp. 397–401.
3. LINE, M. B. In a quotation from *Talking to Librarians No. 3: Maurice B. Line.* On Phillips VC 45 Video cassette/C90 Audio tape. Leeds: Leeds Polytechnic School of Librarianship, 1976.
4. GAWRECKI, D. *Compact library shelving.* Chicago: American Library Association, 1968.
5. OLDMAN, C. M. *and* DAVINSON, D. E. *The usage of periodicals in public libraries.* Leeds: Leeds Polytechnic School of Librarianship, 1975.
6. UNIVERSITY GRANTS COMMITTEE, Working Party on Capital Provision for University Libraries. *Report.* London: HMSO, 1976. *See also* the extensive correspondence on the problems raised by the report in the *Times Higher Educational Supplement*, 30 April 1976 (no. 236) and subsequent issues.
7. SPEYERS-DURAN, P. *Moving a library.* Madison, Wis.: Library Associates of the University of Wisconsin, 1973.

8. HEINTZE, I. *Shelving for periodicals*. Lund, Sweden: Biblioteketjanst for the International Federation of Library Associations, 1966.

9. SMITH, E. S. 'Materials handling in the NLL's new building.' *NLL Review*, 2(4), October 1972. pp. 109–21.

10. STRAIN, R. M. 'A study of usage and retention of technical periodicals.' *Library Resources and Technical Services*, 10(3), Summer 1966. pp. 299–304.

11. COLE, P. F. 'Journal usage versus age of journal.' *Journal of Documentation*, 19(1), March 1963. pp. 1–11.

12. WILSON, C. W. J. *Use of periodicals in the Royal Aircraft Establishment Library 1956–1957*. Farnborough: RAE, 1957 (RAE Memorandum No. 29.)

13. BURTON, R. E. *and* KEBLER, R. W. 'The half life of some scientific and technical literature.' *American Documentation*, 11(1), January 1960. pp. 18–22.

14. SANDISON, A. 'The use of older literature and its obsolescence.' *Journal of Documentation*, 27(3), September 1971. pp. 184–99.

15. LINE, M. B. 'The half life of periodical literature – apparent and real obsolescence.' *Journal of Documentation*, 26(1), March 1970. pp. 46–54.

16. METCALF, K. D. *Planning academic and research libraries*. New York: McGraw-Hill, 1965.

17. COLLEY, D. I. 'The storage and retention of stack material.' *Library Association Record*, 67(2), February 1965. pp. 37–42.

18. BORDEN, J. C. 'The advantages and disadvantages of a classified periodicals collection.' *Library Resources and Technical Services*, 9(1), Winter 1965. pp. 122–6.

19. PIERSON, R. M. 'Where shall we shelve bound periodicals?' *Library Resources and Technical Services*, 10(3), Summer 1966. pp. 290–94.

20. CLOUGH, E. A. 'The binding of periodicals in libraries.' *Library World*, 61(717), March 1960. pp. 185–8.

21. WARD, D. B. 'Periodicals storage re-visited.' *Wilson Library Bulletin*, 34(3), November 1959. pp. 210–12.

22. KATZ, W. *Magazine selection: how to build a community oriented collection*. New York: Bowker, 1971.

23. UNIVERSITY MICROFILMS LTD., *Serials management: the systems answer . . .* High Wycombe, Bucks.: UM, 1975.

24. PARSONS, R. B. 'The economics of microforms as a storage medium in Libraries.' *NLL Review*, 2(2), April 1972. pp. 45–54.

25. COUNCIL FOR EDUCATIONAL TECHNOLOGY. *Copyright and Education*. London: CET, 1973.

Chapter 15
Display

The importance of providing facilities for the adequate display of current numbers of periodicals can hardly be over-emphasized. The greatest use of periodicals occurs early in their life. Much of the impact, and therefore the value, of periodicals in a library would be lost if they were not attractively presented and easily accessible when new. Effective and visible displays in public rooms of the current issues of periodicals received is essential.

The principal strategies of arranging periodicals for display purposes are:

1. Display alongside related subjects on the book shelves
2. Display in a separate sequence or sequences but close to the related subjects in a book sequence
3. Display in a classified sequence parallel to the book sequence but in another part of the room as a separate display feature
4. Display in an alphabetic sequence according to the titles of the periodicals
5. Display in a separate periodicals room, the sequence of periodicals being either alphabetic by title or in subject groups

1. *Display alongside related subjects*

This method stresses the complementary nature of books and periodicals. Too often librarians are tempted to segregate different formats – books, periodicals, microforms, film – for reasons of administrative convenience without regard to the nature of the information they convey. This method is a form of classification prone to the same criticism as that of category 3 below. It is most effective in libraries of well defined and fairly narrow subject coverage, where the total stock is small. It is often the practice in these circumstances to shelve the bound copies of the restrospective files of periodicals with the current copies thus providing constant opportunity for usage of back numbers. When displayed alongside retrospective runs the usual method of housing current issues is in a pamphlet box.

2. *Display in a separate sequence, or sequences, but close to the related subjects in a book sequence*

Where a library is organized into a series of subject divisions, separately housed, the periodical collection may well be split up amongst them according to an estimate of where they will be likely to be most used. The principal difficulty in this system is that users' assessments of which periodicals should be available in which division may be at variance with those of the library staff. If this method is practised it is imperative that complete location lists of all periodicals taken are available in all subject divisions and in a convenient place adjacent to the main entrance; readers seeking particular periodicals are not likely to be pleased if they must spend time seeking them from room to room, or floor to floor of the library.

There will, inevitably, be periodicals which defeat logical allocation to one subject division or another, being relevant to two or more. The weak way out of the dilemma is to place such periodicals in a 'general' category somewhere and thus probably pleasing no one. It is better to place such periodicals firmly in one of its most useful locations, making sure that it is clearly signposted in other relevant sections.

Modern library planning favours the creation of large open spaces subdivided by furniture and shelving to form areas devoted to particular subjects and, as Osborn[1] notes, 'it is possible to create areas at various intervals in which there can be easy claims for readers who wish to browse.' Subject-orientated displays of current periodicals are a very important feature of arrangements of this sort.

3. *Display in a classified sequence*

The basic proposition here is that periodicals are not distributed around the library or to subject divisions as in 1 and 2 (themselves forms of classification), but are kept together in one place and arranged according to an accepted scheme of classification or in subject groups according to a special local practice.

Few libraries display their periodicals in this way because it is difficult to carry out specific classification successfully with such relatively heterogeneous material as periodicals, whose subject content is often even less specific than their titles suggest – and titles are rarely at all specific, for example, *Soap, Perfumery and Cosmetics,* or *Air Conditioning, Heating and Refrigeration News.* Whilst a classified sequence brings together those periodicals of similar subject content, it is often a problem to know where to place items such as those mentioned above.

4. *Display in an alphabetical sequence of titles*

Whether periodicals are kept together or distributed to subject divisions, by far the most common way of arranging them is in alphabetical order by title. It is this method which is most likely to be appreciated by users and to create the least confusion arising from replacing items in the wrong sequence. Its most obvious disadvantage is that periodicals of similar subject interest will only be placed close together if their titles open with an appropriate subject keyword, such as *Mathematics Teaching* and *Mathematical Gazette,* whilst *Journal of the London Mathematical Society* and *Russian Mathematical Surveys* will be placed elsewhere in the sequence. However, purposive readers are usually looking for specific known items and prefer purely alphabetical sequencing to any other. Browsers may well not notice the logic of the sequencing, whatever it is.

It is tempting to librarians to attempt to create more convenient arrangements by keyword, using subtle inversions of titles for the purposes of arrangement and display – thus *Forestry, Quarterly Journal of* and *Neurobiology, Progress in* – but such exoticism is usually self-defeating, confusing both readers and library staff alike. It is a useful device for developing a helpful visible index or handlist of periodicals available, but to use it as a physical arrangement system is to court confusion especially in a large collection.

5. *Display in a separate periodicals room*

There is a great deal of interest and enjoyment to be had from browsing in a large collection of current periodicals. Such a thought might well have been the motive behind the creation of distinct and separate periodicals reading rooms in many large public libraries and academic and research libraries. If this was the motive, it is laudable, but very misguided in all but a few special cases. It is as misguided as the more probable reasons for separation – the instinctive desire of most librarians to seek administratively comfortable solutions to their problems, and the misconception that because formats differ, purposes and uses also differ. If a periodicals collection is selected, as it should be, to complement the bookstock, then there is no justification for the segregation of the current display of periodicals to separately administered areas. Osborn notes the tendency of separately provided periodicals reading rooms in academic libraries to become simply extensions to the main reading room for students eternally seeking comfortable, quiet, study areas regardless of the planned function of a room. The tendency for separately provided 'magazine' rooms to become a magnet for the drifters, the shiftless and the various other categories of social misfit, to the detriment of other, more purposive readers of public libraries, is well documented over more than a century. This form of provision is not as common as it once was.

EQUIPMENT FOR THE DISPLAY OF PERIODICALS

The most familiar type of periodicals display fittings are those constructed such that periodicals can be placed flat with their front covers wholly visible. The shelves are sloped about thirty degrees from the vertical and the periodicals retained in position by a projecting lip on the lower edge of the shelf. This traditional method, and many others, is illustrated in a most significant contribution to the literature of periodicals administration, by Heintze.[2]

A protective cover is often thought to be necessary when the sloping shelf system is used. The purpose is to provide the necessary stiffness to the issues to enable them to stand upright on the shelves and to protect them in use. The protective cover might be a cloth binding, which totally encloses the periodical, or have a transparent front through which the periodical can clearly be seen. Of the two varieties the latter is to be preferred since it allows the original periodical cover to be seen – a valuable mnemonic quality. In the case of the cloth-bound type the periodical title must be lettered prominently upon the front of the cover or, alternatively, in order to preserve the mnemonic quality, a cut out of the title from the front cover of the periodical may be stuck to the cloth cover. Transparent covers are made in either rigid plastic or limp P.V.C. The latter type is most common today.

Protective covers must always be a correct fit for the periodicals they enclose. Periodicals are held in the covers by a string or wire running down the inside of the cover. If the covers are too large, the periodicals will slip about in use, and the retaining string will cut into the periodical spine and cause damage. If the covers are too tight, damage will be caused to the periodicals as they are being put in and taken out. Covers which allow about one 2·5 cm (1 in.) of movement to the periodicals when they are enclosed within the cover should be sought in buying a range of sizes.

The provision of expensive protective covers is often questioned. Apart from their actual cost, which is considerable, there is the additional cost of a good deal of staff time, in placing the periodicals into their covers and removing them when their period of currency has expired. Some sloping-shelf display units are equipped with a metal or wooden retaining strip 15–20 cm (6–8 ins) from the lower edge, behind which the unprotected periodical issues can be slotted and then dropped to the lower projecting lip. In this way the periodicals can be displayed without any protective cover and can support themselves. A disadvantage of this system is that the issues can often be badly damaged by abrasive contact with the supporting strip as they are replaced after use.

Display fittings incorporating back-number storage

Recent back numbers of a current periodical are often as much in demand as the newest issue. It is tiresome and time wasting to both staff and readers if recent back numbers must be brought from a store room each time they are required and then returned after use. One method of making back numbers available has already been mentioned – that of shelving them on open access in pamphlet boxes. Another common method is to house back numbers on flat shelves behind the sloping display spaces, which are hinged at the top to enable them to be lifted to reveal the shelf behind upon which the back numbers are stored. Ideally the hinged sloping shelf should be fitted with a device to enable it to be held in the open position so that both hands may be used to retrieve the stored periodicals. This facility does, of course, add to the already considerable cost of such units. Not all readers are aware of the back numbers being stored behind this type of display fitting unless they are clearly and frequently reminded by printed notices prominently placed on the units. An inconvenience of this type of store is that library staff must spend considerable time in checking and tidying the loose parts which quickly become misplaced with use. Loose parts replaced in the wrong pile are effectively lost until a careful tidying check is carried out.

A compact method of displaying a large number of periodicals

Display shelving of the type described above is expensive both in money terms and in terms of space occupied. Periodicals collections in very large public reference libraries and academic libraries might be of the order of 1,000–5,000 current titles. It is often necessary to find more compact methods of displaying them. A familiar solution is a unit providing a very large number of horizontally or vertically arranged slots large enough to hold the current issue of a single periodical, possibly enclosed in a protective cover. Through this procedure, considerable savings in space are possible, although it has to be said that it is very expensive in terms of the costs of the units. It cannot be said that the result is a display of periodicals, but rather a case where a large number of periodicals are made accessible to readers.

It is usual in employing this method to provide each title taken with a protective cover. Since the whole periodical other than the spine is effectively concealed when it is in its place in the display unit there is no advantage in using transparent-fronted covers. The periodical covers are numbered corresponding to a particular slot in the unit and indexed on a list displayed prominently alongside the unit. Great care is needed to check the unit carefully for misplaced periodicals regularly; a periodical out of sequence is not readily detectable, and many users tend to replace a periodical in any slot which they find empty. A simple method of attempting to limit replacement into the wrong slots and to render its occurrence easier to detect is to provide protective covers in a variety of colours. The different colours can then be allocated to blocks of fifty or so adjacent slots or to different initial letters of the titles of the periodicals taken. Periodicals replaced outside their allocated colour block are then immediately obvious to members of the library staff.

Generally speaking, units with horizontally arranged slots are to be preferred to those with vertical slots. In the former case the periodicals lie flat on the shelves and are less likely to damage themselves through collapsing under their own weight, as they tend to in the units with vertical slots. It is also easier to label horizontally arranged slots legibly and comprehensively. By providing units with slots of about 7·5 cm (3 ins) wide it is possible to arrange for a limited number of recent back issues to be stored in the slot with the current issue. Naturally in this case fewer periodicals can be displayed in a given space.

The units needed for this type of display are very expensive when custom built in wood. Cheaper, less elegant, but acceptable alternative arrangements might be made arranging conventional library book shelving at the rate of twelve to fifteen shelves to a tier as compared to the more usual six or seven. Metal bin storage of the type mass produced for industry as tool storage units might also be used, since they come in a wide range of sizes. Where economy is more important than elegance it is a solution to the display problem to be considered.

Pamphlet box filing

Although mentioned briefly above this method is worth elaborating. It possesses significant merits, not least of which is that it needs no special and expensive display equipment other than the boxes themselves and normal library book shelving units. The periodicals are stored in boxes at the rate of one periodical title per box. The boxes are titled either by spine lettering printed on them or by the use of a cut-out title from the front cover of a periodical issue.

Pamphlet box filing is not especially effective for some of the bulkier weekly periodicals such as *The Economist* or *The Engineer*, nor for the filing of the increasing number of tabloid format periodicals. It is not simply a question of the size of boxes needed for this purpose but the weight of the full box which makes weekly and tabloid periodicals awkward to handle in this way. Most periodicals of monthly frequency will fit into boxes of A4 size or slightly larger.

This means of display need not be regarded as a cheap alternative to be used only when more elaborate arrangements can not be afforded. It is a functional alternative in its own right often much appreciated by library users who are able to carry a box to a reading table and browse through its contents. It is much easier than carrying a bundle of loose parts. Box filing also, of course, affords a considerable degree of protection to the loose parts before binding or when being moved about the library.

A major disadvantage of the method is that it is difficult to maintain the periodicals within a box in their correct order and a periodical misfiled into the wrong box entails tedious searching through many boxes. Checks and tidying of all boxes must be regularly carried out. It is also worth noting that a drawback of this method is that if a box has only a few issues in it, it will result in the parts slipping to the bottom and becoming creased or even permanently damaged. The use of pamphlet boxes incorporating a spring device inside, whilst it assists in maintaining the loose parts in an upright position, adds to the cost of the boxes and seriously reduces their capacity.

A great variety of boxes suitable for the purpose of filing

periodicals exist, from very cheap fibre board types stapled together, to specially made cloth covered items which can be ordered from library supply bookbinders ready titled. A number of types of rigid plastic boxes in attractive colours and having a label holder on the spine to take a typed title card are also available. Many libraries prefer to use boxes designed like slip cases for expensive books. That is to say, boxes open on one of the long sides into which periodical issues can be placed without withdrawing the box totally from the shelf rather than, as with conventional boxes, needing to remove them completely from the shelves, using both hands to hold them. Special fibre board or rugged baskets like rigid plastic containers can be bought for this purpose.

Whether boxes or slip cases should be bought in a variety of sizes to accommodate the different sizes of periodical is an open question. Whilst to buy different sizes can result in significant savings of space by the provision of slim boxes for smaller, perhaps quarterly, periodicals, the appearance of the display is considerably enhanced by the use of one standard size of box. If different sizes of box are decided upon, then three sizes will suffice for most purposes. Quarterlies will usually fit a whole volume into a box 3·75 cms (1·5 ins) wide, most monthlies will be fitted into a box of 5 cms (2 ins) whilst the largest of periodicals can be put into 7·5 cms (3 ins) boxes. In this last case most weekly periodicals will require two boxes to accommodate a full year of issues. David Ward has examined critically various methods of storing the unbound parts of periodicals[3] and is enthusiastic about pamphlet box storage; he is, however, more concerned to examine alternatives to conventional binding for storage rather than display.

NEWSPAPER DISPLAY

The large size and relative frailty of most newspapers means that their display almost inevitably causes problems to the library. Although usually on display for only one day, newspapers are heavily used. The traditional public library method of displaying newspapers is to place them on reading slopes retained by a metal or leather strip placed down the centre fold. Reading slopes for newspapers take up a great deal of space and are most inconvenient and uneconomic as a display medium in any library short of space.

A display which dispenses with the need for reading slopes is the split stick method. The centre fold of the newspaper is clamped between two wooden strips which are then locked together. The title of the newspaper is lettered on the edge of the stick. The 'loaded' sticks are stored in a box-like structure with the two ends resting on the box edges with the newspapers hanging down inside. The newspapers are consulted by lifting them out of the structure and carrying them to reading tables.

Table fittings for the display of newspapers and periodicals

Many libraries have display fittings built into their reading tables. They are usually placed down the centre of the tables in such a way that they form a division between the two sides. Readers consult the periodicals by taking them down from the display and sitting at the table space adjacent to the position of the periodical. The disadvantage is that a reader wishing to consult a number of periodicals must either move from place to place or lean across other readers to collect or replace them, which is irritating to all parties.

INDEXES TO PERIODICALS ON PUBLIC DISPLAY

In order to ensure that the periodicals held by a library are known by the readers to be there, some kind of listing of the material held which can readily be consulted must be provided. At its simplest a typed, or even a manuscript, list will serve the purpose if permanently displayed. Where a library has a large enough collection of periodicals, a separate pamphlet available to library users on request which lists all periodicals taken might be compiled. Such a list might be a simple alphabetical title list or might have a subject arrangement or index. The nature of the periodicals collections of almost any library is such that any listings produced will soon become out of date and must be frequently amended. Whilst a pamphlet for readers to carry away is a useful provision, a master list in the library arranged in such a way that swift amendment can be carried out is essential. Some libraries maintain a master list on cards, one card per title, in a conventional card catalogue cabinet. Whilst this ensures that the necessary revision can be carried out efficiently and quickly and that a full history can be given on the card, it does not enable readers to check quickly in the way that, say, a typed list would.

The problem with typed sheets is that keeping them up to date entails frequent re-typings, and even then messy additions and deletions will be necessary between re-typings. Typed lists do fulfil one criterion for a public index to periodical holdings in that they are easy to consult and comprehensible to readers. They are less likely to fulfil another, at least, over a period of time, which is to provide an up to date list. An admirable development of the typed list is that which allows for neat and swift revision whilst maintaining visibility and comprehensibility at a high level – the visible-strip index. By this method each title is typed or written on a separate strip of card, the strips being designed to take one or two lines of typing and they are, for ease of typing, made up in sheets so that individual strips may be removed from the rest as required leaving a backing sheet and the remaining strips intact. The strips are arranged upon the faces of metal panels with their ends being slotted under retaining flanges. The panels are then mounted on a wall bracket or table top fitment hinged on their inside edges so that the individual panels can be turned over, like the pages of a book. The individual strips can be arranged, re-arranged, withdrawn or replaced in any order at will. It is therefore easy to maintain up to date information. At any given time photocopies of the panels will provide an up to date check list should this be required for any purpose elsewhere in the library. The panels can be protected by transparent rigid plastic covering sheets if required, and prominent tabs fitted on to the outer edges will supply visible signals of, say, the letters of the alphabet for alphabetically arranged lists.

The strips can be obtained in a variety of colours and this can be used as a means of providing certain types of information. For example various departmental locations can be expressed by means of different colours. By using two- or three-line strips a great deal of information can be conveyed about each periodical – for example, full details of holdings of back files, the availability of microcopies and notes of any titles changes which have occurred.

REFERENCES

1. Osborn, Andrew D. *Serial publications: their place and treatment in libraries.* Chicago: American Library Association, 2nd ed. rev., 1973.
2. Heintze, I. *Shelving for periodicals.* Lund, Sweden.: Biblioteketjanst, for the International Federation of Library Associations, 1966.
3. Ward, D. B. 'Periodical storage re-visited.' *Wilson Library Bulletin,* 34(3), November 1959. pp. 210–21.

Chapter 16
The foreign language barrier

In terms of the amount of literature published, English is by far the most significant language, especially in the scientific and technical fields. Although it is not possible to give a definitive statement of the exact proportion of the world's literature which appears in English, it is certainly not less than half. In certain fields of science and technology it may even be as much as three-quarters. A person knowing only English is, therefore, at a considerable advantage in gaining access to new knowledge. There are between 3,000 and 5,000 languages in the world, and the person knowing only one of them is virtually obliged to learn others in order to be fully informed in a specialist subject, unless that one language be English.

Although a substantial proportion of significant literature appears in English it is by no means certain that all of it does (although about 75 per cent of the respondents to a most important survey by Hutchins, Pargeter and Saunders[1] appeared to think that it did). It is therefore of considerable importance that some means be found to improve access to non-English language periodicals for the benefit of English speaking communities and for the vast number of people for whom English is the second or third language.

The facilities for gaining access to foreign language materials are improving all of the time. This includes, naturally, considerable efforts to improve the quality of language teaching at all levels in most countries of the world. In particular, access to scientific literature is improving, and it is this aspect which will be dealt with here. For the humanities and the social sciences the means of access to foreign language materials are by no means as well developed as those of the sciences.

The English-speaking scientist is, then, at a considerable advantage over all other monolingual scientists, but Wood[2] notes that between 70 per cent and 80 per cent of English-speaking scientists included in his survey had felt the need for access to a foreign language item in the past year, and 64 per cent in the previous month. Hanson[3] warns of the dangers of complacency in English-speaking scientists who use only English-language items:

> It does not justify the assumption that because he can read much of the world's scientific literature without language difficulty he can safely ignore the remainder. There are no adequate reasons for believing that high intelligence and capacity for advanced thought or skilled experimentation are monopolized by English-speaking peoples. The only assumption that can be made with safety is that responsible trained workers in one country are likely to produce useful results as their counterparts in others!

A few lines further on Hanson's report says:

> English scientists must face the probability that in the immediate future an increasing proportion of the world's literature will be in languages which few of them can at present read.

The *Chemical Abstracts* Service[4] reveals how the proportion of English-language material is declining in Chemistry by indicating the sources of periodical literature abstracted by the Service (the quantities are given as percentages):

	U.S.A.	British Common- wealth	Russia	Germany	France	Japan	Eastern Bloc
1951	41·1	15·6	8·2	3·1	8·4	4·4	—
1973	26·4	13·1	24·7	6·4	4·3	7·5	5·5

What are the World's major linguistic groups?

An article in the *UNESCO Courier*[5] gave the following twelve languages as being spoken by more than 50 million people in 1965, in order of numerical importance:

1	Chinese	3	Russian
2	English	4	Hindi

5 Spanish   9 Arabic
6 German   10 French
7 Japanese   11 Portuguese
8 Bengali   12 Italian

These are spoken languages; the languages in which most scientific literature is published are somewhat different in the order of their occurrence, thus as Wood shows (figures as percentages):

English	46	French	9
Russian	14	Japanese	4
German	10	Others	17

Hanson believed that the three most significant barriers to English-speaking scientists were Russian, Japanese and Chinese, since he had assumed that most English-speaking scientists can cope with French and German anyway (91·5 per cent of Wood's sample had claimed to be able to read French). Chan[6] is somewhat sceptical about the ability of English-speaking scientists to cope with French and German as they claim but feels that, in any case, they are languages without great significance in the current state of scientific publishing, where Russian and Japanese assume increasing significance. Chan also doubts the efficacy of establishing programmes to teach languages to practising scientists, making the point that such people have enough difficulty in keeping up with their reading of English-language materials without taking time off to learn a language.

It would never be sufficient, however, to develop language teaching as the sole means of improving access to foreign-language material even if it was a cheap and economical thing to do. Some means must be found to make available the results of research for those too busy, or lazy, to learn languages.

The language characteristics of the primary physics periodicals are the subject of exhaustive study by Cooper and Thayer.[7] They reveal that English is the language used solely, or in some degree in combination, in 80·2 per cent of the periodicals they studied with 44 per cent of them being exclusively in English. The International Council for Scientific

8*

Unions Abstracting Board[8] showed that 69 per cent of all scientific periodicals appeared wholly or substantially in English.

The principal areas to examine in considering the ways of breaking through the language barrier are as follows:

1. Guides and co-operative measures for improving access
2. Translations *ad hoc* of individual work
3. Translations of whole periodicals or selections
4. Parallel publication in several languages
5. English-language publication by foreign publishers
6. Current awareness services
7. Automatic translations

1. *Guides and co-operative measures*

The ASLIB Information Department has compiled a detailed guide to services and sources of translation in the United Kingdom.[9] Chillag[10] covers much the same ground as far as United Kingdom material is concerned, although in more detail, and also covers principal European and American sources. He deals with American sources first and in particular the *Translation-register index* produced by the troubled National Translations Center based at the John Crerar Library. In the United Kingdom section of his paper, Chillag mentions first and most prominently his own organization, the BLLD (formerly the National Lending Library for Science and Technology), which provides a comprehensive translation service, a collection centre for translations done elsewhere and an efficient information dissemination system covering all of their translation services.

Translations undertaken 'in-house' by the BLLD are regularly reported in their quarterly *BLL Review* and perhaps 1,000 items a year are generated in this way principally from Russian, Japanese and Chinese. Holdings of translations done by other organizations and deposited in the BLLD total some 400,000 items from British, American and European sources. The dissemination of information about translations services provided by the BLLD is by the *BLL Announcements Bulletin*.

Chillag refers also to the ASLIB-maintained *Commonwealth*

index of unpublished scientific and technical translations, a location list of nearly 300,000 translations established in 1951. In Europe, Chillag refers to a large number of organizations, but the principal institution of note to which he devotes considerable space is the European Translation Centre at Delft in the Netherlands. Established in 1960 under the auspices of the Organization of Economic Co-operation and Development, the Centre acts purely as a clearing house for translations produced elsewhere. The Centre does not prepare translations itself. The Centre is described in a note in *UNESCO Bulletin for Librarians*.[10] Knul[11] elaborates upon the services of the Centre in more detail. A section in the report by Hutchins, Pargeter and Saunders deals with the available guides to translations.

2. *Translations* ad hoc *of individual work*

A British Standard[12] has been produced giving advice upon the preparation of translations, and Sykes[13] has prepared a manual which also includes details of the guides and services available. If a person is aware of the existence of a periodical article in a foreign language which is potentially of value to him, he can do one of two things. He can decide that it would be too much trouble to try to obtain a translation and hope that the material might subsequently be published in English. Wood provides considerable evidence that this is what many people will do in this circumstance. Alternatively he can try to obtain a translation. In very fortunate circumstances he will find that the translation has already been done; if not, he will have to take steps to obtain one. *Ad hoc* translation is expensive – and the more uncommon the language the more expensive the ultimate translation will be. Vickery[14], Liebesny[15] and Scott[16] have discussed the costs of translation, and they clearly show that 'easy' languages cost less than a quarter the cost of 'hard' languages to translate. All three writers warn about the dangers of trying to do translations on the cheap using freelance translators; poor quality work may result owing mainly to the translator's lack of subject knowledge. Many government and private industrial organizations employ their own translators, full time or part time, both to control quality and to ensure swiftness of production of urgent work. Wood mentions that the majority of the 2,000 scientists in his survey stated a preference for the employment of translators by their own organizations, rather than using outside sources. Cook-Radmore[17] from the United Kingdom, and O'Keefe and Jacoley[18] from the United States, both reinforce the warnings about the variable quality of freelance translators. Freelance translators must, of course, be used even by organizations employing their own translators, if they do not have expertise in a specific subject or language areas. Geach[19] lists and describes sources of information on translations available, and also lists directories of translators.

3. *Translations of whole periodicals or selections*

Where the volume of *ad hoc* translation from a particular source is high it might make sense to consider translating the whole periodical regularly. A large number of 'cover-to-cover' translations of periodicals principally from Russian are made into English in the United States and the United Kingdom and, to a lesser extent, in Western Europe.

Besides complete cover-to-cover translations, for example, *Scientific and Technical Information Processing* (Allerton) there are periodicals which publish translations of only the most significant parts of foreign periodicals, for example, *Polymer Science USSR*, or completely new periodicals which amalgamate significant work from a related group of foreign items for example the Rubber and Plastics Research Association's *International Polymer Science and Technology*, which translates from Eastern European, Russian and Japanese periodicals.

Some useful guides to periodicals in translation are:

HIMMELSBACH, C. J. *and* BROCINER, G. E. *A new guide to translated journals : a guide to scientific and technical journals in translation.* New York: Special Libraries Association, 2nd ed., 1971.

SMITH, B. *Journals in translation.* Boston Spa, Yorks.: British Library Lending Division, 1976.

EUROPEAN TRANSLATION CENTRE. *Translation journals : a list of periodicals translated cover to cover, abstracts publications, periodicals containing selected articles and multi-lingual publications.* Delft: ETC. Annual.

BRITISH LIBRARY, Science Reference Library. *Holdings of translated journals (cover to cover translations and translations of selected articles).* London: British Library, Science Reference Library, 1974.

Cover-to-cover translation is expensive and slow. It is doubtful whether some of the periodicals currently published cover-to-cover are really worth the time, trouble and money invested in them. They cost up to £50 a year for quarterlies at 1976 prices and they are usually six months later in appearance than the parent periodical from which they are derived. Whilst *ad hoc* translation is expensive, it has to be pointed out that in cover-to-cover translation the 'cost per interesting page' for material of value to a particular individual might be very high indeed. Some thirteen research associations in the United Kingdom produce cover-to-cover translations from Russian which are published for them by the British Library Lending Division, for example *Coke and Chemistry*, produced by the British Carbonization Research Association. These periodicals are published relatively cheaply at £25 to £50 a year (at 1976 prices) being presumably subsidized either directly or indirectly.

4. *Parallel publication in several languages*

The practice of publishing a periodical simultaneously in several languages obviously ensures wide dissemination of its message but, equally obviously, it is expensive. International associations often publish their periodicals in this way, for example the *UNESCO Bulletin for Libraries* is published in four languages. Also common are periodicals published in one of two or three languages at the choice of the author. Naturally this is most common in bilingual countries such as South Africa but it is to be found elsewhere, for example *Colloquium Internationale*, an ecological periodical with articles in French, English and German; *Libri* is another example. This practice enables the publisher, in contradistinction to simultaneous publication in several languages, to economize upon typesetting costs and if trilingual abstracts are included of all articles the losses to monolingual readers is minimized. The practice of supplying multilingual abstracts even to mono lingual periodicals on the pattern of *Domus*, the Italian fine art periodical, is increasing.

5. *English language publication by foreign publishers*

The pre-eminence of English as the language of science and technology has already been mentioned. This has led to the interesting situation of some publishers in non-English-speaking countries producing periodicals using the English language as the original language of publication. The impulse is purely commercial because English provides a potentially far larger market than would publication in, say, Norwegian. The countries with the strongest tendency to publish in English are the Netherlands, Scandinavia and Japan for example: *Geophysical Prospecting* (Netherlands); *Scandinavian Journal of Haematology* (Denmark).

6. *Current awareness services*

The value of abstracts, especially informative abstracts, is considerable. Wood provides an indication of the amount of foreign-language material available in English-language abstracting services. The quantity of material appearing in *Chemical Abstracts* originally published in non-English languages now approaches fifty per cent and, in these circumstances, the use of such abstracting services enables the non-linguist to pick up at least an impression of trends in other countries. They also provide the opportunity to decide whether or not it would be worthwhile to obtain a full translation. An abstract is much better than nothing in making available information upon foreign-language material and the practice of some abstracting services of publishing fuller abstracts of foreign language items is invaluable.

The principal difficulty in the use of abstracts for breaking the language barrier is that they appear very late – by and large the more difficult the language and the more recondite the subject, the longer the time lag in the publication of an abstract.

Periodicals indexing services also provide some help in that as far as they cover non-English periodicals, the English-language services usually translate the titles of articles and, of course, they group them under subject headings which provide further help in deciding upon the likely uses of a translation. In this case, it is only the barest indication of value which is presented. This is also the case with another source of help – the contents list periodicals of the *Current Contents* type, as produced by the Institute of Scientific Information Inc. from Philadelphia. This particular series is especially strong in the translation of the title pages of Russian and Japanese periodicals.

7. *Automatic translation*

Translation by human hand and brain is expensive, slow and cumbersome in direct terms, and in indirect terms, even more expensive if it is considered that the translator is diverted from more fruitful pursuits by what is, after all, basically a fairly mechanical activity once the language has been learned. Translation by human hand suffers chronic shortages of subject specialists, and of people able to translate from difficult languages.

The possibility of the computer being used to provide translations from one language to another has been recognized for a long time and experimentation and research have been in progress for almost as long as computers have been in use. The potential is enormous although the prospects of early redundancy of human translators is not something to be taken seriously. Despite massive investment of time and talent, the results of the research have been disappointing. As Chan says:

> The most optimistic see machine translation as being useful only as an aid to human translators, either by producing a rough first draft or by providing on-line computer stored dictionaries.

Other writers vary in their opinions from almost euphoric optimism to pessimism even more profound than that of Chan. The major source of difficulty is in creating automatic trans-lations which produce word orders and syntax which faithfully reflect practice in one language from the very different structures of another. The computer has proved excellent at producing swift word for word translations, but they have sometimes seemed as incomprehensible to the non-linguist when translated as they were in the original language. There are those who feel that the problem of syntax is insuperable with the present technology.

The most useful source of references to the literature of machine translation is the quarterly *Information Science Abstracts*. Josselson[20] summarizes progress in machine translation in the United States with reference to Russian/English translation. It is interesting to note that only 22 per cent of the scientists questioned in Wood's survey said that they would be prepared to accept an automatically prepared translation as substitutes for human translation, and even then it would be interesting to know if many of that 22 per cent had actually ever seen a machine-produced translation.

REFERENCES

1. HUTCHINS, W. J., PARGETER, L. J. *and* SAUNDERS, W. L. *The language barrier: a study in depth of the place of foreign language materials in the research activity of an academic community.* Sheffield: Sheffield University Postgraduate School of Library and Information Studies, 1971.
2. WOOD, D. N. 'The foreign language problem facing scientists and technologists in the United Kingdom – report of a recent survey.' *Journal of Documentation*, 23(2), June 1967. pp. 117–30.
3. HANSON, C. W. *The foreign language barrier in science and technology.* London: ASLIB, 1962.
4. CHEMICAL ABSTRACTS SERVICE. *CAS today: facts and figures about the Chemical Abstracts Service.* Columbus, Ohio: CAS, 1974.
5. ANON. 'Two-thirds of the world's books produced by twelve countries.' *UNESCO Courier*, 19(10), September 1965. pp. 15–16.
6. CHAN, G. K. 'The foreign language barrier in science and technology.' *International Library Review*, 8(3), June 1976. pp. 317–25.
7. COOPER, M. *and* THAYER, C. W. *Primary Journal literature in Physics.* New York: American Institute of Physics, 1969.
8. INTERNATIONAL COUNCIL FOR SCIENTIFIC UNION, Abstracting Board. *Some characteristics of primary periodicals in the domain of the Chemical Sciences.* Paris: ICSU, 1969.
9. ASLIB INFORMATION DEPARTMENT. 'Translations in the United Kingdom.' *ASLIB Proceedings*, 25(7), July 1973. pp. 264–7.
10. CHILLAG, J. P. 'Translations and their guides.' *NLL Review*, 1(2), April 1971. pp. 46–53.
11. KNUL, C. M. A. 'Towards a follow up care program for *ad hoc* translations.' *ASLIB Proceedings*, 25(6), June 1973. pp. 220–6.

12. BRITISH STANDARDS INSTITUTION. *Specification for the presentation of translations.* London: BSI, BSS 4755:1971.

13. SYKES, J. B. *Technical translators' manual.* London: ASLIB, 1971.

14. VICKERY, B. C. 'Foreign language serials and translations' *in* Bottle, R. T. *and* Wyatt, H. V., *The use of the biological literature.* London: Butterworth, 2nd ed., 1971.

15. LIEBESNY, F. 'Special fields, patents and translations' *in* Coblans, H., ed., *Use of Physics literature.* London: Butterworth, 1973.

16. SCOTT, P. H. 'Technical translations: meeting the need.' *ASLIB Proceedings,* 23(2), February 1971. pp. 89–97.

17. COOT-RADMORE, D. 'The freelance translator' *in* Sykes, J. B., *Technical translators' manual.* London: ASLIB, 1971.

18. O'KEEFE, W. *and* JACOLEY, R. L. 'Spend your translation dollar wisely.' *Sci-Tech News,* 21(1), Spring 1967. pp. 6–7, 16.

19. GEACH, J. D. 'Indexes of existing translations and translators' *in* Sykes, J. B., *Technical translators' manual.* London: ASLIB, 1971.

20. JOSSELSON, H. H. *Research in machine translation. Russian to English: ten year summary report 1958–1968.* Washington: Office of Naval Research, The Department of the Navy, 1969.

Subject and
selected title index

Author Index